Bridie
GALLAGHER
THE GIRL FROM DONEGAL

Bridie relaxing while on tour in Waterford and Cork in 1957. © THOMAS TOBIN

Bridie GALLAGHER

THE GIRL FROM DONEGAL

JIM LIVINGSTONE

The Collins Press

First published in 2015 by
The Collins Press
West Link Park
Doughcloyne
Wilton
Cork

A CIP record for this book is available from the British Library.

Hardback ISBN: 978-1-84889-257-6
PDF eBook ISBN: 978-1-84889-505-6
EPUB eBook ISBN: 978-1-84889-507-2
Kindle ISBN: 978-1-84889-508-9

Typesetting by Burns Design
Typeset in Walbaum
Printed in Malta by Gutenberg Press Limited

CONTENTS

FOREWORD

*I*t is a great honour for me to be asked to write these few words as the foreword for this book.

I first saw Bridie perform in Annagry Hall when I was about ten years old. To see her glide across the stage in her wonderful gown singing all the songs we came to know through her is a memory I will never forget. Fast forward to 1985, I had the privilege to be part of a concert tour that also featured Bridie.

From the first show Bridie and I hit it off. I suppose the fact that we were both from Donegal was a major plus. I watched her again night after night just as I did all those years before. She had that very special something that you can't put your finger on. I suppose it's called star quality. And Bridie had it in abundance. It was during this tour that I came to know Bridie the person.

She loved to reminisce about her years growing up in Creeslough. I can still see her throw her head back and laugh out loud as we traded stories about funny happenings from home. She liked nothing better than a good laugh. You never had to wonder what she thought because she'd tell you right from the word go, whether you liked it or not. She wanted me to be the best I could be and was always happy to advise me on what to do and, more importantly, what not to do while on stage. Even though we toured together on only that one occasion, we kept in touch in the years that followed right up to her death.

Bridie was the one who paved the way for all of us Donegal singers who came after her. Her music brought her around the world and although she spent her adult life living in Belfast, I feel her heart never left Donegal. I'm so glad that her son Jim has finished this book that Bridie had started. It gives us a peek into the life of an incredible lady who reached the top of her career in the music business but, that said, who never lost the common touch.

DANIEL O'DONNELL

Above: Bridie with her good friend Daniel O'Donnell in 1985.

PREFACE

On 9 January 2012 a very special lady died at the age of eighty-seven. She was my mother, Bridie Livingstone, better known to many people as Bridie Gallagher, the internationally renowned Irish ballad singer, and often described as 'The Girl from Donegal'. In the weeks and months following her passing, so many friends, family and fans asked me was I going to write a book on her life story that the prospect became irresistible. Bridie herself had done some writing many years earlier with that very intention. But as her health failed she never finished it. So I decided to pick up the baton and finish the job: the result is now in your hands.

With Bridie's own written memories to start with, and my own, I also researched published references, including newspaper articles, from different stages of her life and career and interviewed friends and family members who knew her well.

I have attempted to present an honest and interesting account of her life experiences, her achievements, her personality, her strengths and weaknesses, her triumphs and her lows. Some readers will already know much about her life, and others perhaps very little. Everyone, I hope, will find some surprises.

I owe a great debt to many people who have helped and encouraged me in producing this book, especially family and friends of my mother Bridie, the team at The Collins Press, and my colleagues and tutors at Belfast's Crescent Arts Centre, particularly Jo Egan and Ruth Carr.

Most of all, I will be forever grateful for the love and support of my wife Paula, daughters Teresa, Shauna and Nuala, and son Peter. Without their love and support I'd be lost and this book would never have been written.

JIM LIVINGSTONE

Bridie with her son Jim (author) at his First Communion in 1959.

PROLOGUE

'*Two minutes, Miss Gallagher,*' whispered the assistant stage director busy with his clipboard and lists, stagehands scurrying about like silent mice.

Bridie stood motionless in the wings of the vast stage. Both her hands were clasped together in white-knuckle terror like a girl about to board a rollercoaster, and she stared ahead, her mind whirling with thoughts. '*Is this really happening to me? Am I actually going to sing on the London Palladium stage? Please God make it good.*'

She could hear the orchestra playing Rob Murray's big finishing number. She knew that her eight minutes on stage were about to start, eight of the longest minutes in her short show business life. Once Rob was off, Bruce Forsythe, the MC, would be on, building the audience to the edge of heightened expectancy like the pro he was. And then the call to action would come for 'The Girl from Donegal'.

She stepped forward and nervously drew aside the large velvet curtains just an inch to peek out at the cavernous auditorium, blood red and gold, glaring back at her. Rows and rows of glowing white faces singing, swaying and cheering along with Rob as he reached the pinnacle of his act. Was that her mother and father she could see out there? Was that Bob and the children there in the fourth row too? No, they were all back in Ireland. She knew she was alone and felt a pang in her heart. No family there to support and pray for her. No friends to lead the audience in applause. Nobody to hold her tight and reassure her. As so many times before, and many more to come, it would be her alone on stage, striving to win the hearts of the crowd and thrill them with her songs.

Gazing up to the upper circle of seats so high above, she suddenly felt she was looking at Muckish Mountain near home and could even feel the Donegal wind in her face. She saw the school choir with her sister Grace and herself giggling and singing while Miss Cahoun scowled in disapproval. '*Sing up, Gallagher, and concentrate.*' So much had happened since those giddy days twenty years ago and now, holy God, she was about to sing at the world-famous London Palladium.

The orchestra stopped with a flourish. The audience exploded in noise. All became a blur. She couldn't see or hear for a moment. The air around her chilled. She felt her brow rise in sweat. Her mouth was dry. She stole a quick gulp of water, pushed back her coal-black silken hair, fluffed her petticoats and shook her head. Someone thrust a microphone into her hand. It seemed to fit like a favourite glove. She could hear Bruce winding the crowd up.

And then magically she was calm, ready to perform, ready to embrace another audience like all the others and make them hers. She heard Bruce exclaim, *'Ladies and gentlemen, please welcome The Girl from Donegal, Bridie Gallagher.'* She glided onto the stage and was instantly bathed in brilliant warm light. She took her cue from the orchestra and sang *'There's one fair county in Ireland ...'*

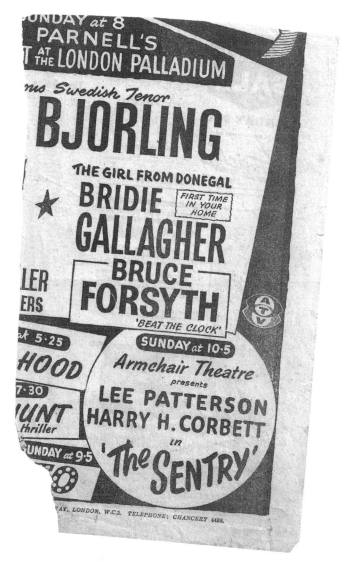

Advert for Sunday Night at the London Palladium from January 1959.

© LONDON EVENING STANDARD

Bridie with concert producer Shay O'Hara at Sydney Opera House in 1977.

Chapter One

THE WHITE GATE

Ah 'tis well to be you that is taking your tae, where,
They're cuttin' the corn around Creeslough the day.

'CUTTIN' THE CORN IN CREESLOUGH', (FRENCH, HASTINGS)

BRIDIE GALLAGHER

*W*hen the phone rang that Thursday morning, on 22 December 2011, it startled us all. We were about to leave for work. Early morning phone calls rarely brought good news. It was Linda, Mum's private carer, who visited her every morning and afternoon. She cooked, cleaned, ironed, washed, shopped, chatted and, most importantly, made Mum laugh. She was really like a daughter to her – the daughter she never had. She had just arrived for her morning call to discover Mum had had a fall, and so she rang me. I didn't hesitate. I ran to the car to get to her house.

Ten minutes later I found Mum lying beside her bed, a blanket over her, and Linda sitting beside her on the bedroom floor. After a quick inspection I could see she was obviously in severe pain and rang for an ambulance. It pulled up a few minutes later and the paramedic came in to make an assessment. Typically, she immediately put on a performance, smiling and joking with the paramedics checking her pulse and heart, even flirting a little while still wincing in pain at any movement.

Twenty minutes later we were in the hospital A&E department where she was seen quickly by a doctor, had X-rays taken and it was soon confirmed she had fractured her hip and needed to be admitted immediately for treatment.

The ward, like so many others, was a long corridor with five 6-bed units and single rooms off the right-hand side, and nurse stations and doctors' rooms off the left. The sickly yellow walls of the corridor were decorated with a variety of oil paintings and prints. The nurses were getting Mum into the first bed. Just across from the bed on the corridor wall was a painting. A painting of a very special scene that shook me. It was one that Mum and all our family knew very well. It was of a little beach near Creeslough on Sheephaven Bay in County Donegal, with a wonderful view looking up to Crockatee Hill at the end of the bay with the towering dark-blue mass that was Muckish Mountain in the distance behind. The place was known as The White Gate. It was Mum's favourite place in the world, half a mile from where she was born.

She was born on the Ards Peninsula, near Creeslough, just half a mile from The White Gate, on Sunday 7 September 1924 and a few weeks later was christened Bridget Ena Gallagher. But she was always called Bridie. Her mother, also Bridget, gave birth in a little cottage on the main road through Ards near Doe Chapel. Bridie lived her first year there with her mother and father Jim, as well as five sisters and three brothers. Her younger sister Maggie was born the following year,

The Stewart-Bam house on Ards, near Creeslough, County Donegal.
© G. KIELY, BALLYSHANNON

making it a family of ten, and they moved to a larger two-storey, four-bedroom farmhouse at Aghallative on Ards, set below a high ridge crowned by the pines of Ards Forest, which has been the Gallagher family home ever since. It was set up a steep rocky lane 300 yards from the main road along Ards peninsula, and half a mile from the 'big house' at the end of Ards, which was then the stately home of the landlords, Sir Pieter and Lady Ena Stewart-Bam. The big house was demolished in the 1960s and replaced by a new Franciscan friary and retreat centre. Bridie was to spend her most formative years in this wild and wondrous place at the foot of Muckish Mountain until she was twenty-four years of age.

Creeslough lies on a gentle green slope bounded by a few small lakes below Muckish with breathtaking views across the narrowest part of Sheephaven Bay, one of the many sheltered inlets on this beautiful Donegal coastline. Along with neighbouring Falcarragh, Dunfanaghy, Carrigart and Downings, it now welcomes a constant stream of tourists from all over the world. They come to enjoy Ards Forest Park, visit Doe

Castle, climb Muckish Mountain and marvel at the spectacular scenery of Horn Head. But for Bridie, from a very young age, her favourite place was that little beach on Ards, The White Gate. She played there as a child, playing hide-and-seek with her sisters and hunting for cockles. Often she just sat on the rocks looking wistfully up the bay towards the dark brooding Muckish Mountain dreaming a young girl's dreams.

The Gallagher house on Ards provided the setting for a happy childhood in which laughter and music played a major part.

The Gallagher family house on Ards *c.* 1930.

'Our home was a big country house with an open fire in the stone-flagged kitchen on which everything was cooked, as well as providing heat. We had no electric, drank water from a spring well, and lived a simple but happy life. There was always someone singing or laughing and often too many people talking at the same time. Mother baked home-made bread every day in a pot oven hung on a crook over the fire. When the dough was put into the black pot oven its lid was covered with pieces of glowing turf puffing whiffs of blue smoke into the room. That beautifully warm sweet baking smell always reminds me of home.'

They were a hard-working family, of modest means, and all active in the local Parish of Doe, especially its sports and music. There was little to suggest in 1924 that this pretty little dark-haired girl of this large family would one day become one of the most famous and glamorous singers ever to come out of Ireland, selling records around the world in vast numbers, starring in many of the great theatres of the world, like the London Palladium and Sydney Opera House, and performing on television and radio shows across four continents.

Her mother Bridget (affectionately known by friends as 'Biddy') and her father, Jim, met as teenagers working at Ards House in 1902. This mansion was built in 1708 and was set amid glorious scenery by the shores of Sheephaven Bay, 3 miles from Creeslough, at the end of the Ards peninsula, looking across to Downings and Carrigart. Sir Pieter and Lady Ena Stewart-Bam, whose 2,000-acre estate encompassed Ards and beyond, right up to the outskirts of Creeslough, were the estate owners and landlords. The Stewarts, Lady Ena's ancestors, were a long-established landlord family and had houses in County Down (Mount Stewart), Argyle in the west of Scotland and Kensington in London. Biddy started work as a housemaid and Jim as pantry boy at the age of fourteen in Ards House. Jim later progressed to head gardener and Biddy became Lady Ena's highly valued personal maid.

'While working for these upper-crust people, Mother and Father learned a great deal. The Stewarts treated all their staff very well and with great respect. Before she married, Lady Stewart also had a beautiful house in Addison Road, Kensington and about 1907 took Mother there for a few years as her personal maid. Lady Ena was very fond of her, and in fact I only discovered many years later that she christened me 'Bridget Ena' in honour of Lady Ena Stewart. She returned to Ards when Lady Stewart married Sir Pieter Bam, a captain in the South African Army, in 1910 and met up with Father again. They fell in love and married in 1912.'

Jim and Biddy lived briefly in two other houses, first at Cashellilly, deep in the middle of Ards Forest, and then in a cottage at Cashelmore on Ards on the edge of the forest. When they made the short move to Aghallative up the road the cottage became the home of an O'Donnell family who became close friends of the Gallaghers.

'Their son, Willie, became a close friend of ours and a good neighbour. He was a frequent visitor to our house, or "raker" as we said in Donegal, and a great comfort during troubled times, always caring for us like younger brothers and sisters.'

Following the Irish War of Independence and tragic Civil War the Stewart-Bam family left Ireland, and their estate on Ards was taken over by the Irish Land Commission. It was broken up into lots, and given to the young families of the estate who, up to then, had been paying tenants. Biddy and Jim were given the large farmhouse and eight acres of land at Aghallative on Ards and settled there in 1925. As well as a large kitchen with an open turf fire on which all the cooking was done using a crook and big black pots, the sitting room and each bedroom had its own fireplace to provide heat. There was no electricity and so light came from candles and a Tilley lamp, which was used only in the kitchen. There was no bathroom or inside toilet. Bathing was done in a large tin bath in front of the kitchen fire and all water came from a well at the back of the house. Modern household conveniences now taken for granted would not appear until many years later.

There was a farmyard to the rear bounded on two sides by stone outhouses, with a byre for four cows, sheds for chickens and ducks, a stable for the horse, a hay barn with a thresher, and a store. At the back of the yard was a steep rock-face reaching up some 30 feet, fringed with gorse bushes and fir trees, at the bottom of which was the house well. At the front of the house there was a small rock garden with large stone steps rising 4 feet up from the lane to the front door. The sides of these broad steps were like two stone benches and were to form the platform for hundreds of family group photographs in the years to come, or

A rare occasion of Bridie milking a cow on the family farm c. 1938. She loathed the job of milking the cows and avoided doing it as much as possible.

just a place to sit and admire the wonderful vista beyond the fields below, looking down on Sheephaven Bay and beyond to Creeslough in the distance.

Jim had trained at Ards House to be a gardener. He bought up a few more acres alongside the original lot given to him. This included an orchard and garden in which he cultivated all kinds of vegetables and fruit. The ten apple trees he planted in the orchard were named after each child in the family.

'My tree bore crab apples – which maybe says something about me as a child.'

As well as working as a gardener, and later a forester, Bridie's father grew potatoes and corn on his small holding. When the corn was threshed in the summer, he brought bags of corn by donkey and cart to the big mill near Falcarragh for grinding – a round trip of 24 miles. Meanwhile Biddy was busy from early morning to late at night in the home cooking, making clothes, cleaning and generally organising her large family. The seven sisters did their bit helping out in the household.

'With no washing machines or modern conveniences we all grew up with each having our own jobs to do around the home and in the garden, which stood us in good stead as the years passed by. Nobody could ever say that the Gallaghers were idle.'

One of her earliest memories was sitting beside her mother watching in wonderment as she made little dresses for her sister Maggie and herself for Sunday Mass on an old Singer sewing machine given to her by Lady Stewart-Bam as a farewell gift. Biddy also made all her own jam, which lasted the whole year and included apple, gooseberry, blackcurrant, strawberry, rhubarb and blackberry. But Bridie definitely preferred working in the house to outside in the fields.

'I loved any job inside the house rather than outside. I always felt the cold very much. Maybe I just hated getting my hands dirty.'

As well as cultivating some crops, the farm had ducks, chickens, sometimes a couple of turkeys, five cows, a couple of pigs, a horse and a donkey. Bridie loathed the job of milking the cows and avoided doing it as much as possible. She also hated gathering potatoes on a cold October day after school.

'I had to gather them following the horse and potato plough. It was hard, back-breaking and filthy work. You certainly couldn't be fussy about your fingernails. I hated it.'

While they were industrious, the family were by no means well off.

Bridie recalled how, if she was lucky, she took a sandwich of bread and jam with her to school. On a Monday, there was often no bread in the house, since the Gallagher household frequently had visitors on the Sunday.

'My mother was so good natured or afraid to "let herself down" once or twice she would give all the remaining bread to Sunday visitors without a thought, leaving us none for Monday morning.'

So on the way home from school that day the young sisters would eat berries from the bushes along the road, especially sloes. Bridie and her sisters also used to creep into neighbours' fields to pick a turnip to eat raw. This was regarded then as a lovely treat, albeit slightly illicit. But she was also resourceful and clearly had developed an engaging personality at a young age.

'When I was about seven I used to call at two different houses on the way home from school, about half a mile apart, and ask for a glass of water. I knew full well that the two old ladies living in these houses would offer me bread and jam, or better still, bread and butter with sugar on the top. That would keep me going until I got home.'

At home dinner of buttered potatoes toasted by the fire with a glass of milk was the staple diet. Meals were very simple then. The girls and younger boys had meat only at weekends – usually chicken or bacon, but during the week there was always some meat for her father and eldest brother Jim, who worked with his father in the forestry. Bridie would laugh loudly years later telling of her mother sitting as usual by the fire, and her older brother John, the youngest of the three boys, rushing in breathlessly from school every single day and shouting: *'What is it today, Mam?'*

Biddy would laugh heartily, never understanding why he bothered asking since it was always the same answer – potatoes and butter. On a Friday this might have been mixed with onions to make 'poundies' as they called their favourite meal. Desserts, like jelly and custard, were only to be had on rare Sundays, when visitors called, or when someone in the family was sick. Bridie could laugh at the memory of her brother Josie, once sick with jaundice and crying: *'Why are you forcing me to have this custard now when I'm sick and can't eat it, when I never get it when I'm well?'*

There was some outdoor work Bridie loved. It was in the hay and corn fields helping with the harvest in the summer. On a warm summer's day, toiling for hours in the fields, they looked forward to Biddy and the

Bridie and her mother Biddy *c.* 1940.

eldest sister Nellie bringing out the tea with hot buttered currant bread and rhubarb jam for the workers in the field.

The Gallaghers were particularly fortunate as children since they often received 'hand-me-down' clothes from the wealthy Stewart-Bam family. Lady Ena was especially fond of Biddy, her favourite maid, and before she left Ards frequently helped the family as it grew. Any clothes

In the lane outside the Gallagher home on the Ards Peninsula, County Donegal, (*l–r*): Rose, Maggie, Bridie's father Jim, Bridie and Josie *c.* 1938.

given were usually of the highest quality. Bridie never forgot how she was once given a lovely bright blue coat with a white fur collar that her elder sister Rose had been given by Lady Ena. She was the envy of all her pals at school.

But the generosity of the Stewart-Bams was not just confined to the Gallaghers. In Ards House every Christmas they held a big party for the children of all the estate families. They had a huge Christmas tree covered with decorations and surrounded with presents for every child on the estate. The children gathered excitedly round the tree and picked their gift before the party, with lots of goodies to eat, started.

When the Stewart-Bams left Ards, the Franciscan Order purchased Ards House in 1927 and established a Capuchin friary. There were no local laundries or washing machines so they asked Biddy to do the laundering of their priest vestments and clothing. She agreed instantly. It was a great opportunity to supplement the family's income. But it was not easy work, especially during wet weather when altar clothes and vestments could be found drying on clothes horses in every single room in the house.

The family had a pony and trap, but Bridie was scared of the pony. Fortunately her younger sister Maggie could handle him well. There were very few cars on the roads then and when the friars needed to go to Letterkenny they had to walk 2 miles from the friary up to the main road to catch a bus outside the 'Rockhouse', one of the original gatehouses of the Stewart-Bam estate. One day, on returning from such a trip, Fr Andrew, one of the Franciscan priests, spotted Maggie and Bridie on the pony and trap on their way to deliver the clean laundry to the friary, neatly packed in a big hamper on the cart. Regarding himself as a bit of a practical joker, he crept up behind the cart and started swaying it back and forth, shouting to Maggie, the driver: *'What's the matter Maggie, can ye not steer that yoke at all?'*

He was doubled up with laughing at his own hilarity but the two young teenage girls were too terrified to utter a word and waited for him to go on his way. Bridie was frightened that day by Fr Andrew, but she was to become very close to the same Franciscan priest for many years, as he guided and advised her throughout much of her adult life.

If Biddy and Jim were away shopping or visiting, one or two of the older brothers and sisters would be left in charge of the 'weeans'. Theirs was a big spacious house where the kitchen also served as a family living room with its traditional dresser in the corner, full of plates of different patterns and sizes. Precious things were put in the drawer of the dresser or behind the plates for safe keeping. The children were always able to amuse and entertain themselves. There was no television or radio in the house until many years later, but everyone could play the fiddle or accordion, or sing and dance. All the girls had dancing lessons in Creeslough Hall on Saturdays. Often, bursting with all this talent, they got old curtains or bed sheets and hung them over the scullery door, secured them with two heavy candlesticks, and put the kitchen table in front of this, thereby creating Bridie's very first 'stage'. They put a chair in front and behind to climb up onto it. Each would take their turn at performing, with Bridie never having to be asked twice to sing.

In the spring and summer on fine days, the girls would go out to the big steps at the front of the house to skip, while the boys played football in the lane, or they would all race to the apple trees in the garden to play.

'We were like monkeys, we spent so much time climbing trees around the house and "walking the gates" – tiptoeing along the tops of gates like tightrope walkers in the circus. Many a fall we had too. Once we were out in the "planting", which was an area of tall trees beside the house, and Grace climbed this large elm tree, but clambered well above her reach and got stuck. All we could hear was her screaming and crying: "Get me

Bridie at the farm gate *c.* 1940 with her accordion. Her mother taught her to play the instrument.

down, get me down – my hip is choked!" – her knickers were caught on the branch.'

When there was snow or a heavy frost they would go up to a sloping field owned by a neighbour, and slide down icy slopes with skis made from the metal rims of old cartwheels. Some of the girls also went bird-watching, looking for nests, but never to steal eggs or destroy them – just to look. Bridie once found a corncrake's nest in the middle of rushes. The little chicks were black and dark brown in colour.

'I foolishly took them home to Mother just, in my innocence, to show her but she scolded me and made me take them straight back again before the parent bird returned. I hated to part with them but I knew better than to disobey Mother.'

On summer days, when the tide was out, the children often trekked down the lane and across a field to the strand of Sheephaven Bay to collect cockles and mussels. The boys would find wood and light a fire on the beach. They would boil the shellfish in an old can and have a picnic with bread, butter and scallions, and of course tea – there were no fizzy drinks then. At other times they would walk further to what is locally called Lucky Shell beach at the other end of the peninsula near Ards Friary. The older boys would collect dulse and carrageen moss for Biddy while the younger girls played in the sand collecting the suppos-edly 'lucky' shells. But strangely, being born and bred by the sea, none of the family could swim. There was no one to teach them.

In 1930, Bridie's paternal grandfather James Gallagher died. He was eighty-four and had lived with the family for a few years prior to his death, his wife having died a young woman many years earlier in 1903. His was the first corpse Bridie, then only six years old, ever saw, and she never forgot the sight at the wake as the old man's remains were laid out in the bed upstairs. Ever after she recoiled at any suggestion that young children should be brought to the bedside to see a dead body. She would shiver at the memory of how her mother brought her and her young sisters upstairs to kneel down by the bedside and say prayers for the deceased. The horror she felt stayed with her for the rest of her life.

Grandfather Gallagher was a lovely old man who used to go for little walks near the house, always carrying a stick. He left his stick in the same place behind the front door on his return every day. Bridie recalled, with a guilty smile, how one day there was a small muddy pool on the road in front of the house.

'I sneaked out with Grandfather's stick and put the handle into the mud and then left it back again behind the door. I then hid with Maggie at the side of the house under the trees to watch Grandfather's reaction. He came tearing after us with the stick, chasing us up into the fields behind. But it was all a bit of fun and he would laugh hoarsely and long at our impudence.'

Biddy's parents, the Sweeneys, lived 5 miles away in a remote cottage in Brocas, at the end of a long steep lane at the foot of Muckish Mountain. Bridie loved going to visit Granny Sweeney with Biddy. Granny was a friendly little lady who told the children stories and gave them little treats. But the girls were always a little afraid of Granda Sweeney.

'I think we thought ourselves a wee bit more grand – at least we had an outside toilet with a river flowing underneath. Nevertheless, whenever we got up to Granny's and got settled in we grew to adore those visits.'

It was not uncommon for neighbours to visit the old couple any night, sitting around the open fire telling stories and sharing local news. It was a byre cottage of one room, with a bed to the side of the open fire. Granny always sat on a stool by the fire.

'There was always a smaller stool by her side on which I sat. The neighbours, with Granda and his brother, Uncle Owen, sat around the other side of the fire on hard-backed chairs. There were no soft seats in that house. The bed in the kitchen always had lovely curtains, which were pulled across when there was nobody sleeping there during the day so that it was neatly cordoned off.'

The cottage also had a half-door so that when the sunshine cast shadows on the door her Granny could tell the time, almost to the minute, just like reading a sun dial. As for Granda Sweeney, Bridie never really felt close to him and always got the feeling that he didn't like children. She could never remember getting a cuddle from him. She recounted cutting the corn with him in the field behind the cottage.

'It was a slow procedure with a scythe. So we children had to hold a stick that was especially cut from hawthorn bush, and trimmed for the job, to pat stalks in place in front of the scythe that Granda swung, as he proceeded along to cut the corn. You had to walk backwards to do this, which was difficult, and if you lost concentration for a second and let the rod drop, Granda would let out a roar that would frighten the life out of us. You felt he might cut the legs off you at any moment.'

Bridie always proudly proclaimed the good education she received at Massinass National School in Creeslough. The teachers were very particular about grammar and diction, which she claimed stood her in good stead in her career years later. She loved school and was always near the top of the class at reading, writing, spelling, geography and Irish. She firmly believed that Irish people should be able to have the chance to learn and speak their native tongue and indeed, many years later in her sixties, she attended evening classes in Belfast to refresh her knowledge of the language. She made good friends at Massinass School, and one in particular was to be life long.

Anna Maria Kelly became her closest school pal and they remained friends for life. They played, sang, danced and played camogie together. At dances after camogie games, according to Anna, both of them became well practiced at telling over-romantic boys: '*You can have a kiss but no trimmings.*' They forged one of those rare friendships that seem to last no matter how little they saw of each other in later years. Seventy years later, with Anna living in Dublin and Bridie living in Belfast, they still maintained regular contact by telephone and letter, sharing their life experiences of all kinds, and once in a while would visit each other for a day of chat, laughter and sometimes tears for lost family and friends.

From an early age at school Bridie's singing ability shone through. If Biddy sent Bridie for a message to the nearest shop a mile away, she always chuckled that she didn't have to look out for her returning as she could be heard singing at the top of her voice as she made her way up the lane to the house. Even when she was about seven years of age, her teacher used to put her at the front of the class to sing for other pupils – she claimed that she hated it, but that could have been false modesty. Later she and her older sister Grace were asked to join the local choir at Doe Chapel, which proved to be something they both loved and enjoyed. Miss Cahoun, one of the two teachers in Massinass, was the organist and her sister Fanny was the lead singer of the choir. This was when Bridie's later reputation for uncontrolled laughter and giggling first came to the fore.

'One night, during October Devotions, the parish priest was celebrating Benediction and we had to sing unaccompanied as neither of the Cahoun sisters turned up, for some reason. So Grace and I started to sing the Latin hymn "Salutaris", but both of us started in different musical keys. We stopped and tried again but it happened a second time. We tried for a third time unsuccessfully, and eventually broke down with a torrent of giggles. It was torture getting through the rest of the hymns that night without laughing, but because we were up in the gallery nobody could see us. We always thanked God it was poor old Fr Gallagher on the altar that night. He was a civil old man who never said a word against us for our giggling. Nonetheless, we waited in the gallery after the service until everyone had left the chapel before coming down and then scurried out to the road home.'

But Bridie was no ordinary school pupil. According to Anna Maria Kelly, she was, in fact, one of the brightest in the class. The two pals excelled at all their subjects, so much so that both were offered extremely rare and valuable scholarships to extend their studies beyond the age of fourteen (then the normal school-leaving age for most children) and attend the Loreto Convent Boarding School in Letterkenny for three years. Sadly, and inexplicably, Bridie was not allowed by her parents to accept the scholarship, then worth £40 annually. Instead, they wanted her to go out to work and earn a living like the rest of her sisters. For whatever reason, Bridie never again spoke of this major educational opportunity denied to her.

But at the time she was, according to Anna, bitterly disappointed. Anna did take up the scholarship and later went on to nursing studies in Dublin and a professional career in health. Were Biddy and Jim wrong to be so short-sighted in depriving their young daughter of such an important chance to further her learning? The fact is that the cultural and economic realities for most families in Ireland in 1938 were usually more focused on finding paid work early rather than pursuing extended education, especially for girls. Bridie's disappointment was only shared with Anna, and no one else, perhaps to protect the reputation of her parents, whom she loved and respected deeply. But it explains perhaps why some thirty years later she went to extraordinary lengths to ensure her two sons received the best possible education. Her further education beyond fourteen was to come by a very different route.

Chapter Two

DONEGAL TO BELFAST

No more beside the sycamore I'll hear the blackbird sing
No more to meet the blithe cuckoo to welcome back the spring
No more I'll plow your fertile fields, a chuisle geal mo chroídhe
On foreign soil I'm doomed to toil, far away from Glenswilly

'THE HILLS OF GLENSWILLY' (M. McGINLEY)

*B*ridie left school at the age of fourteen and went to work in the local post office, which was also a general stores, near the chapel at Doe on Ards. She was paid the princely sum of three shillings per week for a nine-hour working day. The fascination of learning to use the telephone exchange for the small number of people who had a telephone really appealed to her. In her last year at school she went every day after school to work for an hour serving behind the counter. So the transition to full-time work was much less of a difficulty. However, the postmistress, Annie Hunter, was a tiny woman with a fierce temper who would often scold Bridie in front of customers whenever she did something not to her liking. Bridie never got used to that scolding and knew her future lay elsewhere.

But she claimed much later to have learned one important lesson in that first job. That was honesty. At the end of each day, she had to sweep up the shop and tidy the office after closing. One day she found a ten-shilling note and handed it over to Annie. Obviously one of the customers had dropped it. The next day a large man, who was not local, came in and enquired if anyone had found the note, a lot of money in those pre-war days. The postmistress told him that Bridie had handed in the money the night before. Much to her surprise and delight, the man gave her a shilling as a reward for her honesty – a fortune in 1938 for a young teenager. It was a lesson well learned and one that she never forgot.

As she grew into her teens her family on Ards grew smaller. The older brothers and sisters, like most young people in Donegal and Ireland of that generation, began to seek employment and pursue new dreams away from Donegal and Ireland. The eldest brother, Jim, after following in his father's footsteps and working in the forestry, soon got itchy feet and emigrated to England to seek a better life. He trained there and worked as a carpenter, settling in London where he lived until he died. The second eldest brother, John, went first to Garvagh in County Derry to work at turf cutting and then to Kildare and the Bog of Allen. Soon the lure of London drew him to join Jim and he also became a skilled carpenter.

Her three eldest sisters, Sarah, Nellie and Mary, initially worked in local hotels and guest houses. But soon, one after the other, they went to Dublin where they all secured better-paid jobs. Her other two older sisters, Rose and Grace, also worked locally at first until they too left. They went to Belfast to live with a sister of their father, Aunt Mary,

Left: Bridie at Ards House, near Creeslough *c.* 1940.

Below: Bridie *(left)*, and Grace *(right)*, collect the laundry from Ards Friary *c.* 1940.

who lived on the Donegall Road. They eventually moved to Scotland where they settled with their new husbands and were joined by Nellie, who moved there from Dublin with her new husband James after the Second World War.

Bridie's third brother Josie trained as a mechanic at O'Briens garage at Cashelmore, a mile from the family home. In later years, he worked as a lorry driver when a mineral mining company opened up a white sandpit on Muckish Mountain and shipped the silica, used for making glass, to the Pilkington factory in England from the pier on Ards. He later joined his father working in the forestry on Ards, married Bridget

Family and friends cutting the corn *c.* 1940.

Gallagher (no relation) from Cashellily and stayed in the family home at Aghalattive to care for Biddy and Jim as they grew into old age.

Bridie's younger sister Maggie didn't leave home until she married. She and her husband John lived for a time in Clydebank, Scotland, until they decided to come back to Donegal to bring up their family less than a mile from Biddy and Jim. Finally, Bridie's older sister Mary returned to Donegal to marry and begin a family. Tragically, her husband died while she was expecting their only child, James.

As a consequence, Bridie soon had family in Donegal, Glasgow, London and Dublin. It was a large and now widespread family indeed: her brothers and sisters were parents to over thirty children. Throughout her life Bridie was to see all her Gallagher family many times in her travels across Britain and Ireland. It was a great consolation to her to know that she had family nearby no matter where she went across Ireland and Britain.

Meanwhile, she grew more and more interested in music and sport. Apart from all the games played around the house, the four youngest girls in the family – Rose, Grace, Maggie and Bridie – loved to play camogie, one of the fastest and most skilful field games in the world, unique to Irish culture. Nowadays all the players wear protective headgear because of the obvious danger of being hit during play and sustaining serious injury. When Bridie was a girl, no such protective

Creeslough Camogie Team in 1941, *back row (l–r):* Lettie Brennan, Peggy Trearty, Mary Reilly, Grace Brogan, Maggie and Bridie Gallagher; *middle row (l–r):* Frances Brennan, Cathleen and Brigid McGinley, Teresa Conaghan and Nell Ferry; and *front row (l–r):* Teresa McGarvey and Anna Maria Kelly (Bridie's school pal).

gear was used. As a result, players were frequently injured, especially the attacking forwards. This was the role Bridie played well.

There were annual sports days at Creeslough and Portnablagh, which meant a big family outing. Her eldest brother Jim was a fast bicycle rider, apparently winning all before him locally. But her brother John was the star athlete in a rather more esoteric pursuit – the 'slow bicycle race'. He could balance – motionless – on a bike for what seemed like hours without falling off. Her brother Josie was a good footballer, but the girls excelled at camogie. They were very effective forwards and popular with the rest of the team and spectators for their flair and skill.

One day the Creeslough camogie team, including Maggie and Bridie, was playing the Gweedore team. It was a game with added significance in that the Donegal County selectors were watching the match to pick players for the County Minor team.

'The game had barely started when a big red haired girl from Gweedore tackled me and split open my skull with her hurley. That was me finished that day.'

Bridie recovered quickly but she never forgot (or for that matter forgave) that girl. But more happily at one of these sports days, she persuaded her slightly older friend Grace Anne McFadden to ask Biddy if she could go to the camogie dance – her first dance, at sixteen. Her mother agreed, as long as Grace Anne looked after her. Bridie was over the moon and went with Grace Anne and her own sister Grace, having spent all afternoon getting ready. They had great times playing camogie, travelling to different places all over Donegal. But as young girls, they really looked forward to the trips, not for the game or the big teas after the match but the camogie dance that followed. She loved the popular music of the time (Vera Lynn, Bing Crosby, Anne Shelton, etc.) and at these dances she soon began to venture onto the stage and sing a song with the band.

Her mother Biddy was a beautiful singer and would sing ballads of all sorts. The first songs Bridie remembered being taught were 'The Hills of Glenswilly' and 'The Little Old Mud Cabin on the Hill'. Biddy also introduced Bridie to the delights of the button-key accordion, which she learned to play quite well, but it never appealed to her as much as singing. While many of her family sang and played, Bridie always credited her mother as being her first real inspiration to sing.

Records of that time, while immensely influential, were rare to find in most houses simply because record players were so difficult to get and were very expensive for a family like the Gallaghers. But fortunately they were able to compensate for this disadvantage. She and her sisters Maggie and Grace used to visit a neighbour's house at Cashellily, in the middle of Ards Forest, the same house their parents had lived in when they first married. The girls had to make their way through the dark forbidding forest along a rocky path to the house owned by another, unrelated, Gallagher family. The girls, aged between fifteen and nineteen, didn't have a torch or a hurricane lamp, but as a guiding light used a candle lodged in a potato inside a jam jar held by a long piece of string. It was clearly not great and on more than one occasion the girls found themselves terrified in the darkness holding on to each other when strong winds blew out the candle. They would scream for help and usually one of their brothers or Mr Gallagher, the new owner of Cashellily, would come to the rescue, guiding them to safety.

'I often had nightmares about walking through the wood in the dark. It was madness, I know, but the fact was, the Gallaghers at Cashellily had a record player and records and, most importantly, boyfriends waiting for us. The excitement and thrill of getting there was irresistible.'

In the house at Cashellily they played records and danced for hours. There were always plenty of visitors, most of whom came by road on bicycle or foot from around Doe or Creeslough, and some even walked across the Back Strand from the next peninsula when the tide was out. The records were often played by twelve-year-old Bridget Gallagher of the Cashellily family, who kept the wind-up player going and changed old 78 records like a modern-day DJ while the older girls and boys danced the popular steps of the time – waltz, quick-step and, increasingly the American-style Jitterbug and Lindy Hop.

It was listening and dancing to the Gallaghers' record player that reinforced Bridie's love for music even more. The records were varied, although noticeably short on Irish music and heavily influenced by American music: they included Vera Lynn, Anne Shelton, Joan Regan, Betty Driver, Joe Loss, Bing Crosby, Glenn Miller Orchestra and the Primo Scala Accordion Band. But among all this she was particularly fond of a musical family group called The McNultys who originally came from Donegal but had emigrated to America. They recorded songs such as 'Killarney and You', which became a big favourite of Bridie's. Indeed it was the first song she ever sang in public and one of the first she recorded some years later.

Her first real stage performance was in 1940 when she was sixteen. She was asked to perform by Fr Andrew, the Franciscan friar in Ards Friary who, years before, had frightened Bridie and her sister Maggie on the donkey and cart. It was at a charity show in aid of the Franciscan friars on Ards held every year in the Creeslough Hall. She sang 'Killarney and You', 'Believe Me All Those Endearing Young Charms' and 'Juanita' as a duet with her sister Grace, accompanied by Hyodie Hunter on the piano. He was a brother of Annie Hunter, the postmistress. Bridie described Hyodie (his proper name was Hubert, but he acquired the nickname Hyodie because the children could not pronounce Hubert) as a lovely man whom she adored. He was obsessed by music of all kinds, and ready to teach or help anyone wanting to perform. He would often be seen striding across the strand on Ards from Creeslough, swimming or gathering cockles and mussels. Along with the persistent persuasion of Fr Andrew to go on stage and sing, Hyodie was the other important childhood influence on Bridie's singing, and he introduced her to older songs she would not usually hear on the radio with her friends.

'If you met him on the road he was always singing and would wave and have a ready smile for anyone. He taught me so much about music and song and made performing such fun.'

Ironically she didn't remember enjoying singing at school. One of

Bridie with five of her six sisters (*l–r*): Grace, Mary, Sarah, Bridie, Nellie and Rose
c. 1941.

her teachers would regularly ask her to sing the teacher's favourite song, 'The Moon Behind the Hill', which Bridie then hated. At that time, like her teenage peers, she considered it too old-fashioned. If she had any early ambitions of singing on stage, she dreamed of herself as a pop singer, certainly not a singer of Irish ballads. In fact, this particular song was later to become one of her most popular recordings (so much so that she recorded it twice).

She started singing in public more regularly from about the age of seventeen, encouraged by Fr Andrew, who could see she had talent, to participate in local concerts. Then she started singing at dances when local bands would invite members of the audience up to the stage to sing a song. Very quickly these bands realised that Bridie was particularly good. She sang songs other young people liked. She sang in tune and could sing comfortably and in time with a band, a feat that many singers found difficult. One of the band members, and one of her first boyfriends, Willie Kelly from Creeslough, recalled that when Bridie was at a dance the band knew she could be relied upon to come up and sing if invited. She had the confidence required and never had to be asked twice. Eventually, one of these bands, The Cleveland Quartet, led by her second boyfriend, Bill Gallagher, offered to pay her one shilling if she occasionally sang with them at dances. At this time one shilling was, for many girls particularly, a typical pay for one day's work. So a shilling for a night's singing was quite attractive.

The band, however, had to depend on Bridie making her own way to the dances, usually with one of her sisters on foot or, if very lucky, by taxi. The band's only transport was bicycles. Incredibly, they carried their instruments in all weathers on tiny trailers attached to two of the bandsmen's bicycles. Naturally this meant the band's travels were limited in distance to dance halls in the general area of Creeslough, Carrigart and Dunfanaghy. Bridie was undoubtedly one of the most attractive girls in the area and the object of many boys' attention on the dance floor. She had a reputation for great beauty, good dancing and sparkling personality. Willie Kelly fondly remembered her laughter as a special feature of her personality: *'She had a laugh that I could only describe as loud but sweet and never to be forgotten.'*

Willie also recalled, with a glint in his eye, the night Bridie agreed that he could take her home for the first time after a dance at Creeslough, which essentially marked the beginning of their brief teenage romance. This entailed Bridie sitting on the crossbar of Willie's bicycle as he pedalled energetically from the town downhill to the Rockhouse on Ards, where they would alight and he would walk her up the hill along Watson's Road to the bottom of the lane leading to her house at Aghalattive, in the hope, presumably, of stealing a goodnight kiss. There was no question of leaving her right to the door because, as Willie remembered, that would risk the wrath of Biddy.

Later, Bridie also sang with the Boyle family band from Dungloe, known as The Butchers (they actually had a butcher's shop near the town). She was now paid a few shillings for each night's performance and could even afford a taxi from Creeslough to Dungloe where she would stay overnight with the mother of the Boyle boys. When she was eighteen she stepped up a rung to sing with Paddy McCafferty's Band from Ballybofey. This was real progress, because they were very popular, not just around Donegal but in counties beyond, more professional, and they specialised in Glen Miller-type music, which Bridie adored. She managed to fit in these ventures while still working during the day as a domestic servant in a local hotel for just over five shillings a week. She left the post office after only one year.

In 1942 the Eamon O'Shea Travelling Show was touring Donegal and happened to be looking for a girl singer to join their troupe. They staged a talent competition in Creeslough Hall. The eighteen-year-old

Bridie hadn't entered the competition in advance but was in the audience that night. Bill Gallagher, Willie Kelly and other friends led by Fr Andrew encouraged her to enter the competition. So up she went and sang the Vera Lynn song, 'Yours', and promptly won the competition. She was mobbed by her friends and felt ecstatic at this dramatic turn of events. She won a small money prize but more significantly she was invited to join the touring show for a few months by Eamon O'Shea himself. Her immediate impulse was to agree. The opportunity sounded so exciting and romantic she felt she had to take it. But instead she told him that she would need her parents' permission to travel away from home, which would not be easy to get.

Undaunted, Eamon visited the Gallagher house on Ards the very next day and explained to Biddy and Jim how talented their daughter Bridie was, in his professional view, and that if they agreed Bridie could travel with his show, she would be cared for personally by his wife. In addition to feeding and accommodating her, he was prepared to pay Bridie seven shillings a week. This was a significant weekly wage for a young woman at that time. Biddy hesitated at first, but when she was told there was a close family friend, John McCarry from Creeslough, also touring in the show as a fiddler, she relented, confident that John would see to it that their daughter was well looked after. So off Bridie went, touring around Donegal and Sligo.

'I certainly got the corners knocked off me on that first tour. It lasted three months and I just loved every minute and learned so much. I had to take part in everything to do with the show – sketches, drama, even playing the drums when the drummer became ill or selling raffle tickets. The shows were drama and variety, and at the beginning of each performance a trio played while the audience took their seats. Every night I did my own little spot billed as the "Girl with the Golden Voice" or the "Captivating Crooner". But eventually I became very homesick. John McCarry, true to his word, helped me pluck up the courage to tell the O'Sheas that I wanted to go home, and they agreed.'

Back home in Creeslough she continued to sing occasionally at dances while working during the day in another hotel. While she was disappointed that her first venture onto the professional stage had been short-lived, she still loved home life, the dancing and the fun with friends, and didn't yet have high ambitions beyond that life. She continued to perform in the local concerts and in fact received her very first notice in a newspaper (the *Derry Journal*) in 1946 when

Grace *(left)*, and Bridie *(right)*, with boyfriends *c.* 1942 in Creeslough, County Donegal.

she appeared with Maura Briody in Creeslough Hall, again for the Franciscan friars. The local boys were certainly glad to see her back and resumed their competition for her attention. One boy in particular made a major and unexpected impact on her life.

He was Frank (not his real name) who lived near Creeslough. Frank and Bridie met at a dance in Creeslough Hall and soon became firmly established as boyfriend and girlfriend. But apart from not being a musician in a band, she knew this boyfriend was different from the ones who had gone before. She fell madly in love with him, as did Frank with her. He was handsome, smart, very courteous and kind, a great dancer, and full of fun and laughter – everything it seemed that Bridie had dreamt of as a future husband. He also had a good job with decent prospects working as a clerk in an office in a nearby town. Finding the right man to settle down with and raise a family, rather than any sort of career, was for most girls like Bridie the main ambition in life. It was one that they were strongly encouraged to pursue by family, Church, State and society in general. So she felt very special in Frank's company and began to imagine for herself a new life ahead. Among their close friends they fast became 'The Couple', destined for marriage. They went everywhere together and quickly found they had a common love of music and dancing, and a shared ambition to travel to faraway places. After about a year they both finally committed to the idea of marriage after Frank proposed. There were problems for the young couple madly in love and wanting to marry. It was Ireland in 1947, they were both in their early twenties, they had little or no money or secure financial prospects, and, most significantly of all, she was a Catholic and he a Protestant.

Ireland has suffered centuries of political, religious and economic turmoil. One of the consequences of this turmoil has been sectarianism, by no means unique to Ireland, but a feature nonetheless that has scarred so many lives. Bridie was a typical young person growing up in Ireland. She generally obeyed her parents, her teachers and, as a Catholic, the priest, and kept to the rules. She attended Mass and other religious duties regularly and conscientiously. But she also had a spirit within her that made her challenge herself, authority and society's norms. Frank was very much the same. They were both determined to marry and have their happiness together.

For the first time in her life she had fallen deeply in love with a man. She knew her parents would probably be unhappy that he was a Protestant, but she had a naive confidence she could persuade them that this good man was right for her. Likewise, Frank felt exactly the same. Sadly, they never actually got as far as announcing their engagement publicly. Both sets of parents found out what was happening and forbade the loving couple from marrying. No one knows why. The parents may not have acted out of any form of sectarianism, and perhaps may have feared the obstacles and even dangers that might lie ahead for them if they should marry and live in what was, and sadly still is in some areas, a divided society in Ireland. Whatever the motives, the outcome was clear. There was to be no marriage and the couple faced a dreadful dilemma. They both loved and respected their parents and did not want to go against their wishes, no matter how strong their feelings for each other. But they also loved each other deeply. The pressures on them must have been enormous. They were devastated. It was the worst kind of situation for a loving couple. They had little money, family opposition, and a community, churches and society that would never support them in marriage. So very reluctantly, and tragically, they went their separate ways, never to meet again. Whatever the reason, this beautiful, bright, ambitious and talented young woman decided her future now lay beyond the shores of Donegal and she left her home county. Frank also left Creeslough, a heartbroken young man, to live in Scotland, not to return for many years. Bridie left Donegal, Ards and The White Gate, and travelled to Belfast to live with her Aunt Mary on the Donegall Road.

She never again spoke with her family about this sad event in her life. In fact, writing many years later she simply explained her decision to leave Donegal in 1948 as being 'to go to Belfast for a holiday and perhaps to find work'. She made no mention of her love for and devastating break from Frank. Perhaps it was too painful a memory to recall, or perhaps she did not want her parents, to whom she always remained loyal and respectful, to be the subject of criticism. She had known much happiness growing up on Ards, taking her first tentative steps on the stage, and making good and lifelong friends. But there was also sadness – a sadness that she had earlier been denied an extraordinary educational opportunity and that she now had suffered heartbreak in love. She was to begin a new chapter in her life, determined to find success and happiness.

She caught the train for Letterkenny at Creeslough station on the old Lough Swilly line. Biddy, Jim and her sister Maggie were there to wave her off. From Letterkenny she went to Strabane by the Donegal Railway Company, and finally to Belfast by the Great Northern line, arriving at the Great Northern Railway station on a cold March evening in 1948. It must have been a long and perhaps sad journey. A young woman of twenty-four, unable to marry the man she loved, and now destined for Belfast, a large, smoky industrial city that could have been a million miles from Donegal in her eyes. She never stopped loving her mother and father and, despite the hurt suffered, had left on good terms. She left Biddy and Jim behind telling them she was going to Belfast 'for a holiday'. She was nervous and feeling very alone because she knew in fact that this was not to be a holiday. She planned to stay with her Aunt Mary to whom she had written three weeks before, and was hoping to get work as a domestic housekeeper like her sisters Rose and Grace who were already in Belfast.

She wept when she saw her older sisters waiting on the platform for her. The long journey had taken its toll and the anxiety and hurt from the events of the previous months, and leaving home, boiled over as the three hugged long and closely. Grace had moved to Belfast the previous year and was working as a housekeeper for a local optician, Mr Prescott. Rose was working for a lady in a very grand house off the Malone Road. To have familiar and friendly faces there to meet her was all that Bridie needed to help regain her composure and steady herself for a new life in this strange city.

The change in culture and environment was enormous. She had only once before been in a large city, visiting her sister Sarah in Dublin for a weekend two years earlier when she sang with the McCafferty Band at a dance. The tall smoking chimneys, large city centre buildings, bustling and honking traffic, strange accents, even the elegant gas street lights, were all a new and intoxicating mixture to this young migrant. But once she settled in Aunt Mary's place she soon adjusted to the new ways of living, guided closely by Grace with whom she now cemented a strong sisterly bond that was never to be broken.

Within only a few weeks Rose came to her with news. She had decided to move to Glasgow to be near her boyfriend, Denis Herraghty, who was from Dunfanaghy near Creeslough but now working in Scotland (they soon married). Initially Bridie was downhearted at losing her big sister to Glasgow. But Rose had more exciting news. She had persuaded her employer to consider taking Bridie on as her replacement. And better still she could have her own room and live in her employer's very grand house. Bridie was thrilled.

After a brief introduction a few days later, at which the employer, Miss Annie Harvey, asked a few questions and cast a careful eye over this young woman from Donegal, Bridie got the job and started working in Miss Harvey's large house in Marlborough Park South, off the Malone Road, for a wage of thirty shillings per week. The Malone area has always been synonymous with wealth and regarded as the most salubrious part of Belfast. As it turned out, the new housekeeper was especially fortunate to find herself working for a lady who treated her with kindness and fairness for over three years.

Miss Harvey was an elderly lady whom Bridie described later as very genteel in manner, constantly fussing about keeping a clean and tidy house, but who could be quite prickly and bad-tempered if she found work not done to her exacting standards. Miss Harvey would literally run a finger along sideboards and shelves to check that dusting had been done to the required standard. But she liked Bridie's promptness, enthusiasm and willingness to work hard, and quickly grew to like and trust her, so much so that she even took a motherly interest in any young men that the young housekeeper met on her nights off. So it was that Bridie got a good job, a comfortable place to live and a fancy address with a decent employer.

It had been a major transformation in Bridie's life, moving from a remote, sparsely populated, rural community in Creeslough to the large and bustling city of Belfast, living and working away from home and her parents, knowing no one except her two sisters and aunt, with no friends to dance with nor local hall to sing in at parish concerts, no beach like The White Gate nor green fields of Ards but dark, smoky, unfamiliar streets. How could she find happiness and joy here?

Chapter Three
THE GIRL FROM DONEGAL

Her fair charms without equal, from the Nore to the Moyle
Oh, sweet maid from lovely Derry on the banks of the Foyle.

'LOVELY DERRY ON THE BANKS OF THE FOYLE' (J. J. McCREADY)

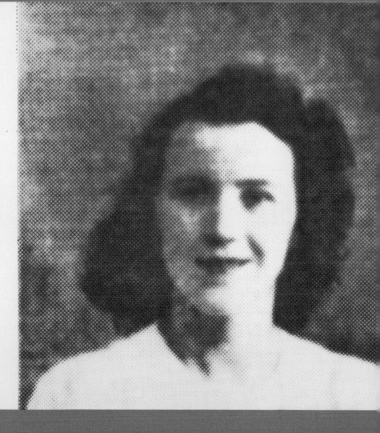

* **Bridie Gallagher**
The Captivating
Crooner
*

*S*ome weeks after arriving in Belfast, Grace and her Belfast boyfriend, Walter Wallace, took Bridie to a Sunday night variety concert at St Mary's Hall in Bank Street. Belfast had several very good theatres, but only one was open on a Sunday night. Bridie had already discovered one aspect of Belfast life that was very different to Creeslough – everything seemed to stop completely on a Sunday. In Creeslough, or bigger towns like Letterkenny, shops would certainly close, but sports and entertainment would be prominent activities for everyone on a Sunday. Belfast was very different. It had a much more puritan culture and was to remain so for many years with all 'ungodly' activity banned on a Sunday. One of the few exceptions was St Mary's Hall. It was owned by St Mary's Catholic Parish Church and was the only venue open for musical entertainment on a Sunday. Interestingly, the church was built 150 years earlier using money given by Belfast Presbyterian and Church of Ireland communities for the then quite small Catholic population in the city who had no church.

Variety music-hall shows were the most popular entertainment for the great mass of people in cities in the first half of the twentieth century and had played a significant role in preserving people's morale during the great terror of both world wars.

'I felt I had died and gone to heaven that night. I had never before experienced a truly professional variety concert on a proper stage. I just loved the colourful costumes, music, dancing, comedy and excitement of variety theatre I found that night in the old hall. My tour a few years previously with the Eamon O'Shea Travelling Show appearing in dingy parochial halls or even tents, paled into insignificance.'

Phone 66674

★

Bridie Gallagher
The Captivating Crooner

★

46 Marlborough Park South
Belfast

Bridie's first business card in 1949. At the time, Bridie was keeping house for Miss Harvey in Marlborough Park South. She used this address on her card with her employer's blessing.

She had been to many country dance halls and toured with a travelling show around Donegal towns for a few months. But to see properly lit stages dressed with sumptuous curtains, a smartly dressed Master of Ceremonies, sometimes five or six musicians playing a wide range of instruments in a band, hilarious and often risqué comedians, gorgeous dancers performing exciting and glamorous routines, and beautiful singers wearing evening gowns was breathtaking and thrilling. She wanted to be up on that stage.

She was well and truly bitten by the show business bug that night like never before. There were concerts every Sunday night and they were very popular. Bridie became a regular fan. It is fascinating to note that the audiences at these concerts were drawn from all parts of Belfast, not just Catholic west Belfast. Protestants and Catholics filled the hall without any difficulty. Indeed it was well known that some popular Protestant performers would often appear on these Sunday night concert bills using assumed names, to avoid criticism from their Orange Lodge, even though virtually everyone in the audience knew their real identity.

After several months, at the end of one of these Sunday night concerts, Bridie approached the suited man on the door who she thought looked important and just might know the manager. She asked him whether there were any auditions for new singers. That man was Gus Hughes, who ran his own printing business by day, and variety shows by night. Gus and his partner Billy Matthews produced the packed shows at St Mary's Hall every Sunday night. His nephew Eamonn Holmes was to become a very popular television presenter in Britain. At that time there were more variety shows in Belfast than Dublin, so artists used to travel north to appear in them. While Grace and Walter waited for Bridie outside, Gus took Bridie by the hand back into the hall and asked the pianist, who was putting away his music, to stay behind for a few minutes to audition Bridie. She sang a Vera Lynn song and Gus knew immediately that this girl was good. He told her he would let her know his decision the following Sunday. True to his word, and after discussing the matter with his partner Billy, Gus told Bridie they had decided to give the 'wee girl from Donegal' a try on the show the following week. Bridie thanked him excitedly and ran out to tell Grace and her boyfriend the great news.

On that first show in Belfast she appeared low down on the bill. She was a newcomer performing for no fee, singing a few Vera Lynn and

Bridie (*centre*) and cast in an early Belfast concert *c.* 1949.

Anne Shelton songs. She was received quite well by the audience, even though they didn't know her. Gus and Billy were very pleased and asked her to perform again two weeks later, only this time for a fee of five shillings, reckoning that the girl had the potential to become 'a draw'. The pianist playing that night was called Gerry O'Rawe. His father, Harry, also produced weekly variety concerts in Larne, Lisburn and Ballyclare. Gerry duly told him about the beautiful new girl singer from Donegal and a few weeks later Bridie appeared in her first of many concerts in Larne, again for a five-shilling fee – plus a return train ticket from Belfast to Larne.

The news was getting around fast among the agents that there was a new act in town. Soon Harry Baxter, the biggest Belfast agent, who had offices on the Dublin Road, heard the good reports about the new girl. She was very pretty, with a sparkling and quaintly innocent personality. Most importantly, she sang with a voice that was different.

Harry's agency ran variety shows and dances all across Northern Ireland every Friday and Saturday night and some weeknights. So if an act was chosen to be on his books, they could be guaranteed plenty of regular work. Harry lost no time and signed Bridie up to an agency contract within a few weeks. She quickly found herself in demand right around Northern Ireland with bookings nearly every weekend, usually now being paid a ten- or even fifteen-shilling fee.

She was still living and working at Miss Harvey's who, as it happens, was delighted that her young housekeeper had found early success on the stage. She herself loved the theatre and immediately decided to do what she could to support her talented young employee. She even

PROGRAMME

(1) **CITY OF BELFAST LADIES' PIPE BAND**
   PIPING, MARCHING and HIGHLAND DANCING

(2) **HARRY RAWE'S "VARIETY CAVALCADE."**

FRANK McFADDEN,	—	King of Comics.
POLLOCK & WILKS,	—	B.B.C. Musical Act Supreme.
ENA MACK,	—	Dainty Little Comedian.
CHRIS KANE,	—	Prince of Yodellers.
BRIDIE GALLAGHER,	—	Queen of Song.
JIM GILLESPIE,	—	A Wizard on the Banjo
BILLY BURNS,	—	A Scotsman from Belfast.
SHIRLEY CRAIG.	—	Brilliant Soprano
LILA EWING,	—	The Ever Popular Accordionist.

At the Piano—Gerald.

Show produced and presented by Harry Rawe.

(3) **CITY OF BELFAST LADIES' PIPE BAND in Piping and Marching.**

(4) **BROCK'S FAMOUS 'Crystal Palace' FIREWORKS DISPLAY.**

God Save The King

Concert programme from Larne Town Hall in 1949. Bridie is listed as 'Queen of Song' in Harry O'Rawe's 'Variety Cavalcade'.

helped make stage dresses for her. More extraordinarily, she allowed Bridie to use her Marlborough Park address as her contact address on a little business card that she'd had printed by Gus Hughes to give to prospective promoters or theatre managers. The thirty shillings she now earned from weekly shows effectively doubled her total weekly wages. She could afford little treats and extras unheard of in Creeslough like eating in restaurants, going to the cinema and, best of all, going to see real stars, like Jimmy O'Dea and Delia Murphy, at Belfast's Grand Opera House or Empire Theatre.

Then one day, romance entered Bridie's life again. She went to do her usual shopping for Miss Harvey one Saturday along the busy Lisburn Road. She noticed him with some friends standing at the corner of Tates Avenue. He was tall, handsome, smiling and smartly dressed in a white shirt, grey flannel trousers and a navy blue blazer. His dark hair was swept back, glistening with Brylcream, and, along with the other boys, he held a cigarette just the way Humphrey Bogart did in the movies, between thumb and middle finger, puffing blue smoke into the air and chortling at their coolness.

The next Saturday he was there again and, to her surprise this time, he shouted, 'Hello.' She blushed and walked on quickly, looking at the footpath and trying not to look at him, secretly excited at this good-looking boy noticing her. The following Saturday as she passed with her bags of shopping he shouted to her again. She blushed even redder but this time could not stop a giveaway smile creeping across her face before she hurried on. That smile seemed to give him added confidence. The next Saturday she was on a bus, this time heading for the city centre. *'The bus stopped just past the corner of Tates Avenue and I saw him standing there as usual. He looked up and spotted me at a window on the upper deck. I turned away instantly. Before I knew it he had jumped on the bus, run up the stairs and sat down behind me in an empty seat. He started chatting and joking and was very funny. Bob Livingstone was an eighteen-year-old apprentice coachman living with his parents in Cussick Street off the Lisburn Road, just half a mile away from Miss Harvey's in Marlborough Park. Then, without warning, he asked me would I like to go to the pictures. I was filled with a mix of excitement and terror, still a stranger in Belfast and very unsure of myself. But something made me say, yes. I think it was his smile.'*

They arranged to meet the following Friday night at the Majestic Cinema on the Lisburn Road. And for the next two months they met almost every Friday to go to whatever movie was on at the cinema. At the end of each night Bob would walk Bridie up the Lisburn Road to Marlborough Park and Miss Harvey's.

By this time in 1949 she was performing almost weekly on the circuit of concert halls around Belfast. Bob came along to see her sing one night at St Mary's Hall and just loved her singing and the buzz of this new discovery for him – show business. Soon he never missed a show, and was always by her side, carrying her bag, getting the taxis and generally watching over her like a guard dog.

He told Bridie he was unhappy at home and did not get on well with his mother. It had not taken long for Bridie to realise that Bob was a Protestant. But they didn't talk about religion or politics; just movie stars, songs, work and their ambitions. She certainly didn't tell him about her previous forbidden love for a Protestant boy back in Donegal and how badly her parents had reacted. But she could understand why he was unhappy, especially if he had mentioned to his mother that he was courting a Catholic girl.

'I grew very fond of him, and yes I loved him. He came with me to all the shows, and after a while it seemed as if he was always at my side; a part of my life. But it was a very innocent courtship. We were young, naive, and full of starry-eyed love.'

She continued working for Miss Harvey and singing at weekends around halls of all kinds in variety concerts, but now increasingly with Bob escorting her. This was either on the Harry Baxter circuit or for Harry O'Rawe in Larne and Ballyclare. Harry O'Rawe's daughter Vera recalled often meeting Bridie and other acts at the train station on York Street to give them their train tickets to Larne for the show that night and then travelling back on the eleven o'clock train that night after yet another packed show.

But Bridie was to go to a special show of a world-famous entertainer one night that had an enduring impact on her singing on stage. That was in July 1951 when she went by train to Dublin to stay with her sister Sarah and see the great Judy Garland perform at Dublin's Theatre Royal.

The theatre was the biggest in Ireland, holding audiences of up to 3,000 people. Press reports at the time recorded that it was the people in the audience who chose Judy Garland's songs for her that night, shouting up requests time after time. The *Irish Press* reported: *'At the Theatre Royal last night, the dynamic film star obliged with the old film favourites many having an Irish tinge.'*

Despite being this great and glamorous star, Judy was dressed simply in a black figure-hugging dress, and constantly engaged in good-humoured repartee with the people who had flocked to see her.

'Miss Garland got down to business, flung off her shoes and got her fans to sing with her "Over the Rainbow", and "A Great Day for the Irish",' the *Irish Press* noted.

Bridie was enthralled by her easy and friendly stage manner and how she chatted with audience members, wandering back and forth across the vast stage. Singers then usually stood in the middle of the stage with a microphone on a stand. Judy carried a hand-held microphone and roved about the stage, during and between her songs. Bridie was amazed to find that in the middle of her performance this great star was throwing off her shoes and crying *'My feet are killing me'* and the audience burst into adoring laughter and applause. She was particularly impressed that, in this vast auditorium, Judy had the ability and confidence to perform some songs accompanied only by her personal pianist Buddy Pepper, rather than the full orchestra.

Bridie soaked it all up and learned much that night, especially that Judy Garland had mastered the art of combining a great voice with sparkling personality, warm rapport with her audience, strong songs and good musical accompaniment. Now Bridie had seen Judy's act live on stage – one of the world's truly great variety acts and one that was to shape Bridie's own future stage act. She drew endless inspiration from that magical night's performance by Judy and used it to nurture her own stage act, honing it and fine-tuning it week after week on the local circuit.

Earlier in the year Bob had ended his apprenticeship and started working full-time as a mechanic. He and Bridie still went out every week to the cinema or a show, and he continued to go to all her shows to support her. Gradually they fell deeper in love. They were comfortable with each other and came to rely on each other for advice, help, support and tenderness. But they both knew they were playing with fire. She was a Catholic girl from the Irish Republic. He was a Protestant boy from Belfast whose father, Fred, was an Orangeman and whose mother, Lizzie, held very strong views about Catholics and Protestants even mixing together at all. They were living in a city in which men and women of different faiths who fell in love and considered marriage risked criticism, hatred and even physical violence from all sides of the political and religious divide.

Eventually, one day, while walking in Cranmore Park, Bob proposed marriage. Bridie was thrilled and extremely happy but soon fell quiet at the prospect of telling her parents, and Bob his. Then Bob dropped a bombshell. He told her he had thought about nothing else for weeks beforehand and had made his mind up that he was going to convert to Catholicism so they could marry. He knew his parents, especially his mum, would be furious but it was the only way he could see them getting married. Bridie was stunned. This surely was the greatest act of commitment any girl could expect from a man professing love and seeking marriage. She immediately said yes.

(l–r): Bob and Bridie with Grace (Bridie's sister and brides-maid) and Josie (Bridie's brother and Bob's best man) at their wedding on 6 September 1951 in Creeslough, County Donegal.

Bob began attending classes at Clonard Monastery in west Belfast that same month and completed his conversion to Roman Catholicism in June 1951. Bob's parents reacted very differently. His mother was devastated. She was vehemently against his religious conversion, and just as strongly against his marriage to Bridie. His father was, perhaps surprisingly, much more supportive. He had met Bridie and had quick-ly grown very fond of her. Even though he was a loyal Orangeman he viewed the love between two young people to be of greater importance than any religious difference. He was challenged by his own Lodge whether he would do anything to stop the marriage. But he made it clear he would not stand in the way of the couple. Bridie loved Fred, and in turn he loved her deeply for the rest of his life.

Bridie and Bob married in Creeslough on 6 September 1951, the day before Bridie's birthday. It was a sunny day and her old boyfriend Willie Kelly, who had just returned from working in England, drove them from Doe Chapel to a wedding breakfast in Dunfanaghy. Bridie's brother Josie was the best man, her sister Grace was bridesmaid and her sis-ters Mary and Maggie were in support. About twenty of Bridie's friends from Creeslough were there but none of Bob's Belfast friends or family attended the ceremony. Nor indeed, sadly, did Bridie's parents Biddy and Jim. The photographs of the wedding celebrations are of scenes of great happiness but with a tinge of sadness. The absence of both sets of

Bridie and Bob's wedding party on 6 September 1951.

parents was an aspect of the day that reflected the times in which they were living. The absence of Bob's parents was perhaps to be expected, but Bridie's parents' non-attendance, despite Bob's conversion to Catholicism, is more difficult to understand and must have been upsetting. But this time Bridie was determined to marry the man she loved no matter what objections were raised. She showed for the first time the independent mind and determination of a maturing young woman.

After a meal, some music and dancing, the happy couple were driven, again by Willie Kelly, to Letterkenny where they boarded a train to Dublin for a four-day honeymoon. They stayed in a small bed-and -breakfast there and spent their first day walking all around Dublin city centre. They met another honeymoon couple called Geoffrey and Anne, from England, and they went around everywhere together as a group. Both couples soon discovered that they were not alone in being nervous about starting married life, not least in sharing a bed with a partner of the opposite sex. They laughed and joked in the pubs and as a result reassured each other immensely in adapting to this new way of living.

All too soon the honeymoon was over and they said farewell to their new English friends. They didn't see each other again until ten years later, when Geoffrey and Anne came to see Bridie perform in a West End theatre in London.

The new Mr and Mrs Livingstone arrived back in Belfast and settled into a flat in University Street, which Bob's younger sister Frances had arranged for them. They had thirty shillings between them to set up

Bridie and Bob
on honeymoon
in Bray, County
Wicklow,
September
1951.

their marital home, having already paid one month's rent in advance. While Bob continued his work as a mechanic, Bridie had stopped working as a domestic for Miss Harvey, but continued to visit the old lady from time to time until her death some years later. She now divided all her energy between making their new home in University Street as perfect as possible and singing her pop songs in local concerts, although she was still a minor act on any bill.

Early in 1952 she discovered she was pregnant and they began to prepare for the arrival of their first child. With the small savings they had put aside from Bridie's growing earnings from concerts (typically at that time £2 per show), Bob put a deposit down on a small two-up-two-down red-brick terraced house in Carmel Street just around the corner from their flat. Bridie, of course, had to reduce her concert work and by the late spring she stopped performing altogether. On 20 October 1952 I was born in the Jubilee Hospital. I was christened James Francis, after Mum's father and Dad's sister. The new family moved straight into 61 Carmel Street that week, where we lived happily for the next seven years.

By Christmas Bridie was back singing on the concert circuit. The extra money to complement Bob's wages was a big bonus for a young couple in those rationed years following the Second World War. Soon it meant they could actually afford to buy a little car – a Fiat. But being away from home for a night meant careful planning to look after baby Jim. They had good neighbours next door (the Presleys) and friends

Above: Bob and Bridie with baby Jim (author) outside their home in Carmel Street, Belfast.

Left: Bridie with baby Jim (author) in 1953.

close by (Tommy and Evelyn Ward, a couple they played cards with for entertainment some evenings) who all helped out. But life was a hectic round of Bob's work by day, Bridie's weekend concerts, baby needing constant attention, Bridie dressmaking, Bob fixing neighbours' cars in the 'back entry', a house to be cleaned and cooking to be done.

And then one cold night in Derry, at the beginning of 1953, an event changed Bridie's singing career, and her life, forever. She was booked by Harry Baxter to appear on a variety show in St Columb's Hall in Derry. I was almost one year old and she had only recently got back onto the concert circuit after a break of six months. She had arranged with a neighbour's daughter to babysit because Bob was working late nights at the engineering works. Harry had told her the potentially exciting news that London agents might be at the show and it could be a chance for her to move up the show business ladder as the new Vera Lynn from Ireland.

She travelled to Derry by a taxi provided by Harry, with two other Belfast artists performing on the same show. It was a two-hour journey along bumpy roads for what was a monthly variety concert. It had been going strong on the last Sunday of every month since the end of the war. With her return to the concert circuit, Bridie was very popular on this particular concert bill, as well as many others around Northern Ireland, all promoted by Harry. Her nightly fee was now £3 and she was slowly gaining the status of 'minor local star'.

Bridie was still relatively naive and even innocent of the big bad world that she so desperately wanted to experience. The presence of London agents that night could be her chance to get to England, get a record contract and get better work in bigger theatres, but she was also terrified at the thought of failure. She had experienced some of the nasty side of show business where petty jealousies could often arise between competing singers or artists: stage shoes mysteriously disappearing in dressing rooms, make-up being 'accidentally' lost, precious sheet music getting damaged. Friends consoled her by telling her that such occurrences usually meant her talent was obviously overshadowing others and so she should be pleased.

Lelia Webster, her voice coach, had said the previous week that her voice was improving all the time and her programme of songs was very strong – just what would impress London agents. She planned to sing two Vera Lynn hits and one by Deanna Durbin in Derry. All had strong choruses and melody lines with a variety of tempos. But she would start, of course, with her signature song, which for some years had been 'My Blue Heaven' (recorded by Bing Crosby).

Three hours after leaving Carmel Street she was composing herself in front of the make-up mirror she had to share with the other four girls in her dressing room. As her time moved closer she felt the tension rise up through her body. And then what Bridie heard next filled her with horror. She could hear two local Derry girls singing on stage and they had started with one of the songs she had planned to sing. Bridie fell back into the chair and sat trembling, unable to speak and with tears starting to run down her cheeks. A few minutes passed, there was modest applause and then the band struck up again. This time Bridie slumped against the dressing table, devastated, as the female duo sang yet another of her three chosen songs. She could hear others in the dressing room around her tutting about unprofessional behaviour, and some patted her on the back in consolation.

'I was flabbergasted. How could they be so unprofessional, so unfair? Everyone's programme had been agreed earlier. I just saw my performance disappear before me. And certainly any chance of being spotted by those agents was gone. I had to get word to the pianist leading the band that I would change my programme.'

She ran out into the corridor for privacy. Looking out a window at the moonlit River Foyle she thought she was finished as a singer. Nearby stood Jimmy Irvine, the taxi driver, puffing on a Gallaher's Blue cigarette. *'I didn't even see Jimmy standing there but then heard him tell me those girls were just jealous and that I shouldn't let it worry me. And then he reminded me that some nights he drove me to shows he could hear me singing old Irish ballads. He urged me to do a few of the ballads instead. Nobody was doing them.'*

She thanked Jimmy for his kindness and quickly realised his advice was sound. At least she would be different from anyone else. There was nothing to lose now, anyway. Why not be different? She ran into the dressing room and fumbled in her bag for the old music book her mother had given her. She picked three good songs and at the concert interval asked the Derry pianist if he could do these songs instead for her act. Fortunately, he was expert enough to play anything put in front of him.

So, on she went twenty minutes later and surprised the entire audience and the other performers by not singing her usual pop songs. This time it was 'The Whistling Gypsy', 'Killarney and You', and 'Goodbye Johnny Dear'. She had caught everyone by surprise. But when she finished the first song the audience erupted with roars and cheers of approval. By the time she finished her third and last song the Derry crowd was ecstatic.

'I took two curtain calls and backstage afterwards there were back-slaps, kisses, hugs and thumbs up from everyone. Back in the dressing room I was shaking, but I knew something important had happened. The London agents never did come round after the show. That was disappointing. They were looking for a new Vera Lynn after all. But that night in Derry, I found something much more important: a new act. I would no longer be a pop singer, but an Irish ballad singer.'

Bridie's newly discovered stage persona quickly attracted widespread attention. Her new focus on Irish ballads rejuvenated songs too long forgotten, and attracted growing interest among audiences. Very simply, it made her unique among girl singers at that time in Ireland. She got busier and busier. She was invited to sing at the highly prestigious Memorial Show for the victims of the SS *Princess Victoria*, which sank in January 1953. She was in demand for concerts in parish halls, Orange halls and town halls.

In another major career step, she was invited to join James Young's

Show at the Legion Theatre in Bangor, County Down, in her very first summer season show. It was for fourteen weeks including rehearsals. I was nine months old, still in a big high black pram. Bob was working with the Clarence Engineering Company, earning about £5 a week. The summer season earned Bridie £7 per week, and more than doubled the family income. They were now even able to buy a second-hand piano, then a real luxury for most, but for Bridie it was increasingly a professional necessity for rehearsals and learning new songs. But such a busy life required hard work and organisation.

'I was always an organised person. So as Bob came in the door from his work I had his dinner ready on the table, Jim fed and ready for bed. I had my little case with dress and make-up packed ready to go out the door, and run for a city centre bus to catch the transport, provided by James Young, to go to Bangor. The show started at eight o'clock and finished before eleven. Then it was straight home and get ready for the next day. It was exhausting but worth it, and I loved it. James and his partner Jack Hudson had great taste and worked like demons on everything they did, so I learned an awful lot from them about production, stage sets, costumes, how to grab an audience and win their affection.'

Bangor's Legion Theatre was not very big, seating less than 200 people, but no expense was spared in doing what was necessary to present and produce high-quality shows. They spent hours decorating the hall and stage before the opening, and hired beautiful stage curtains. They also had flowers everywhere inside the hall, making it very pretty and welcoming. It was a full-production variety show with sketches, speciality acts and musical scenes each night. There was an interval halfway through the show when a raffle took place. All the artists, except the star, Jimmy, sold tickets for prizes, and the audience was always large and very appreciative.

Other performers included Jimmy Kennedy, the tenor singer who played his part in scenes and sketches as well as his own singing spot. There was Marie Cunningham, with whom Bridie forged a lifelong friendship. Marie had just returned home from touring England with the Big Bill Campbell Show and had learned much about the business in Britain while still only in her early twenties. She kept Bridie and others entertained with stories of her hilarious exploits touring in Britain. She and Bridie shared a little makeshift dressing room at the side of the stage with Jean Murphy. Jean and her husband Sammy, a double act billed 'Four Flashing Feet', sang and tap-danced. Marie played the accordion in her spot and acted in comedy sketches with James Young and Jack. A few years later, Marie was to gain international recognition as Ruby Murray's gifted accompanist, touring the world with Ruby at the height of her fame. All the cast was required to sing in the musical scenes. One night, as Bridie was taking part in a sketch with James Young, she took a fit of giggles and ruined his punchline – a cardinal sin. Apparently she was wearing a dress with a low-cut neckline and James had taken a sly glance at her cleavage and started to sing 'Down in the Valley'. The *Northern Herald*, in its review of the show, reported '*Easily the most popular of the supporting company was Bridie Gallagher, described as the girl with a tear in her voice and a twinkle in her eye. The dark haired Bridie appeared in a billowing gown of white and charmed the audience with her sweet voice. She received several well deserved encores.*'

That autumn Bridie was engaged by Harry Baxter to support the great Delia Murphy on a short tour of town halls across Northern Ireland. Bridie found Delia to be a quiet and charming woman, with a unique character. From Bridie's point of view, Delia was the original Irish ballad singer and had a style all her own with a lovely west of Ireland accent. She was in awe of this marvellous and humble woman, and asked her if she would mind her singing some of her songs. Delia was delighted and immediately encouraged Bridie to sing all the ballads she could find. From then on Bridie included in her act many of Delia's songs, such as 'The Spinning Wheel', inspired by the generosity of the woman who epitomised Irish ballad singing at its best.

The following year, 1954, brought more important developments. The most important was Bridie's second pregnancy. She and Bob discovered in August that she was to have a second baby in early 1955. As before, Bridie had to cut back on her programme of concerts, finally stopping work by November. But this was not before she had performed in many more shows, travelling all over Northern Ireland and even on a short trip to England with the James Young Show. She was honing her craft – learning how to engage audiences, work a stage, build a repertoire, refine her stage dress sense, improve her movement through dance and even how to make best use of make-up. She was now transforming from a part-time singer into a fully fledged professional stage artiste. All she lacked was wider recognition outside the north of Ireland. That recognition finally happened – in the form of Bridie's first record.

She had had one previous audition earlier that year at Waltons in Dublin at which she sang two songs for the late Leo Maguire. He was polite and listened intently, then told her nicely to 'go away, have her voice trained, and perhaps come back to him a year or so later'. She was disappointed and wondered if that was the end of any recording career. Then just six months later, one freezing Sunday night in December 1954, there was a knock on the door at Carmel Street. It was John Davy, who represented Mervyn Solomon from Beltona Records in Belfast and had brought along Dick Rowe from the parent company Decca Records in London. He explained they wanted to do a test recording with Bridie and some other girl singers and asked if she would be interested. At first she was downcast as she looked down at the bump beneath her maternity dress and looked back at John.

'I told them they must be joking. I was expecting my second baby. John Davy just scratched his head and said nobody would see me. It's a record after all. So what's the problem? We all collapsed in laughter. He was right of course.'

With only a little persuasion Bridie agreed to record a demo. Arrangements were made and a date was set in early January 1955 for the recording session. Bridie, now heavily pregnant, chose two songs that she loved. On a Sunday afternoon, she and Bob, having left baby Jim with his Auntie Frances, made their way to a hall that for most of the week was the Jewish Institute off the Antrim Road. There were no professional recording studios in Belfast at that time other than those used by the BBC. Mervyn Solomon, who owned Beltona Records, regularly got his staff to set up recording equipment in this little hall in Fleetwood Street behind the Mater Hospital. It was used for recording all types of music – pop songs, Orange flute bands, Irish accordian bands, and now Irish ballads. Bridie arrived to find a four-piece group of musicians led by Tommy James on piano, with George Newman on accordion, Billy McAlpine on double bass and John Maguire on drums.

It was all very relaxed. There was a short rehearsal when keys and tempos were fixed and the songs rehearsed. Then the English producer from Decca Records announced the beginning of recording. Bridie, for whom recording was a very new experience, was surprisingly in a very relaxed mood, and treated the whole process like a normal show rehearsal. She didn't think anything significant would come of her 'heavily pregnant' recording, for which she was paid a fee of £3.

As it happened, when Dick Rowe of Decca Records heard her singing

Bridie's sons, Jim (author) (*at the back*) and Peter (*at the front in the middle*), with friends outside their house in Carmel Street, Belfast, in 1956.

'A Mother's Love's a Blessing' and 'I'll remember You Love in My Prayers', he was very excited and reportedly welcomed the result as the 'new voice' they were seeking. It was Dick who first described Bridie as having 'a tear in her voice'. One month later, with her second baby due in days, she signed her first recording contract.

Bridie gave birth to her second son, Peter, on 3 March 1955. The recording company was quite prepared to wait until Bridie was fit and able to return to stage after her new baby's birth. Bridie and Bob also realised that, with her recording contract in place and growing demand for her to sing, they needed to do something to help with the two little boys they now had. The answer came in the form of Mary Kearns, a nineteen-year-old from an orphanage in Derry who was recommended to them as a live-in nanny by their parish priest. Mary soon became a much-loved member of the Livingstone family, staying with us until 1965. Bridie spent the next nine months focused entirely on her new baby Peter and her fast-growing toddler Jim.

But once she was ready, the single record was re-recorded with more musicians and released in April 1956. 'A Mother's Love's a Blessing' became an instant hit. Bridie had now 'arrived' on the bigger scene. In a matter of weeks, her name was being broadcast almost daily to millions by BBC Northern Ireland, Radio Éireann and BBC Scotland (which had a large Irish emigrant population, mainly from Donegal). Things would never be the same for the Livingstone family in Carmel Street, Belfast.

Chapter Four

TOP OF THE BILL AT LAST

It's my own Irish home, far across the foam,
Although I've often left it, in foreign lands to roam,
No matter where I wander through cities near or far,
Sure me heart's at home in old Ireland,
In the County of Armagh.

'THE BOYS FROM COUNTY ARMAGH' (TRADITIONAL)

*B*y the summer of 1956 Bridie's recording of 'A Mother's Love's a Blessing' had been released in Ireland and Britain by Beltona Records, a subsidiary of Decca Records, on a 78-rpm format. In January 1957 it was released as a 45-rpm single. The recording, with the other ballad 'I'll Forgive but Never Forget' on the B-side, received many radio plays and wide popularity, selling in many thousands, especially in Scotland with its large Donegal emigrant population. Bridie was in demand like never before, now from everywhere in Ireland and, for the first time, Britain. Bookings seemed to flood in and as a consequence her performance fees doubled to £15 per night. Her billing also rose. More and more, she was near the top of the bill and being treated as a rising star by the public and promoters. She still had no professional management but Bob did his best to negotiate financial terms with promoters all over the country. He relied heavily on advice from their friends in the business, like Marie Cunningham, James Young and Gus Hughes, whom they trusted. But it was becoming a strain, with Bob's lack of any real business training.

In June Bridie was contracted to appear in a new ballroom in London, the Buffalo Club in Camden Town, which had been opened

Bridie on stage at Dublin's Theatre Royal in 1956.

Bridie waiting to perform at Theatre Royal, Dublin, in 1957. She saw Judy Garland perform there in July 1951 and was delighted to be asked to perform there herself.

by a little-known building contractor called Bill Fuller. Her fee was £16 plus travel and hotel expenses. Four years later she was to renew her relationship with Mr Fuller, not in London but much further away in the US. This was a key development because it meant Bridie was now being contracted to appear outside Ireland in her own right and not as part of a touring show, such as the James Young Tour to Britain a couple of years earlier. She was now performing weekly in theatres and dance halls, and her fame was growing and attracting the attention of more agents and promoters, as well as newspapers. She was the rising star of Irish show business.

Then she got the call to perform on the stage of the Theatre Royal in Dublin – that same stage on which she had watched the great Judy Garland perform five years earlier. She felt dizzy at the prospect but took it in her stride. She journeyed to Dublin by train and stayed with her sister Sarah and family in Stillorgan for the week. Bob stayed with the children in Belfast where the eldest had just started primary school. She wasn't the top of the bill, but she didn't care. As far as she was concerned, singing on the Theatre Royal stage was a major success in itself.

Despite being relatively unknown by the Dublin audience, she proved to be a great success that week in July, mainly because of the Irish ballads she sang in her act. 'A Mother's Love's a Blessing' was still attracting almost daily plays on the radio, not least because it was an Irish ballad unheard for many years. These songs were not commonly performed in concerts then, nor played on the radio, certainly not since the heyday of Delia Murphy and Count John McCormack twenty years before. American popular music had dominated the airwaves since the 1940s.

In the audience every night that week was Anna Maria Kelly, Bridie's old school friend from Creeslough, who was now a nurse and married and living in Dublin. She was a regular and loyal audience member when Bridie appeared in the Theatre Royal, or any other theatre in Dublin for that matter, even though, as Anna recalled, she was invariably mortified when Bridie called out her name from the stage: '*Are you there, Anna Maria?*' Bridie would ask this with the whole 3,000-strong audience searching for the elusive Anna Maria, who was sinking lower and lower in her seat with embarrassment. She always sang 'Noreen Bawn' for Anna as it was written by her uncle.

On the first four nights of the six-night run, Bridie got a message from the stage door manager that a man called Nelius (short for Cornelius) O'Connell was asking to speak with her. But each night after the show she was rushing to get the last bus to her sister Sarah's house in Stillorgan. She hadn't time to talk with anyone. On the fifth night Sarah and her husband Paddy were in the audience. They called round backstage after the show to congratulate her before taking her home in Paddy's car. Nelius O'Connell was standing again at the stage door, this time with an enormous bouquet of flowers. When Bridie appeared, he introduced himself and asked politely if he could bring Bridie and her party as his guests for supper to the Irish Club in Parnell Square. It was then a famous and very popular club in Dublin, of which he was the manager. None of them had been to the club before and it sounded too good a treat to turn down. So Bridie agreed and off they went.

While they dined, Nelius didn't waste his time in making his bid to be Bridie's first professional manager. He talked incessantly about how

Bridie with her first manager, Nelius O'Connell, in 1956. © THOMAS TOBIN

he would like to manage and promote Bridie all over Ireland and Britain, his past experiences in the business, the sorts of venues he felt he could get her into, the sort of fees he regarded as feasible to demand, his contacts with newspapers and radio, how he wanted to work exclusively with her and no other artiste, and how he regarded it as essential that she had her own personal musical accompanist. At the same time they had a lovely supper and enjoyed the late-night entertainment.

About midnight, it was time to go home to Stillorgan, so Bridie thanked Nelius for his generosity and told him she would think seriously about his offer of management, but she needed time to consider and discuss it with Bob back in Belfast. He seemed very experienced, enthusiastic and full of ideas about how her stage career could blossom further. She spent all the next day discussing what she should do with her sister and then phoned Bob before the last show. They had agreed some months before that she needed to find a proper manager but were both unsure how to get one. Bridie was impressed with Nelius' style and ideas, and Bob was reassured by her confidence and no doubt persuaded by her obvious determination. The next day, before taking the train back to Belfast, she rang Nelius and told him she would be happy to work with him and would like to meet up again soon, along with Bob, involved for years in promotions, dances and bands, but never with a single artiste.

He was from Tipperary and had been in business of various kinds

Bridie's first professional photograph, taken in 1956.

for some years. He was well known in show business circles and had promoted many variety concerts and dances, as well as being the manager of the prestigious Irish Club, which was widely regarded as the premier nightspot in Dublin. He recognised Bridie's talent and potential to attract audiences, and wanted this young new singer to begin by appearing at the Irish Club before touring around Ireland and then Britain, where there was a large Irish emigrant population eager for Irish entertainment.

A few weeks later Bridie and Bob travelled to Dublin to meet him, this time for coffee and cake in the plush Gresham Hotel, and to agree the terms on which they would work together. Surprisingly, perhaps, it was to be based on a verbal agreement. No written contract. There was a simple understanding that Nelius would do all the bookings, make all travel and hotel arrangements, and take a management fee of 15 per cent commission for his trouble after all expenses were paid. He insisted Bridie needed her own full-time musical accompanist, who would have to be paid well, and also that she should only appear in the best theatres or largest dance halls. Bridie got more excited by the minute. She felt that her career was now really moving onto a new professional footing. She was exhilarated. And then Nelius dropped his bombshell.

He wanted her to start by coming to Dublin and appearing six nights a week at the Irish Club for six weeks to launch her career into the 'big time'. As the club was in the centre of Dublin and a popular venue for many important people in show business and the media, Nelius believed this would provide a sound and high-profile platform from which to launch his new starlet's career onto a higher level.

In the previous five years of performing, Bridie had never been away from home and her children for more than one week. It may seem un-believable now, but she had never contemplated that the 'big time' could mean being away from home for long periods of time. Her two sons were only four and one years of age. She hated being away for that week while at the Theatre Royal, but six weeks? She needed more time, and asked Nelius to wait until she and Bob had time to consider the matter. She promised she would give him her definitive answer within a week.

'It was a very difficult decision for me at that time. In fact it made me quite sick. I had two young babies and I had to face the prospect of being apart from them and Bob a great deal more than I had thought before. We sat up all night talking and trying to decide what we should do. We finally decided three days later that we should give it a try at least. We innocently thought there might be ways we could all perhaps travel together sometimes. More importantly, we thought it would mean we could earn the sort of money that would help give the boys the start in life that we never had – a nice house, good schools, good jobs, lots of opportunities.'

Many years later, journalist and friend Tom Tobin asked her if she ever regretted that decision. She thought for a moment and then surprised Tom. *'Oh yes. Many times, many times. The success and money was great, and maybe we would never have got all the nice things in life that we did without it. But while it was the right thing to do for my career, there were many times that I regretted that decision because I did miss so much of my boys' childhoods. I can never get that back or get used to it.'*

In September 1956, having given Nelius the answer he was hoping for, Bridie began her six-week run of appearances at the Irish Club and was an immediate hit. She attracted constant press interest during her run, much of it encouraged and promoted by Nelius through his numer-ous press contacts. It was, of course, exactly what Nelius had banked on. Soon inquiries from promoters all over Ireland came flooding in and Nelius started negotiating engagements in all the best venues. Quickly, the name 'Bridie Gallagher' became very well known and soon there were extraordinary stories of people travelling great distances to see her perform. One memorable example was the seventy-year-old man from Skibbereen who cycled 15 miles over the hilly roads of west Cork to see the new star singing his beloved Irish ballads.

Nelius hired pianist Thelma Ramsey, originally from Larne, to be

Bridie with her close friend Tom Tobin in 1957. © THOMAS TOBIN

Bridie's accompanist. New stage dresses were bought in Dublin and a new hairstyle created. Up to that point Bridie had worn her black hair curly and shoulder length. Now it was cut in the American bob style, which was to remain her basic style thereafter.

By the end of that year she found herself almost continually on tour with only occasionally a few days at home in Belfast. Nelius booked concert dates all over Ireland and, as Bridie's popularity grew and grew, this eventually led to her first concert tour in Britain with the Hawthorne Ceilí Band from Arbroath in Scotland. She was gaining more and more attention in the press while all the while developing her stagecraft. Having a permanent accompanist like Thelma gave her added confidence and meant that she was always able to rely on good musical backing wherever she went. It was one less thing to worry about in giving a good performance. The tour of Britain in March 1957 was arduous, with travel each day from one city to another by train, check-ing into hotels, finding places to eat, maintaining her stage clothes in pristine condition, keeping in touch with Bob and the boys at home by telephone (hers was one of the first houses in her street to get a telephone installed), having press interviews in each town, doing the shows and trying to relax in strange environments.

For Bridie, the biggest and most memorable concert at that time was in Glasgow's St Andrew's Hall. By then, three of her sisters had moved to Glasgow to live, and they and their husbands were in the audience that night. Bridie always remembered the tension of having to face an audience of 3,000 people, made all the more powerful having her sisters there, and knowing that the vast majority of the crowd were originally from Donegal.

'I sang a special song for them that night, "The Hills of Glenswilly", which was our mother's favourite. The result was I broke into tears half-way through, and so did many of the audience. I recovered and finished the rest of the programme. It was a very traumatic but wonderful night. I was so proud that my sisters could see me on that enormous stage, so far away from Creeslough Hall.'

But then the tour came to an end and an exhausted Bridie, Thelma and Nelius arrived back in Belfast only to find disagreement. Due to both Bridie and Bob's lack of business acumen, and a large degree of naivety, they frequently found themselves misunderstanding financial deals made by Nelius for Bridie. This led to a growing and persistent bickering, and a gradual souring of the business relationship. No one issue caused the split from Nelius but eventually by September it became inevitable.

'Nelius was a good man and good manager for me. He taught me many important things about the business and was the man who started my journey up the show business ladder. I am proud we never stopped being friends.'

While the split from Nelius was not anticipated or planned, Bridie and Bob also knew other management companies were eager to sign her and manage her career. She had privately been approached several times by Philip Solomon in Belfast regarding management. Philip – or Phil as he became known to Bridie – was the younger son of a family well known in business circles in Belfast. Several family members had ties with the music business in particular. His father Maurice and uncle Harold Peres founded Solomon and Peres in the early 1920s. Maurice and Harold Peres became two of the biggest shareholders of Decca Records and Phil's brother Mervyn founded Emerald Music, an independent record label, specialising in Irish, Scottish and Celtic music. Phil started his show business career in the 1950s as a publicity agent for the singer Ruby Murray, who reached the top of the UK singles chart with 'Softly, Softly' in 1955. Together with his wife Dorothy, whom he had married in the early 1950s, he also handled the publicity for concert tours by artists like Jimmy Shand, Jim Reeves, Acker Bilk and Chris Barber.

In 1958 Phil and Dorothy moved to London, where they handled the publicity for a wide range of performers, such as Gene Pitney, Kenneth McKellar, Louis Armstrong and Mantovani. Phil also started managing The Bachelors, a trio from Dublin who specialised in close-harmony versions of evergreens and were very successful in the mid-1960s, scoring seventeen British top ten hits between 1963 and 1967. Bridie was already under contract to Phil's brother Mervyn for recordings at Beltona (later to become Emerald) in Belfast. When Phil heard she was parting from Nelius he immediately contacted her with an offer of six weeks' work at £200 per week, or £30 per night – an offer she couldn't refuse. She was to tour Northern Ireland initially with the famous Scottish singer Kenneth McKellar but importantly she would receive equal billing. In effect, this meant her name would be just as prominent as Kenneth's, already an established television and theatre star.

Success followed success when Phil Solomon took over her management in late 1957. There followed three of her busiest years, filled with playing the biggest theatres, increasingly as top of the bill, international travel and new recordings, along with higher and higher earnings. He was the supreme wheeler-dealer with business contacts everywhere. He understood how show business worked better than anyone in Britain or Ireland at that time and knew how to maximise success for his artists better than most.

'I frequently didn't even know how much I was earning and I was surrounded by a small army of people who all had to be paid. I soon had to rent a suite of offices in Bedford Street, Belfast, with a personal manager and administrative staff attending to fan mail and general business, and a personal secretary, Mollie Neeson. Business was incredible, with audiences in thousands, of a kind never seen before in Ireland.'

Bridie Gallagher shows, with their vast crowds, were regular events, and in time became legendary. One venue in the summer of 1958 stood out – the unlikely setting of the village of Kilmainham Wood in County Meath. With Bridie's undisputed popularity, the promoter realised that the local hall was too small, so a large marquee tent was erected, designed to hold up to 1,500 people. But on the day over 6,000 people turned up and paid going through the gate into the field where the tent was. The crowd, most of which was outside the tent in the field, became so excitable when the band started up that the stanchions of the marquee tent began to lean dangerously to one side. The show had to stop immediately. There was a real danger the marquee could collapse with disastrous consequences. The organisers sent for the police to escort

Bridie posing with her new catch in Cork in 1957. Her husband Bob was actually doing the fishing! © THOMAS TOBIN

Bridie through the crowd and back to a local hotel while action was taken to make safe the enormous tent.

Disaster had been averted but how could she possibly perform now? Undaunted and keen to avoid the wrath of the crowd, the promoters manoeuvred a large flat back lorry, which had earlier delivered the big tent, into the middle of the field and then directed the band musicians to set up their gear on the lorry. Bridie was flabbergasted when the promoter suggested she sing from the back of the lorry. Fortunately, the weather was fine. She also realised, having seen the crowd, that this could be the only way of performing to the people that day. So after some adjustments to her programme and make-up she was escorted back to the field to sing from the back of the lorry to the crowd.

'It was a frightening but exhilarating experience. People said then I took it all in my stride but I certainly didn't feel calm at the time. I had just bought a beautiful pink sequined dress in London for the occasion – the nicest dress I ever had, ballet length with full skirt. In the scrimmage of people trying to shake my hand, the dress was badly torn – so there wasn't much profit for me that day. But I didn't care. Singing to that vast crowd in that tiny village will live with me forever.'

Five years later she was invited back to Kilmainham Wood by the local parish priest and given the honour of planting a tree to commemorate that extraordinary night in 1958.

Another enormous crowd appeared in Macroom in County Cork. Bridie checked into the local hotel in the afternoon to rest after a long drive from Dublin. Before long the small town was thronged with people. At the dance hall, they packed in the crowd like sardines. The police became worried for people's safety, but nobody was prepared to challenge the enormous crowd intent on seeing The Girl from Donegal. She was told the next day by the local police sergeant that over 5,000 people were estimated to have descended on the town that day for the show. It was rumoured that the crowds actually drank the town's bars dry.

Business continued to boom and Bridie appeared at venues all over Ireland and Britain while, at the same time, recording new material with Beltona. The most successful was 'The Boys from County Armagh', which was taken from her first LP and released as a single in late 1957. The LP was called *The Girl from Donegal*, taken from the title of another song on the album. Thereafter, with Phil Solomon's advice, she took this as her billing title and signature song. From then on she started every performance with one verse and chorus of that song. She was now introduced everywhere as Bridie Gallagher, The Girl from Donegal. But it was 'The Boys from County Armagh' record released in 1957 that was to bring international success and soon become synonymous with the name Bridie Gallagher. Every radio station played it every day, often several times. Indeed, one radio commentator in RTÉ remembered the day when a frustrated listener rang to complain and ask, *'Deh yeas only have Bridie Gallagher records in yer library collection?'*

One day in early 1958, Phil announced confidently to Bridie that he was going to put her on the London Palladium stage. When she laughed incredulously and said he must be joking, he was indignant and stated robustly he would bet her a car that he could do it. Bridie still thought he was kidding.

After Phil took over her management, demand for appearances became so great that she was contracted to different venues and promoters either individually for theatre and dance appearances or heading a full package variety show, complete with dancers, singers, speciality acts and musicians. Promoters would book the package show for a period of weeks at a time and organise venues in their own particular area of Ireland or Britain.

A very enthusiastic County Waterford promoter, Tom Tobin, booked The Bridie Gallagher Show, as it was billed, for four memorable weeks of one-night stands in counties Waterford, Cork, Clare and Limerick. The cast of the show was based in Dungarvan, County Waterford, for the duration. Tom combined the role of promoter with journalism and was later to become editor of the *Limerick Leader* newspaper and, along with his wife Kathleen, a very close friend of Bridie's until his untimely death in 1989.

Tom rented a most unusual dwelling place for the entire company to stay. It was a holiday home comprising three former railway carriages that had been put together as one long coach on a site near the beach and converted into chalet accommodation – the perfect 'digs' for a young and lively band of entertainers. So they christened it their Happy Holiday Train.

The girls occupied the bunk beds at one end of the coach and the boys the other end. There was a dinette and sitting room in the centre. Bridie was initially booked into a local hotel, but decided that she preferred the company of the show gang and moved in to stay with the girls in the Happy Holiday Train. She often talked of the many laughs they had during these four weeks. Since it was self-catering, the cast had a meeting at which it was decided that the boys would do the cooking and shopping, and the girls would do the cleaning and washing up. Tommy Moran, a wonderful crooner in the mould of Bing Crosby, and comedian Sammy Shortt, who were surprisingly very good chefs, agreed to do the cooking and all ten in the cast, including the star Bridie, chipped in and formed a pool to pay for groceries. There was a different menu every day. They had a good breakfast and always looked forward to the main meal in the afternoon, before heading off in the two cars and one Commer van to each nightly venue, located all over the southeast and southwest of Ireland, to perform. Sometimes this meant a two-hour journey, but sometimes a lot less. When venues were nearby they had more time to spend on the beach, playing cards, maintaining tans, or rehearsing new routines. Those four weeks saw the cast living together in a very confined space with surprisingly few disputes or arguments. They became a very close team of professionals. It was a closeness that was to carry them through five more years of touring together.

In those days, anywhere south of Dublin was new territory to some of the company, so they had some fun finding venues with very basic maps that often lacked a lot of local detail. There was Adamstown, for example, in County Wexford, with a beautiful hall set miles from any obvious landmark or road sign. The convoy circled around for some time before they finally found the hall. There were thousands of people there, with apparently as many outside as inside the hall. There were actually some people perched on the high windowsills of the hall peering in at the audience and stage. The show was a terrific success, and afterwards the troupe headed for the Happy Holiday Train, tired but very satisfied with the successful night. They got there at about two in the morning. Tommy Moran moaned how ridiculous it was. *'Big business every night's great. But when will we have a bad crowd so we can get an early night?'*

On another night the venue was Goaten Bridge, the only open-air ballroom in Ireland. It had walls but inexplicably no roof. The place was a terrific attraction for dancers from all over the southeast of Ireland. It was run by a man called Sean Maher who later emigrated to Australia. This unique ballroom on the border of south Tipperary was surrounded by trees. On this particular night there were, yet again, thousands of

Bridie's children, *(l–r)* Peter and Jim, in 1958.

people there, as many outside as inside. Bridie had to push and shove to get to the stage where the band had already been playing for some time. There was a makeshift stage made up of builders' planks, with crevices and cracks between the planks. As Bridie moved around the rickety stage during her performance, one of her stiletto heels got stuck in a crack. *'I was stuck and had to stay stationary until the song was finished. When I tried to release my foot, the heel broke. I continued on to sing another song undaunted, knowing my loyal troupe were creased up in laughter in the wings, until the same thing happened with the other heel. I pretended not to notice, but after finishing the song I tried to get free and broke the second heel. And now the audience were laughing. There was nothing for it but to join in with the laughter and, like Judy Garland many years earlier in Dublin, I laughed loudly and flung my shoes in the air. I finished my show in bare feet.'*

Phil Solomon had stipulated in all contracts that no hall or venue was to hold fewer than a thousand people, but as Tom Tobin did most of his bookings by phone, he had no idea what some of the halls were like physically. When he asked about capacity he would be told: 'Of course we can take 1,000 people. No problem.' When they arrived in a place called Quilty in the heart of County Clare, they unknowingly passed the venue three times. The troupe drove down the main street of the village and stopped to ask a woman where Quilty Hall was. She answered: 'It's up the road'. They went up past a small pub and again asked a man and he said it was 'down the road'. They decided eventually to ask in the pub – and there at the back they found 'Quilty Hall'. It was no more than a small extension behind the pub with four bare walls and little or no seating, and looked quite incapable of holding more than 200 people. The ancient piano was so out of tune that some notes didn't play at all. Luckily Kenny Thompson was on the tour and had his accordion. Bridie took a look at the place and rather petulantly insisted they were not playing there no matter what. The rest readily agreed (some even hoping this might be their long-awaited night off). The owner of the pub pleaded with her and the troupe to calm down, offering them all drink and tea.

While they discussed the problem, hundreds of people suddenly descended on the pub, wanting to see for themselves if it really was the great singer Bridie Gallagher in their town. It transpired they had not believed the posters advertising her performance in Quilty as being even remotely possible. They were all so glad to see Bridie and the cast that Bridie quickly realised they had no alternative but to put on a show despite the tiny size of the hall. As it turned out, it was a great night of fun, music and laughter, thanks to the kind-heartedness of the people of County Clare, helped along by the very liberal application of the licensing laws by the pub's owner. The following day it was unanimously agreed by all the cast to christen the hall 'The Quilty Opera House'.

Bridie continued touring, appearing either solo in the best theatres or with her own package show, guided by Phil's expert hand. No part of Ireland or Britain was excluded and as a consequence her record sales rose and rose. She made frequent public appearances, opening shops and festivals and even attending dinners of prominent organisations as a special guest. She was now the top of the bill. Wherever she went, large excited crowds could be guaranteed. Phil had managed to push her performance fee higher and higher to the point where the standard fee was now £100 per night, equivalent today to almost €3,000.

Back home in Belfast, Bob was running his own taxi firm and the boys were both at primary school. Mary Kearns was proving to be worth her weight in gold, looking after the boys as if they were her own and in the process keeping a happy home. Bridie was still able to get home most weeks for a few days, despite extensive and exhausting travelling, and valued that precious time with the boys, who were growing fast. But there were still challenges to be faced. Her popularity was confined to Ireland and Britain. There were important venues that she had not yet conquered. Phil knew that her music and talent was capable of transcending international boundaries and was determined to get her to the very top of the show business tree. His promise to put Bridie on the stage of the world's greatest theatre was about to become a reality.

Chapter Five

THE INTERNATIONAL STAGE

From Derry quay they sailed away and bade farewell to all
And now they're in America far away from Donegal.

'THE STAR OF DONEGAL' (TRADITIONAL)

*A*fter twelve hectic and exhausting months, Phil Solomon's promise became a reality. Bridie was engaged to perform at the London Palladium on Sunday 4 January 1959, a major highlight of her career. The news came as a bolt out of the blue to Bridie in October 1958. Phil had said nothing to her in the intervening months since his brag, as Bridie saw it, that he would get her onto that famous stage. She was thrilled beyond imagination at the news. She knew that great names in show business had graced the Palladium's stage, like Bob Hope, Gracie Fields and Frank Sinatra to name only a few, and what an important achievement it was for all performers. It was widely recognised at that time as the pinnacle in show business worldwide for an artist to perform on that special stage.

She was the first Irish ballad singer ever to appear on the London Palladium stage. This was long before the days of stadium and arena concerts, instant Internet communications and twenty-four-hour news and celebrity culture. It was an era when success and reputation in show business was measured less by record sales and size of audiences and more by the status of venues at which artistes performed. So Bridie found herself about to join a distinguished and highly select group of performers who had starred at the London Palladium, which a few years later was to include The Beatles. In both the public and professionals' minds it established a performer as a star. No other venue could be guaranteed to convey that accolade. For Bridie this really was the peak of her career, reached after ten years as a professional performer, and one she had never dreamed of as being possible.

It was a day and night she would never forget. She was nervous and remembered the build-up to it over several weeks being electric. In the four weeks before, she performed in concerts in England and recorded her third album of songs at Abbey Road Studios in London under the direction of George Martin (later to become best known for his association with The Beatles), at the same time as organising musical arrangements for her Palladium performance. The whole experience remained etched on her memory.

'We went shopping for a new dress and I tried on several in Young's of Bond Street. I decided on a beautiful ballet-length, pale green dress which was beautifully beaded. It needed a little alteration so we said we'd call back for it just the day before the Palladium show. To my horror, when we called back for the dress, they had sold it to somebody else. I was disgusted, but I proceeded to fit on yet more dresses and finally decided

Bridie opens one of many Cavendish Furniture Stores in Northern Ireland (1959).
© BELFAST TELEGRAPH

on another green dress. It, too, was ballet-length with a much fuller skirt, a sort of bouffant tucked in all around the bottom of the skirt, with a big red rose below the waist and off-the-shoulder broad straps. It was not a patch on the first one, and I thought it was a bad omen.'

She was booked into the Mayfair Hotel just off Berkeley Square. She had stayed there before on a couple of occasions when recording albums. Mervyn Solomon, Phil's brother, used to ask the hotel reception for a call at six in the morning so that Bridie's voice would be clear enough for recording sessions starting at ten. On the morning of the Palladium show it was no different, not that Bridie needed it, as she could barely sleep all night with anxiety. She remembered being so overwrought that Phil's wife Dorothy prescribed a comforting breakfast – gazpacho, a beautiful fresh chilled tomato soup, topped with fresh cream. Bridie was on call at the theatre for ten o'clock for rehearsal, staying in the theatre all day, except for a short lunch break.

She had to sing three songs, 'The Girl from Donegal', 'The Boys from County Armagh' and a song recommended to her by Max Bygraves called 'I Found You Out', a singalong pop song. (In Bridie's view this was one of the best recordings she ever made.) Her performance was set at eight minutes and she was paid £200.

'Jussi Björling, the Swedish tenor, was top of the bill and I was second top. I will never forget the lovely introduction Bruce Forsythe gave me, the loud roar when I went on stage; the glamour of the famous Tiller Girls dance troupe, Val Parnell and his wonderful orchestra, and of course the fun Bruce had with Beat the Clock.'

To her delight, Jussi Björling came up to Bridie's dressing room to pay her a big compliment. *'Miss Gallagher, you have a very rich and beautiful voice, so take care of it and I wish you luck.'*

She was overjoyed and honoured to receive praise from such a top-class singer. Bruce Forsythe wrote to her some years later recalling that wonderful night and Bridie's great performance. She had made a major impact, not least because of the large television audience watching the show on ITV (sadly not in Northern Ireland where the only television channel was the BBC; UTV had not yet been established), and from that night onwards she knew she had achieved what so many other stage performers had not.

The very next day, with only a few hours of sleep after the Palladium show, Bridie flew from London to New York with Dorothy Solomon as her aide and Sheba Kelly as her new pianist for her first tour of the US. Their flight from London took thirteen hours, which seemed like an eternity. Before arriving at LaGuardia Airport in New York, they first touched down briefly at Shannon Airport in Ireland, and later at St John's Airport in Newfoundland for refuelling. The three women were very tired when they arrived in New York, only to find themselves being met by journalists, press photographers and two welcoming parties representing the different and competing promoters who had booked Bridie for performances during the three-week tour.

Each party had booked Bridie into a different hotel: one had booked the Statler Hilton (now the Hotel Pennsylvania) and the other the Park Sheraton Hotel (now the Park Central Hotel). After half an hour of argument between the parties, it was finally decided that they would stay in the Statler Hilton, the hotel booked by Dublin man Harry McGuirk,

Bridie *(in centre, holding the bag)* sets off for her first US tour in 1959 with Sheba Kelly *(blonde lady to Bridie's left)* in January 1959. Bob, Bridie's husband, is on Bridie's right while Bridie's manager Philip Solomon *(front right)* stands with Vivienne Stewart, a dancer on The Bridie Gallagher Show, beside him.

for the first week of the tour when most of her appearances were in New York and New Jersey. Then they were scheduled to fly to various cities for shows before coming back to New York and staying at the Park Sheraton Hotel as booked by Kerry man Bill Fuller who was promoting the majority of shows and events on the tour for Bridie. Bridie had met

Bill three years earlier when he brought her to his club, The Buffalo in Camden Town, London, when she was really only beginning to make the grade and being paid a fee of £16. Now she was the star, straight from the London Palladium performance and earning a nightly fee of £200 plus all expenses.

Her opening show in New York was for Bill in the famous City Centre Ballroom, just off Broadway. So many people turned up she had to have a police escort to and from her hotel. The band that night was led by Paddy Noonan, and he ensured Bridie's accompaniment and performance was perfect, to the delight of the thousands of Irish emigrants crammed into the ballroom. That same week she also did many radio and television interviews as well as concerts at the St Nicholas Arena Hall and the Jaeger House Ballroom in New York for Harry McGuirk. She then flew on a whistle-stop tour from one city to another, taking in Boston, Philadelphia, Chicago, San Francisco, Los Angeles, Sacramento,

Bridie performs with the Martin Costello Band in New York on her 1959 tour. The photo was probably taken in the City Center Ballroom in Manhattan.

Bill Fuller, Bridie's main promoter in the US. Bridie always said Bill was a gentleman and she was delighted when he introduced her to Pat Boone in 1959.

Pittsburgh and Toronto, before returning to New York in the third week for final shows and public appearances.

In her teenage years Bridie had listened, enthralled, to gramophone records and learned songs that had been recorded by the famous McNulty Family. She was thrilled to find that on this first tour in 1959 she was to appear on a show with the same family group in the St Nicholas Arena, New York, but this time with her as top of the bill. The McNultys were an Irish family who had emigrated to America long before. On that night the McNulty grandmother played the concertina, her son and daughter sang and danced, and her grandson Peter played the fiddle and other instruments.

Bridie also found herself in great demand by television and radio stations for interviews. The Joe Franklin television show *Down Memory Lane* was a regular appearance for her virtually every time she toured America. His show was immensely popular with millions of Irish-American viewers and presented a great opportunity to plug new records and gain publicity for Bridie's personal appearances. Dorothy Hayden Cudahy had her famous radio programme *Irish Memories*. Her ancestors were from Kilkenny and she had played Bridie's records even before they met: they founded a firm and long-lasting friendship. Harry McGuirk himself, the promoter who ran the Jaeger House Ballroom, also had a radio show *Shamrock Time* for Bridie to perform on. So there was no shortage of coverage during any tours to the US.

Her itinerary was hectic and tiring but she still found time for a little relaxation and viewing other performers, especially on Broadway. What she did not expect was to meet some of her music and screen idols in person. For her at that time, Pat Boone was a wonderful artist whom she admired and she loved listening to his music. While staying at the Park Sheraton Hotel, near Central Park, Bill Fuller arrived one afternoon after Bridie had returned from Chicago and announced, in his broad Kerry accent: *'C'mon on now, lads, get yer best gear on, we're going out.'*

Bridie always said that Bill Fuller *'really knew how to treat a lady'*, and that when he brought you out on the town *'the sky was the limit'* (although he also struck a hard bargain when a contract was being negotiated). Bridie thought they were going out to dinner so she put on her best 'little black number', made popular by Marilyn Monroe. He had a big limousine waiting and they were whisked off to NBC television studios in the Rockefeller Center to find that they were to attend Pat

Boone's recording of his television show. Bridie was flabbergasted. At the end of the show Bill Fuller asked rather nonchalantly if she would like to meet Pat. Bridie went weak at the knees. Whatever her newly acquired status as a star, in her eyes Pat Boone was a proper star of global fame.

They went backstage and Pat came out to meet them wearing a bright red tracksuit. Bridie felt quite faint and had perspiration rolling down her face and across her hands. But she delighted to find that this quiet, genial star put her at ease very quickly. He was charming, kind and very unassuming. He even said he had heard a lot about Bridie's tour success. It turned out that he lived next door to Bill Fuller in New Jersey, and they often chatted together.

But there was a double surprise that night that stunned Bridie. Pat had Ginger Rogers as a guest on the show that they had just finished recording. Bridie had only seen her in films and, like so many others, adored her as a great actress, dancer and singer. Pat motioned Bridie to follow and they went into the actress's dressing room and found a fabulously beautiful woman chatting to friends. She turned out to be a charming and even humble woman. Bridie was fascinated by her relaxed appearance and down-to-earth style but, most of all, her fabulous beauty and charisma. She learned a lot that night about how true stars carried stardom and never forgot their kindness, generosity and humbleness.

'When Ginger teamed up with Pat Boone during recording she looked like a teenager with little three-quarter-length jeans, flat shoes and a little top, dancing effortlessly around on the set. She was the most beautiful and talented woman I ever met. She showed that night that performing was a serious business that required hard work and dedication, but also that stardom needed to be carried with gratitude and care.'

On that and the other tours to follow Bridie met many other celebrities, such Perry Como, Frankie Laine, Jimmy Durante, Johnny Mathis, Johnnie Ray and Johnny Cash. *'I had the pleasure of performing in Bill Fuller's Carousel Ballroom in San Francisco (later to become the Fillmore West) with Johnny Cash and June Carter in the mid-1960s. It was the most fantastic ballroom I've ever played. It was massive, with wonderful lighting, and an amazing golden ceiling. Johnny was great that night despite the turmoil in his life for some time before, and was very kind to me. He later married June and found happiness and even greater success which was richly deserved.'*

Bridie (*front left*) dancing the twist with the club's professional dancers at New York's Peppermint Club in 1960.

Sheba Kelly (*left*) and Bridie (*second from left*) with friends at the Copacabana Club New York (1960).

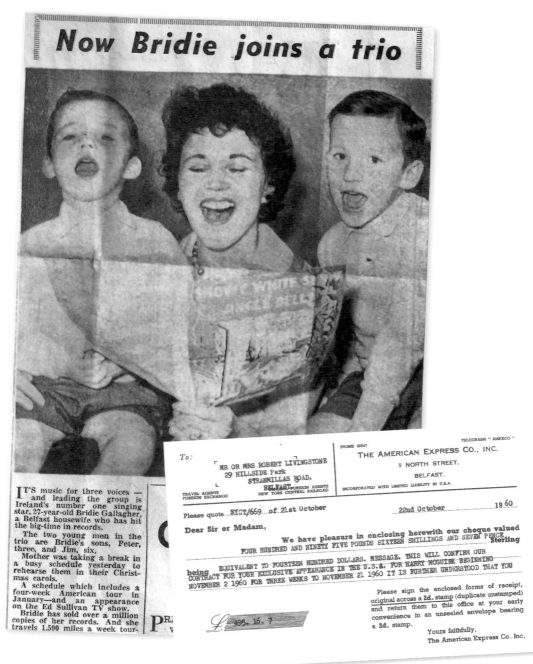

Now Bridie joins a trio

IT'S music for three voices —
and leading the group is
Ireland's number one singing
star, 27-year-old Bridie Gallagher,
a Belfast housewife who has hit
the big-time in records.

The two young men in the
trio are Bridie's sons, Peter,
three, and Jim, six.

Mother was taking a break in
a busy schedule yesterday to
rehearse them in their Christmas carols.

A schedule which includes a
four-week American tour in
January—and an appearance
on the Ed Sullivan TV show.

Bridie has sold over a million
copies of her records. And she
travels 1,500 miles a week tour-

PHONE 26847   TELEGRAMS " AMEXCO "

THE AMERICAN EXPRESS CO., INC.

9 NORTH STREET,

BELFAST.

To:
MR OR MRS ROBERT LIVINGSTONE
29 HILLSIDE Park
STRANMILLIS ROAD,
BELFAST.

TRAVEL AGENTS   FOREIGN AGENTS
FOREIGN EXCHANGE   NEW YORK CENTRAL RAILROAD   INCORPORATED WITH LIMITED LIABILITY IN U.S.A.

Please quote NYCT/669 of 21st October   22nd October   19 60

Dear Sir or Madam,

We have pleasure in enclosing herewith our cheque valued
FOUR HUNDRED AND NINETY FIVE POUNDS SIXTEEN SHILLINGS AND SEVEN PENCE Sterling

being EQUIVALENT TO FOURTEEN HUNDRED DOLLARS. MESSAGE. THIS WILL CONFIRM OUR
CONTRACT FOR YOUR EXCLUSIVE APPEARANCE IN THE U.S.A. FOR HARRY MCGUIRK BEGINNING
NOVEMBER 2 1960 FOR THREE WEEKS TO NOVEMBER 21 1960 IT IS FURTHER UNDERSTOOD THAT YOU

Please sign the enclosed forms of receipt,
original across a 2d. stamp (duplicate unstamped)
and return them to this office at your early
convenience in an unsealed envelope bearing
a 2d. stamp.

Yours faithfully,
The American Express Co. Inc.

Above left: This article in the *Sunday Express* in 1958 featured a photo of Bridie with
her two sons. It was pre-publicity for her appearance at the London Palladium in
January 1959. © SUNDAY EXPRESS

Above right: Advance payment from Harry McGuirk, a New York promoter, for
Bridie's second US tour in 1960. This was the first advance Bridie ever received.

London Metropolitan Music Hall on Edgware Road. It later became known as the Metropolitan Theatre.

Bridie would often recall, on her second visit to the States in 1960, meeting up with the Clipper Carlton Showband from Ireland who were on tour at the same time.

'We all had a night off so Hugo Quinn and the boys took me out to dinner in the Copacabana Night Club where Jimmy Durant was doing cabaret. What a show he put on, surrounded by eight girl dancers. We had some great laughs.'

In the total of fifteen trips to North America she played in venues right across the US and Canada, always to great acclaim. On her second visit in 1960, the promoter was again Harry McGuirk. This trip stood out for one important reason: it was the first time she received a down-payment in advance of the three-week trip, a total of £495, equivalent today to more than €12,000. Another memorable highlight was on her fourth tour in 1963, when she was honoured to lead the St Patrick's Day parade in Chicago.

After that first US tour in 1959 she returned to Britain to spend a couple of days in London on her way home to Belfast, to prepare for a four-week season at the London Metropolitan Theatre, which was to be followed by a nationwide tour of all the great theatres across Scotland and England. Somehow or other she had to fit in a recording session for an LP in London as well. Wherever she appeared there were capacity audiences and rave reviews. The tour ended with another wonderful climax – her first appearance at the Royal Albert Hall, London, for which she was to gain the record for the biggest ever audience – 7,500 happy people. Standing room was allowed on the night, and it was needed. One of Bridie's closest friends, Vivienne McMaster, who led the dance troupe in her show, recalled how the police had to bring mounted officers to marshal the crowds trying to get in to see Bridie that St Patrick's night.

While the London Palladium just three months earlier was the obvious pinnacle of her career, as it would be for any artiste then, she never forgot how nervous she was at the Albert Hall. There were so many supporting artistes on the show that it seemed to go on forever. All the artistes, groups, musicians and dancers went down so well with the audience that their performance times were greatly extended by applause.

Phil Solomon came into her dressing room to check if everything was all right. *'Of course everything is all right but for God's sake please get me on to do my spot as my nerves cannot stand it any longer.'*

Phil thought for a moment, and went to see Deirdre O'Callaghan in her dressing room. Deirdre was a beautiful and talented harp player and singer, performing very quiet and delicate traditional ballads. As she was next on the programme, he instructed her to *'Get on, Deirdre, and play that harp like it were a banjo until I get Bridie on.'*

Poor Deirdre must have been horrified. But she was a great professional and never flinched. She went on and did a much condensed version of her act.

Bridie finally got on stage to be met with thunderous applause in the great dome-like hall with smiling and cheering faces on all sides. It was fantastic and Bridie performed her best show ever, in her view.

'Although I appeared at the Albert Hall a few times since, it has never been quite the same. All of Ireland seemed to have been there that St Patrick's night in 1959. Although I was nervous before the performance, once I was on stage the enormous crowd carried me forward and I could have sung all night.'

Phil Solomon was undoubtedly her most influential and dynamic manager. Their professional relationship lasted only three years, but in that brief period Phil, a master of public relations and business negotiation, catapulted her to the greatest heights in show business, securing her first major concerts in every city in Ireland and Britain, including the Albert Hall, her first great tours of the US and, most significantly,

Bridie on stage in Ireland in 1960.

her appearance at the London Palladium in 1959. But Phil was not an easy man to work with. He demanded excellence at all times, was a stickler for punctuality, told Bridie very little about contracts signed on her behalf until after the event, and could be ruthless in pursuing the best deals with promoters. Bridie never viewed this as to her detriment

Bridie smiles while making an appearance in the US in 1961.

as she realised that his business acumen was what was needed to be successful in a very competitive business. The regrettable split from Phil started in late 1959 but it was 1960 before it was finalised. It was unique in that it occurred in a blaze of publicity, court action and controversy.

It was October 1959 and Bridie was to appear as the star at the Theatre Royal, Dublin. The theatre was fully booked out weeks in advance with its capacity seating of around 3,000. There were two shows on the day in question, one in the afternoon and one at night, with cine-variety in between. A new act from England had been booked onto the show by Phil with Bridie as top of the bill. It was Billy Fury with his band, then an up-and-coming pop act from London. He hadn't been to Ireland before but had already achieved some limited success in England, which had been going through the early rock 'n' roll phenomenon, and Phil was convinced that he would attract an important new young audience that would be to Bridie's advantage. Indeed Bridie herself was excited at the prospect of having this rising young pop star on the same bill.

After the afternoon matinee show, the manager of the theatre came to Bridie's dressing room in a very agitated state. He complained that Billy Fury was 'being a very naughty boy and bringing too much explicitly sexual behaviour into his act'. Bridie had only met Billy the day before at rehearsals, which were quite brief and did not involve anyone doing a complete act; it was more an opportunity to check their sound and stage settings. The manager made it quite clear to Bridie that if Billy Fury's act continued in this manner, he would pull the curtains on him. Bridie didn't know what to do but simply said she was not responsible for other acts and suggested he contact Phil Solomon.

When Billy was personally warned by the theatre management, he phoned his personal manager Larry Parnes in London, who instructed him to continue doing his act as usual. And that night he did exactly that. The theatre manager, as promised, duly pulled the curtain down in the middle of his act. Uproar ensued, among Billy and his band, and indeed his young Dublin fans in the audience.

Billy Fury's act at that time included him performing a song lying down on the stage – and, according to the manager, simulating the sex act. In 1960s Dublin, and probably most venues in Britain, this was viewed as very bad taste and not acceptable by the standards of the day. People had seen Elvis and Cliff Richard 'grinding their hips' but Billy's antics appeared much more explicit.

The fateful decision was nothing to do with Bridie, but since she was the star, everyone wanted to know what she thought, and what she was going to do, not least because a few days later the same show was scheduled to open in Cork City Hall. As it happened, Bridie was on good terms with Billy and his group, even though she hadn't seen much of them before. After rehearsals earlier in the day, Billy had come up to her dressing room and presented her with a beautiful box of lace hankies embroidered with red roses. She was very touched by his kindness and thoughtfulness, especially from such a young man.

The next day, the newspapers all had big headlines such as 'BRIDIE IS FURIOUS' and so forth. People assumed the curtains had been pulled on her orders. In the public's mind, or more accurately that of the newspaper editors, she was the top of the bill, it was her show, and so she was responsible for anything that happened. In the days that followed, her office in Belfast received scores of phone calls and letters with mostly favourable comments about her, mainly from people she did not even know. She had letters from priests, nuns and politicians, as well as genuine fans. They were all commending her for not wishing to associate herself with such a 'tasteless and offensive act', despite the fact that she had actually done nothing. It all became very difficult, confusing and extremely upsetting. They were scheduled for Cork City Hall later that week, but with all the letters and the press reports, she was in a quandary as to the best course to take.

Back in Dublin's Gresham Hotel, where they were staying the next night, there was a lot of animosity for some hours between Phil and Bridie, with Bob at her side. She questioned Phil how the show could possibly go to Cork with all the bad publicity received and face further upheaval. She assumed that, after the fuss died down, Billy Fury would be back in slightly more liberal England where his antics might just be acceptable, but she would be left living and working in conservative Ireland, and even more puritanical Belfast, where such behaviour by any singer on stage was definitely regarded as unacceptable. She also felt embarrassed herself and, without being moralistic about it, she did personally find Billy's antics unacceptable, although she thought he was a beautiful singer.

At the very mention of not doing the Cork show, Phil exploded, warning Bridie she would not get paid one penny for any of the shows if she didn't go to Cork.

The next morning Bridie and Bob retreated to their Belfast home to think things through. It was a very serious dilemma and one that needed cool heads, away from the heat of battle. Their house was besieged by the press, all wanting to know if she would go to Cork and, more importantly, if she would do the week-long Grand Opera House show in Belfast a couple of weeks later in which Billy had also been billed in support of Bridie. It was a big story and a big problem for Bridie.

Twenty-four hours later, having sat late into the night discussing the matter with Bob, and having taken advice from trusted friends and her solicitor, she made her fateful decision. She wouldn't go to Cork. It was a momentous decision for her. It was to be the first and only occasion in her long career that she refused to perform a show for which she had been contracted. She was deeply traumatised by the whole affair and was wracked with misplaced guilt for a long time about her decision. Most of all, she felt embarrassed and hurt for the people of Cork that she would not be there. Indeed, she still felt that sorrow and pain thirty years later when she wrote about these events in her journal, and never stopped feeling sorry for the people who had been disappointed. This was in spite of the fact that at the time she received very supportive letters from fans, politicians and clergy, congratulating her 'on her stand', and a letter from a police commissioner in Cork assuring her of a great welcome back to Cork any time.

In Cork the City Hall was full and Billy Fury was there along with other acts, but no Bridie Gallagher. There was, not surprisingly, more uproar and the people who had turned up demanded their money back. The show was cancelled. It was a disaster and Phil immediately issued a statement that he would sue Bridie for significant damages amounting to many thousands of pounds.

Back in Belfast the *Belfast Telegraph* and other papers reported the events and posed the question would Bridie appear at the Grand Opera House the following week, given that Billy Fury was also billed on the same show. As it happened, his management had obviously had enough and ordered Billy back to England. Bridie duly did the two-week-long show without Billy to sell-out audiences and great acclaim. It was clear that the people's sympathies were with her and not Billy or Bridie's management. It is interesting to note that Billy's act continued to attract adverse publicity for some months until eventually, as reported in English newspapers, he agreed to tone it down. Soon after, his career and fame soared with many great hit records following.

Legal proceedings were initiated by Phil against Bridie and the case lasted almost a year, until finally, in October 1960, it was settled out of court on terms agreeable to both parties. Naturally she did not get paid for the Cork show and agreed to pay her own legal costs, but she was paid for the Dublin and Belfast shows. The out-of-court settlement was a relief for everyone. Bridie particularly did not fancy the prospect of a public mudslinging in a courtroom.

However, to the surprise of many, she honoured the many dates that Phil Solomon had booked after these events in November 1959 for up to twelve months. Phil and Bridie both knew there was money to be made and it was in no one's interest to cancel lucrative business. But the end of her contractual relationship with Phil did eventually come that October in 1960 after three hectic but fabulous years. Interestingly, she remained in a close working relationship for many more years with his brother Mervyn in Belfast who owned Emerald Records.

She met Phil and his wife Dorothy many times after this when in London, but they never worked together again. Once, in 1974, at a dinner to celebrate her birthday in London's Talk of the Town in Leicester Square, Phil and Dorothy joined Bridie's party. He bemoaned the fact that they had ever split up. He knew there was so much more success they could have achieved together. Bridie wholeheartedly agreed. The dispute that resulted in the business split, and the painful legal action, was not enough to permanently end the underlying friendship and mutual respect that had been established during those three busy years.

Chapter Six

THE BRIDIE GALLAGHER SHOW

For driving on my jaunting car from Roscommon to Kildare,
From Dublin down to Castlebar and from that to County Clare.
From Cork to Limerick and Athlone then home by Mullingar,
You can view the lakes of Killarney, from my Irish Jaunting Car.

'THE IRISH JAUNTING CAR' (CREAN)

*B*ridie was in the front passenger seat of her Sunbeam Rapier convertible car, which Phil Solomon had presented to her twelve months earlier after her London Palladium appearance. It was June 1960, and Phil and she had more or less parted company professionally, although the court case was still pending for breach of contract. Bob was driving and they were on their way to Bundoran, a popular seaside town on the borders of Donegal, Leitrim and Sligo. Their two boys, myself and Peter, were in the back seat under the careful eye of Mary Kearns, the live-in housekeeper. The holiday resort was to be the location of that year's summer season show, The Bridie Gallagher Show, which was due to run for twelve weeks until early September.

The family car was being closely followed by the Commer van with the dancers and equipment, driven by Sammy Shortt, and two more cars with musicians and other acts that made up the cast of the summer season variety show. They were eagerly anticipating the next twelve weeks performing to families from all over Ireland and Scotland spending their summer holiday in bed-and-breakfasts, caravans and hotels.

The previous five years had been a whirlwind of concert- and dance-hall appearances for Bridie, promoted first by Nelius O'Connell and later Phil Solomon. It had been a meteoric

Bridie at the London Metropolitan Theatre in 1959.

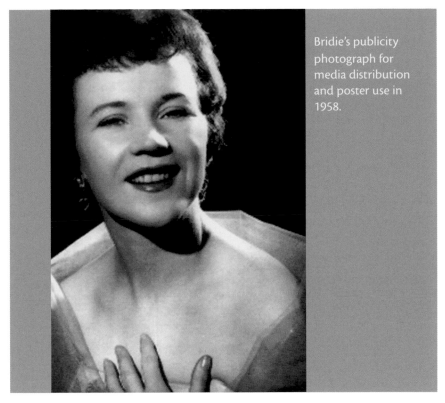

Bridie's publicity photograph for media distribution and poster use in 1958.

rise for The Girl from Donegal and up to now Bridie had mostly been appearing in her own right as a top-of-the-bill artist in theatres all over Britain and Ireland. The year 1959 had been a phenomenal period for her with extraordinary highlights like the London Palladium, her first of fifteen tours to the US and Canada, and London's Albert Hall. But solo appearances in concert halls or variety shows, while being the main form of engagement during these years, were not the only ones. She had, on occasions, toured with a supporting variety show group, usually organised and promoted by Nelius or Phil. Eventually, in 1960 she established her own variety show troupe, which toured extensively and successfully for almost five years. Some of the troupe were regular members like Vivienne Stewart (dancer), Pat York (dancer), Tommy Moran (singer), Pat McGuigan (harmonica player), Frank McIlroy (tenor) and Sammy Shortt (comedian). Bridie had first met Vivienne in 1953 on the SS *Princess Victoria* benefit concert and they remained close friends. She was a brilliant dancer, especially at tap-dancing of all styles, and many years later she established her McMaster School of Dancing in Bangor, County Down. Her students featured in many

Bridie at the Holiday Coaches in Dungarvan, County Waterford, in 1958.
© THOMAS TOBIN

The 'crooner' Tommy Moran performing in The Bridie Gallagher Show in 1960.

pantomimes in Belfast's Grand Opera House from the 1980s onwards. Pat York was also a great dancer and talented musician, who later emigrated to Canada where she formed her own theatre company but never lost touch with her pal Bridie. Tommy Moran was one of the most beautiful male singers to come from Belfast, with handsome looks and a golden deep voice like Bing Crosby's, who always made girls in

Bridie's dance troupe led by Vivienne McMaster (née Stewart) in 1960, *(l–r)*: the Johnston sisters *(far left* and *far right)*, Vivienne Stewart, Miriam McComb, Mollie Richie and Mollie Neeson.

the audience swoon. Pat McGuigan was a wizard on the harmonica who emulated the great Larry Adler and, at the same time, kept all the cast in stitches with his infectious laugh and naughty antics. Frank McIlroy was a magnificent Irish tenor whom Bridie adored listening to from the wings of any stage. Sammy Shortt was a very tall, extremely funny man, on and off the stage, with a gormless look on his face but a smile and laugh that could light up the biggest room or theatre. He was invariably the instigator of many outrageous practical jokes on cast members, including Bridie, who often felt the need to reprimand him but invariably ended up laughing at his irresistible charm.

But on one memorable occasion in Killarney the cast got their own back on Sammy. Pat York and the girls dared him to find them one

Sammy Shortt, the comedian in The Bridie Gallagher Show, in 1961.

afternoon in a game of hide-and-seek They told him they would hide among customers in a variety of pubs in the town and his task was to find them: his prize was a kiss for each catch. So off they went and thirty minutes later he followed. But, unknown to Sammy, they had taken off by taxi to a pub outside town. Poor Sammy visited a dozen Killarney town pubs and had a drink in each while searching, but naturally found

Comedian Frank Carson (*left*) and compère Billy Livingstone (*right*) in 1961.

Bridie rests while signing autographs for fans in the US in 1961.

none of the girls. He arrived back at the digs around tea-time, a little the worse for wear for drink, only to face the wrath of Bridie who threatened to sack him for being drunk before a show. True professional that he was, he went on stage that night and stole the show with a hilarious performance that saved his job and mollified an angry Bridie.

Week commencing 20th February, 1961

The
Bridie Gallagher Show

•

1. OVERTURE
2. LILY COMERFORD IRISH DANCERS
3. END OF MATCH. "SAMMY & CO."
4. FRANK McILROY. "THE VOICE OF IRELAND"
5. HOW A WAR STARTS. "SAMMY & CO."
6. KAYE BROS. "THE TWO ROYAL SCOTS"
7. FRASPA & RENATO. "FLYING HIGH"
8. MAGGIE MURPHY'S HOME. "SAMMY & CO."

9.   I N T E R V A L

10. LILY COMERFORD IRISH DANCERS
11. NO MUG OUR SAM. "SAMMY & CO."
12. TOMMY MORAN. "A VOICE TO REMEMBER"
13. PAT McGUIGAN. "HARMONICALLY YOURS"
14. FRASPA & RENATO. "SENSATIONAL SLACK WIRE"
15 SAMMY & TOMMY. "THE TWO PLAYBOYS"
16. BRIDIE GALLAGHER. "THE GIRL FROM DONEGAL"
17. GRAND FINALE

LESLIE BERESFORD AND HIS EMPIRE ORCHESTRA

STAGE MANAGER · · · } *For Empire Theatre* { · HERBERT STILLING
ELECTRICIAN · · · · }   { · · HARRY GARGAN

Above: Empire Theatre
programme from
February 1961.

Right: Metropole Theatre
Glasgow programme
insert from 1961.

Music sheet of Bridie's new release in 1959.

Empire Theatre Belfast programme cover from 1960.

Poster of Bridie's final show in Belfast's Empire Theatre in May 1961.

Others artists came and went from the cast depending on other contractual commitments and the size of theatres, such as Tom Raymond (comedian), Frank Carson (comedian), Jackie Wright (comedian), Connie Stewart (comedy mime act), Frank Murphy (tenor), Jack Kirwan (comedian/magician), Kenny Thompson (accordionist), the Alexander Brothers (Scottish singing duo), Deirdre O'Callaghan (singing harpist), as well as more dancers, speciality acts and musicians. All the acts were immensely talented and ensured that The Bridie Gallagher Show was always a major attraction wherever it performed.

Ordinary working people in Ireland and Britain in the 1950s relied mainly on three outlets for entertainment – radio, dances and theatre variety shows. Television was the preserve of the very few rich people who could afford a set, and mass audiences through this new medium were not evident until well into the 1960s. Variety shows had evolved from the musical halls that grew and flourished from Victorian times. They became the staple diet for the masses looking for music, fun and glamour.

Shows were produced in all the great theatres and were usually designed to appeal to family audiences, although some were of a more adult and sophisticated nature. But they were also presented in local church or town halls by touring troupes, just like the Eamon O'Shea Travelling Show that Bridie had joined in 1942 in Donegal. From a business perspective they provided a platform for Bridie to perform for twelve months of the year. Like other stars, she tended to confine her solo appearances to winter and spring months. Many big theatres in cities would run a skeleton programme or close altogether during the summer months, primarily because the paying customers were away elsewhere on holidays, the long evenings of daylight encouraged people to stay outdoors, and theatre premises needed maintenance work done to prepare for another winter season. So touring with her own variety shows was essentially aimed at following the customers who had left towns and cities and gone to the seaside in the summer.

'My very first summer season as Top of the Bill was in the Abbey Cinema in Ballyshannon for twelve weeks in 1958. The show lasted two-and-a-half hours every night with an interval. The cast included Brendan Carlin, Gerry Gibson, Frank Murphy, Mary Wallace, Al Burrows, Vivienne Stewart, Pat York, Mollie Richie and Sammy Shortt. It was good business but also great fun. We worked as a great team and in the process all became very good friends.'

Advert for Bridie's first summer season with her own show in Ballyshannon in 1958.

Each artiste already had wide experience from appearances in shows all over Ireland and Britain. Bridie reckoned she had had the best teacher, namely James Young with whom she had worked in Bangor, County Down, for a summer season in 1953. She regarded him as a genius and in her view *the only man who I ever saw on stage who could make you laugh and cry in the span of one short performance*. However, he was not an easy man to work for. He was a perfectionist and demanded the very best from everyone around him. He expected everyone to muck in and work as team, with no exceptions. Bridie, now with her own show, was determined to emulate his approach to stage production, direction and promotion.

It was a great personal responsibility to have a touring show on the road. The financial costs of production and maintaining a cast on the road were high, as were the risks. Her business records from that time demonstrate that a typical wage bill in 1960 for the touring show involving twelve cast members was £250. Cast members usually paid for their own meals and accommodation and looked after their own tax affairs. A typical week's door takings and profit from a nightly raffle for a box of chocolates in a summer season like Bundoran amounted to some £300, leaving Bridie with a personal profit of about £50. At this time in her career Bridie was typically able to command a minimum nightly fee of £100 plus expenses for a performance. So a profit of £50 for a week would seem, at first sight, not to be a very cost-effective result for such a big 'star' at that time. However, the fact is that during the summer months, all Top of the Bill performers had to deal with the reality that the normal performance outlets ran reduced programmes. The real business benefit of a summer season was not the money made at the time but the scale of exposure. An artist could be seen by many more members of the 'paying public' during a summer season than at any other time of the year. This was an opportunity to advertise future performances in cities and towns during the winter months and pro-mote new records just released or about to be released. Every summer season was an investment in the future for Bridie and other stars like her, designed to pay dividends later in the year.

Each show group would typically consist of a good comic, a feed for a comic who would often double as an MC for the show, an accordion/piano player, drummer, guitarist, a male tenor or female soprano or both, six dancers, a novelty or speciality act (usually referred to in the business as a Spec Act) such as mime, magicians or puppeteers

London Metropolitan Theatre programme from 1960.

Pavilion Theatre Liverpool programme from April 1959.

Metropole Theatre Glasgow programme cover from October 1961.

– and Bridie, the Top of the Bill. Everyone in the company would do their own act and take some part in comedy sketches or musical scenes. In addition, everyone played a part in setting up the show in terms of dressing stages with curtains and scenery, organising sound and lighting systems, taking turns at the box office, and selling tickets during the interval raffle.

A show programme would usually include an opening scene of music and dance involving all the cast members and ending in a fanfare for the star Bridie, who would then welcome the audience to the show and wish them an enjoyable evening. This would be followed by a musical act or singer, then a comedian possibly doing a routine with a straight man 'front of curtain' while behind preparations were being made for the next act, the Spec Act. This would be followed by a comedy sketch 'front of curtain' and then finally Bridie would end the first half with a short twenty-minute spot before a fifteen-minute interval, during which raffle tickets would be sold by members of the cast. The second half would open with the dancers doing a tap routine and often singing as well. Then the comic would do another front-of-curtain routine. This could be followed by a tenor or crooner performance. Next could be a favourite feature for Bridie, usually referred to as 'a scene'. This involved the entire cast in a costumed drama/musical sketch, based often on a song such as 'The Spinning Wheel', 'Monastery Garden' or 'Maggie Murphy's Home'.

'I remember doing the "Monastery Garden" one night, dressed as a nun and singing "Ave Maria". At the side of the stage one of the cast, unknown to the audience, started to joke with me, whispering loudly off stage: "They'll never make a bleedin' reverend mother out of you, Bridie." Of course, being a giggler it was torture for me and the other girls on the stage dressed as nuns trying to finish "Ave Maria" without laughing, which some in the audience then might have regarded as blasphemous. The cast were forever playing tricks of some kind on each other and me. Not very professional, I know, but it helped the team spirit and made for some very happy tours.'

After the scene the comic would do another front-of-curtain spot while the stage was dressed for the final star act when Bridie would take to the stage for her longer and final appearance. During this performance she would often add to her repertoire in response to requests sent up by audience members during the interval. This was always warmly welcomed by audiences as it made the performance all the more personal and memorable to them. It was, however, difficult for musicians who often played without sheet music. It was an important education for any aspiring professional musician. Playing by reading music was an essential skill. But playing 'by ear' without music and with only a knowledge of the song's melody was what made the difference between a good band musician and a great one.

Once Bridie had finished her final spot and left the stage, the MC would thank the audience and perhaps have a final spar with the comic before introducing the finale. This would often use a theme song like 'It's a Great Day for the Irish' and see the dancers doing a short routine and then introducing each of the show's acts, with Bridie taking the final call. She would close the show by making a final thanks to audience and cast. The cast would join hands with Bridie at the centre for a final rendition of the theme and the curtain would be drawn. Most nights there would be what is called a 'false tab' where the curtain was drawn back to give the cast another chance to reprise the theme and receive another round of applause. Given the family nature of the entertainment and audiences, the show would usually end by ten o'clock at the latest.

It was hard work for everyone involved. All the acts would rehearse new routines each week. For summer seasons in particular, it was always the object to attract audiences to return for a second or third show in a family's two-week holiday. So it was important to ensure that dance, comedy and singing routines varied week after week. There was constant maintenance and repairs to be made to props, equipment and costumes. And all the while for Bridie there was the task of planning twelve months ahead with her manager for future shows, recordings and personal appearances. Following the split with Phil Solomon, one of his staff, Joe Cahill from Dublin, took up the reins of management very successfully.

The show, of course, also needed to be marketed and advertised. In some seaside towns there could often be more than one competing variety show or circus. So some of the boys in the cast would spend several hours every day hanging new posters all over the town and, in particular, driving up and down the main street or promenade with a loudspeaker mounted on the roof of a car announcing that night's show, times, prices and special deals. On one memorable occasion in Bundoran, where her show featured as a summer season on six different years, Fossett's Circus came to town for a week competing with the show. On that sunny July afternoon there was the comical sight and sound of two cars facing each other in the main street blaring their sales pitch at each other like jousting knights or gladiators.

There were risks in producing summer season shows for Bridie that the cast did not have to worry about. The profit margin was typically low and a wide variety of circumstances and events could often conspire to reduce audience attendances. In the late 1950s and early 1960s most people on holiday travelled by bus or train and stayed in bed-and-breakfast accommodation or caravans. Thus they had no access to transport during the actual holiday other than buses. Car hire was a rarity. So if it rained heavily many would decide not to go out in the evening. Paradoxically, if the weather was very sunny and hot, this also could reduce audiences, as some preferred to spend the long evenings on the beach or in the open. Given the vagaries of weather in Britain and Ireland, one can understand that people would often prefer to make the most of the sometimes rare fine weather that did come along. For the variety show producers and artistes the weather could always be an unreliable and fickle friend.

Other misfortunes that could, and did, happen from time to time were deaths and funerals of parish priests, ministers or politicians, electricity cuts or strikes, or, in one terrible year, an outbreak of foot-and-mouth disease. In all cases the cast members would have to be paid despite shows having to be cancelled or curtailed. Bridie, as the promoter, just had to absorb the loss. Thankfully these disruptive events were few and far between. But she did, nonetheless, have to supplement her earnings by simply working even harder than everyone else.

While summer season shows often involved performances on seven nights of the week, Bridie would frequently finish the first half of the Sunday night show with a long spot and then jump into a car to be driven sometimes up to a hundred miles to perform a guest spot at a dance with a showband. From Bundoran, for example, she did this regularly, travelling to Galway, Ennis in County Clare, or Portrush in County Antrim, each time earning her standard fee of £100. In a good week this boosted her personal weekly profit to a total of £150. In a bad week affected by weather or some other misfortune, the money would subsidise the summer season show. Whatever the outcome Bridie worked very hard, but of course never showed it on stage.

'Audiences want to believe I'm living constantly in some luxury. The truth is it's a constant slog rehearsing, learning songs, travelling, missing meals, packing and unpacking, sleeping when you can, but always

having to smile when in front of the public. It's a tough life, but it can be a wonderful one.'

She took her summer season show to Bundoran on six occasions. The second, in 1961, held very special memories for her. One of the regular cast was Pat McGuigan, who previously had worked as a plumber in Belfast. Pat was a musical genius on the harmonica. She spotted him one night performing at the Empire Theatre in Belfast. She was about to go on tour and needed a novelty act for the show. Pat had just come second at the World Amateur Harmonica Competition and played in the style of Larry Adler. He also had the ability to play guitar and a tiny harmonica, about an inch long, which he held in his mouth, at the same time. Many years later he gained prominence as the writer of 'Men Behind the Wire' and for forming a band called Barleycorn. He was a popular musical act and toured with Bridie's show for several years. He was also a talented songwriter.

Another notable member of the company was the singer and raconteur Eamon O'Shea, the very same man who, almost twenty years earlier, had taken Bridie on her first professional tour in Donegal. Now he was working for Bridie. Pat and Eamon were arguing one night in Carroll's bar in Bundoran after a show as to which of them could write the better song. Bridie was listening to them and jokingly pointed out she was planning material for another LP and whichever one of them came up with the best song, she would record it. And so the fiercest competition began to the great delight of all the cast, who started waging bets on the winner. Two weeks later they both came up with two excellent songs. Pat's was 'The Castlebar Fair' and Eamon's was 'Heaven Around Galway Bay'. To their joint delight, Bridie recorded both of them. Although those laying bets were not so pleased at a drawn result.

That same year Eamonn went on to write and publish 'Come Down from the Mountain Katie Daly', which has been popular internationally ever since. It was a strange situation for Bridie to be working with, or, more correctly, employing this man who discovered her at the talent competition in Creeslough in 1942. She knew him privately as Herman and not Eamon. This was his assumed stage name. In fact, he had been born in Germany. For obvious reasons he assumed an Irish identity when touring Ireland in the middle of a world war.

Of course, travelling constantly on the road with a touring show had its challenges. Keeping her hair styled as it had been developed by top professionals in London could be difficult, but the girls in the company

PROGRAMME

Bob Livingstone

presents

The Bridie Gallagher Show

★

OPENING	THE FULL COMPANY
PAT YORKE	MUSICAL MOMENTS
JACKIE WRIGHT	THE BLONDE BUMSHELL
LEO MADDEN DANCERS	TRADITIONAL IRISH DANCERS
CRIONNA ROWE	A LITTLE DASH OF DUBLIN
JACKIE WRIGHT & CO.	COMEDY SKETCH
MARY LANGLEY	CHILD STAR FROM ARDOYNE

Introducing Guest Artistes of the evening :
From the Grand Opera House Pantomime " Old King Cole "
(By kind permission of Geo. Lodge, Esq., O.B.E., J.P., and Tom Arnold)

MR. PETER YOLLAND	Producer
HARRY BAILEY	" Old King Cole "
HARRY SHIELS	Queen Aggie
HILDA DIXON	Nemo the Gypsy
VICKI LAINE	Princess Melissa

Syd Durbidge presents TOMMY KELLY
(ACCOMPANIED BY IRIS TATE)
Ireland's Greatest Little Entertainer in New Successes.
(Musical Instruments supplied by Musical Centre, Grosvenor Road)

Personal Appearance of FREDDY GILROY
(European, British and Empire Bantamweight Champion)
By kind permission of MR. JIMMY McAREE

INTERVAL AND LUCKY PROGRAMME DRAW

PAT YORKE	MORE MODERN MELODIES
JACKIE WRIGHT	CRAZY COMEDY WITH THE COMPANY
FRANK McILROY	A VOICE TO REMEMBER
THE CY BRENT TRIO	MUSIC IN THE MODERN MANNER
SAMMY SHORT	SIX FEET OF FUN

The Girl from Donegal . BRIDIE GALLAGHER

Above: Forum Cinema programme from December 1959.

Right: Bridie performing in England *c.* 1962.

were all multi-talented in that regard and helped each other. Her costume dresses also demanded care and maintenance. She spent large sums for exquisite dresses in London, primarily from Bond Street. She wanted to appear everywhere with the most unique and lavish gowns. She knew her audiences wanted this glamour and, indeed, she was often told that a lot of the women used to come to her concerts not only to hear her sing but to see what she was wearing. To transport and care for these outfits 'on the road', she used a large wooden trunk that could accommodate up to twelve dresses at a time, some with petticoats and hoops. With the help of the girls in the show, she kept them clean, repaired and always ready for any performance.

Ironically, dresses and clothes in general, in a totally different way, were to provide her with an extra income outside show business during the 1960s. As the work rolled in, her gross earnings, apart from summer seasons, were topping £500 per week in the early part of the decade, equivalent today to almost £10,000 or €12,000. Of course the taxman took good care of much of that. She was advised by her accountant to buy some sort of commercial business as a way of reducing her tax exposure. So, with Bob's advice, she acquired a launderette business at Ardoyne, Belfast, in 1960. At that time there were very few homes with a washing machine, and the nearest launderette was more than a mile away on the Shankhill Road. A huge official opening was organised by Bob, at which some of her touring show, including the comedian Sammy Shortt and singer Tommy Moran, originally from the Crumlin Road, performed, culminating in Bridie herself singing to a large crowd gathered on the small square at the shopfront. Hundreds of people turned up along with the customary press and, in fact, such was Bridie's popularity that some of the local factories and businesses in the district closed for the duration of the opening ceremony.

She owned her 'beautiful' launderette for just over ten years, employing three or four local people. It did very good business initially but declined gradually as other competing launderettes opened on almost every main road in the city. Eventually, by 1970, she sold the business. By then most homes were being fitted with washing machines and the demand for launderettes had dropped dramatically.

Wherever they went Bridie's entourage was easily recognised around the country, as the show's transport wagon, a Commer van, had Bridie's name emblazoned in large block capitals on both sides. But sometimes public recognition was the last thing she wanted. One embarrassing

Bridie backstage at Dublin's Theatre Royal in 1960.

day, driving along the roads in the midlands of Ireland, lived with her for a long time. Three cars plus the wagon were travelling in convoy as usual. Bridie's car, driven by one of the cast boys, was at the tail end of the convoy. She began to wonder why her car was getting a particularly loud reception from waving townspeople as they passed through towns and villages. She later learned from one of the dancers that the wagon in front of her car had a pair of large knickers stretched out on the front window. Some of the boys of the company shouted, *'These are Bridie Gallagher's knickers.'*

She never discovered who owned the big bloomers, but knew they were not hers, nor indeed who the culprits were, though the range of suspects was small. She was initially annoyed but quickly folded in laughter when the other girls described the looks on people's faces in each town and village.

After such extensive touring there was usually a short break of a week or two when everyone went back home to see their families, and have clothes properly cleaned, ready for the road again. The Bridie Gallagher Show also toured England, Scotland and Wales, playing in hundreds of theatres through the early 1960s. Wherever they went Bridie invariably had to perform one or two extra dates each week, usually as 'double dates', such as the cabaret at a dance. This often meant her ending her concert performance and then driving at break-neck speed to another city or town up to 50 or 60 miles away for a late-night performance.

One memorable night in Her Majesty's Theatre in Aberdeen, a gentleman came to the stage door after the show and asked if he could speak to Bridie. A messenger came up to her dressing room to ask if she would meet him as apparently the matter was urgent. When he came in she was worried at first that he brought bad news. However, he turned out to be a very kind and friendly man who expressed great delight at being allowed to meet Bridie.

He was a very successful building contractor. He lived in a most beautiful mansion outside Aberdeen with his very elderly and ailing mother who came originally from Killarney. He told Bridie that his mother's dearest wish was to meet Bridie and hear her sing a song for her. He offered Bridie £100 to do this after the show ended that night or some time when it suited Bridie best. She was so overcome by the man's sincerity and devotion to his ageing mother that she agreed to do so the following afternoon since the show was not performing the next night. She made only one stipulation, that she could bring the rest of the company with her and give his mother a proper show. The man was completely stunned, never expecting more than one or two songs from Bridie and certainly not a full variety show.

So the next day the entire company entertained the old lady and her family for almost an hour in a fabulous house. The businessman was so overjoyed, he arranged a dinner party for the whole show. He wrote regularly to Bridie for many years after, never forgetting her kindness in return.

In 1961 The Bridie Gallagher Show toured the entire British Isles, until it reached the climax at the famous Metropolitan Theatre on Edgware Road, London. Sammy Shortt was the comic for the show, working in partnership with wee Jackie Wright. Since Sammy was handsome, six-foot-four with black wavy hair, and Jackie was only five-foot-three with a shiny bald head, they made a hilarious combination that often had audiences laughing when they came on stage, before they even spoke. Many years later Jackie became a celebrated part of Benny Hill's team in his internationally successful television series.

The cast also included The Alexander Brothers in their first venture outside Scotland, the Lily Cumerford Dancers from Dublin, Billy Wyner (a comedy pianist) and Tommy Moran as a male crooner who was popular with the ladies. It was booked for four weeks with a possible extension of another week. As it happened the theatre was completely booked out for the whole five weeks, breaking all box office records, which had stood from the days of the legendary Marie Lloyd seventy years before. Bridie was presented with the Golden Key to the theatre as a result.

It was one of the longest periods she had ever been away from home and she was constantly pleading with Bob and the management to let her fly home to see her children, but they kept putting her off time after time. Little did she know Bob had a plan. He kept saying he would try to book a flight on a Sunday. To her great amazement and delight on the third Saturday night, as she was finishing her final spot, the manager of the theatre, Mr Mullin, walked onto the stage to present her with a beautiful bouquet. He said he had an announcement to make. First of all he praised Bridie for the marvellous business she had done, and the pleasure given to so many people. Then he said they had a special thank-you treat for Bridie, and duly called her two little boys, myself and Peter, from the back of the auditorium.

'I can see them yet walking down the aisle of the theatre and onto the stage. Of course I broke into tears. It is a wonderful scene I shall never forget. The entire company and theatre audience were crying too as they stood up to give a standing ovation. The tears rolled down my cheeks with joy, and so did my black mascara, but nobody noticed. There was happiness in everyone's face. Jim was nine and Peter just six. When I think that they were in London all day with my housekeeper, Mary Kearns, and I didn't know a thing about it. I was so overjoyed and so was everyone else. The boys stayed for a few days in London with her in the luxurious Mayfair Hotel. It was their first time travelling by plane, first time in London, first time in a fancy hotel and first time on stage. It was an event the whole family never forgot.'

One of Bridie's favourite summer seasons in the 1960s was spent in the Derby Castle Theatre on the Isle of Man. It was a very popular holiday resort and proved to be one of her most successful seasons both financially and commercially. She rented a house overlooking the sea in Douglas so that she, Bob and the children could be together. The great joy for Bridie with summer seasons was that they provided this precious family time for at least eight weeks when she could be with her two little boys. They, in turn, had wonderfully long summer holidays in many different resorts, and often had new friends to play with – the children of other acts on the show. That particular season Frank Carson from Belfast was the young comic on the show in Douglas and he brought his lovely wife Ruth and their children for their holiday too. Because the Isle of Man attracted thousands of holiday visitors, and especially families, from all over Ireland and Britain, it was a great showcase for Bridie, and indeed the other acts, and led to many follow-up bookings for appearances.

She had great memories of that season with its fun and the exploits of all the cast. The boys of the company used to play cards during the show in the dressing room when they weren't on stage. Bridie's act naturally closed the show each night, followed immediately by the finale requiring all the cast on stage. The boys had worked out how to time their card-playing by her programme. Her second last song was always 'Goodbye Johnny Dear', which included the lyric 'Write a letter now and then, and send her all you can'. It was naturally Frank Carson, the comedian, who used to order one of the younger lads to *go down there and see "did Johnny send the money home to his ma yet"*, – the signal for them to stop the cards and get ready for the finale.

One of the greatest treasures Bridie received that season was a portrait of herself painted in oils by Frank De Mumford. He and his wife Maisie were a speciality puppet act on the show – The De Mumford Puppets. Not only were they a terrific act, which appeared in Las Vegas, London and Paris, Frank was also a very talented designer and artist. He invited Bridie to sit for him while he did her portrait. She had three sittings in the flat that Frank and Maisie had rented in Douglas for the summer.

Her hair was jet black and short and she wore a royal-blue beaded dress with a white mink stole. The large 3-foot by 4-foot portrait was exquisite when finished, and Frank and Maisie invited all of the show company for a party to exhibit the portrait for the first time. Bridie initially hung the large portrait in their Bedford Street office where it

Portrait of Bridie painted by Frank De Mumford in the Isle of Man in 1959. She initially hung the large portrait in her Bedford Street office before moving it to the dining room of her home in Belfast.

was admired by hundreds of visitors. Later she hung it in her home's dining room in Belfast. Visitors and journalists would always comment on the fabulous portrait, a portrait that captured her beauty and style as an artiste.

My brother Peter and I had a marvellous time holidaying in Douglas. The nanny, Mary Kearns, took us out if our parents were busy in the theatre. When Bob's father Fred, Granda Livingstone, came to stay for his July holidays, the fun factor rose dramatically. Trips to the beach and rides on the horse-drawn trams were supplemented by visits to bingo halls and wrestling matches in the arena adjacent to the Derby Castle Theatre. Aged nine and six, we would gladly have stayed on the Isle of Man forever.

Bridie's last summer season was, appropriately enough, in Bundoran in 1969. She returned after a gap of six years to top the bill in a planned eight-week season produced by Billy Livingstone (no relation to her husband Bob) in the new parish hall. She loved the show immensely, with great friend Barney Fitzgerald and his band providing first-class music, Patrick O'Hagan, the wonderful Irish tenor (whose son Johnny Logan went on to win the Eurovision Song Contest several times), Danny Small, as usual, the most eloquent Master of Ceremonies (who in years to come gained well deserved fame as the MC at the televised World Championship boxing fights of the great Barry McGuigan in Belfast and London), local Irish dancers, and other quality acts. But what made the season most memorable was the outbreak of rioting in Belfast and Derry followed by more deadly shooting in August. Many of the families holidaying in Bundoran were from both cities, and the news of riots (often quoted as the start of Northern Ireland's Troubles), burning houses and deaths made many return home immediately in fear and dread. The summer season show had to be cut short. Sadly, it was the beginning of thirty years of turmoil and death that was to affect everyone living in Ireland.

Another notable season brought phenomenal success and tragedy at the Metropole Theatre in Glasgow in 1961. The theatre had been booked out long in advance for the five-week run. But disaster struck one Saturday morning after only two weeks. The company were in the theatre for the normal weekly rehearsal preparing new acts and scenes for the following week. They broke up for lunch hour and retired to nearby pubs for food and drink. Forty minutes later one of the stage-hands crashed through the door of the nearest bar, in which most of the company was eating. Breathless and white with shock, he shouted that the theatre was on fire. Everyone dashed up the street to find traffic halted, a crowd being held back by police, and enormous clouds of black acrid smoke billowing from the old theatre. They all stood dumbfounded on the footpath opposite. As they watched the theatre burn, Bridie and her cast were broken-hearted. It was a much-loved theatre in the city and its destruction was a severe blow to everyone. But there was nothing they could do. All the show's costumes and personal belongings were still in the dressing rooms and clearly at risk of being destroyed. The five-week season of The Bridie Gallagher Show seemed obviously at an end.

The cast retired again to the pub to ponder the tragedy and their future. An old woman who sold newspapers every day on the street corner opposite the Metropole happened to be a dog-breeder specialising in miniature dogs, particularly Pekinese. She came into the pub carrying a small box and approached a very disconsolate Bridie at her table. She was Irish and apologised for interrupting the group, and then proceeded to place the open shoebox on Bridie's knee.

'Missus. I love your singing and I'm so sorry for your trouble. Would you like this wee pup to cheer you up?'

Bridie was amazed and shocked. Her immediate reaction was to tell the old woman to go away. But as she cuddled the tiny bundle of brown fur with big round black eyes and a tiny little pink tongue, she just could not let it go. Without any thought about where she would keep the little pup she just fell in love there and then with the tiny bundle of joy. She asked the woman how much the pup cost. At first the woman said it was a gift, but Bridie insisted and paid her £5. The assembled company were surprised, to say the least, at the seemingly irrational act by Bridie, but not as much as Bob. It was a pedigree male Pekinese with a most unusual reddish brown colouring. She immediately christened the little fellow Flame, in honour of the Metropole Theatre fire. Bridie loved the little dog with a passion, and took him everywhere with her that tour, much to Bob's consternation. Her little boys back in Belfast were less concerned with the news of the fire and more excited at the prospect of getting their first dog. But Bob put his foot down about touring a Pekinese dog. The following week, the pup was transported to Belfast when Bob paid a short visit home.

Two days after the fire, Bridie and the company were relieved and overjoyed to discover that, due to the magnificent work of the firemen, most of the dressing rooms area of the theatre and its contents were saved. It was the main auditorium that was very badly damaged. The Metropole Theatre fire was very big news in all the newspapers and on news programmes. As well as the obvious concern for the future of the theatre, many pressmen asked what Bridie would do now. Her manager, Joe Cahill from Dublin, was always ready to conjure a plan no matter what the circumstances. He quickly contacted Jonnie North, the manager of the theatre in Inverness, and between them they organised a tour of Scotland's main towns for the entire show, to start the following week. They didn't need much publicity owing to the big news of the fire. Theatres and halls all over Scotland were only too eager to get The Bridie Gallagher Show, which had featured so prominently in the news for days before. As one newspaper put it, the show was not only a tour de force, but now forced to tour.

The show travelled all over Scotland, even to the Orkney Islands where the people gave Bridie and her cast a great welcome. It was in the autumn so the highland scenery was magnificent to admire as the company toured about. As for the changing colours of the trees around Fortwilliam, Bridie found them unbelievable. It made a scene of rare perfection to be imprinted on her memory for many years.

Shortly after the impromptu tour of Scotland, Joe Cahill booked Bridie to appear in cabaret at a dance in Tipperary. She travelled to Dublin with her pianist Thelma Ramsay to be met by Tom Costello (later Johnny McEvoy's manager). They arrived at the venue and were greeted by a throng of people. They were taken into a nearby family home adjacent to the ballroom. There was a sumptuous meal awaiting them, and a beautiful bedroom to change in (not always the norm on the road). By show time there was pandemonium. They couldn't get into the hall with the vast crowd surrounding it. The gardaí were there in small numbers, but could not control the crowd.

Somebody made a suggestion that Bridie should sing from the top window of the house to help quell the noisy crowd who could not get into the hall. Bridie agreed. A microphone was rigged up from the up-stairs window and she proceeded to sing a few songs from there with Thelma on accordion, much to the delight of the people in the street. They were overjoyed and probably felt that they had one up on the people inside the ballroom who had paid, getting their brief perfor-mance for free. It did the trick and the crowd in the street started to move and Bridie and her cast were able to go inside to do the full show when extra police arrived to provide an entry.

By 1965 the ballroom scene in Ireland with its quite unique Irish showbands had become big business, and was growing competition for Bridie. These bands relied heavily on performing music emanating from the US and Britain and there was relatively little locally written material produced. But for many Irish young people, these very skilful and entertaining bands provided the only means to experience live the pop music of the famous American and British artists who rarely visited Ireland at that time. This was stiff competition from a new genre, but with the aid of good management (Joe O'Neill from Dublin took over from Joe Cahill after he emigrated temporarily to the US in 1963), Bridie was able to hold her own by doing more and more guest appearances at dances along with the showbands and, as a consequence, fewer and fewer theatre concerts. Many of the theatres around Ireland slowly declined in popularity and many closed forever while ballrooms became bigger and bigger, and so did the crowds. Bridie was one of the first solo artists to make such guest appearances at dances and so she continued to play to audiences of thousands night after night. It was Monday to Sunday inclusive. She was lucky to get the odd night off. It was hard going but she thrived on it, provided she could go home now and again.

Thankfully, touring her show around halls and theatres in the 1960s was more often a pleasant, if tiring, experience. It also continued to involve significant highlights. With the rise of showbands, Bridie had to work hard to compete. But in a fascinating merger of two very different styles of Irish showbands and Irish ballads, she performed for a second time at London's Albert Hall in 1966 but this time sharing the bill on St Patrick's night with one of Ireland's new stars, Dickie Rock and the Miami Showband. Bridie's musical backing was provided by the Skyrockets Showband from Enniskillen with whom she toured extensively for several months. Bridie admired Dickie immensely and, while they came from very different musical styles, they had a wonderful time performing together on one of the world's most magnificent stages.

The touring was demanding both physically and psychologically, especially being apart from the children. But for Bridie, the greatest benefit was performing to and seeing her fans all over Ireland, Britain and America. It consolidated her reputation with a legion of fans worldwide and her place in their hearts and minds as their Girl from Donegal. But as Bob Dylan sang at the time, '*the times, they are a-changing*'. The wonderful era of variety theatre, from the First World War onwards, was coming to an end in every city and town. Bridie's meteoric rise to fame had been built around concerts in halls and theatres in Ireland and Britain. The 'Swinging Sixties' had come to the fore, televisions were found more and more in every home, and people's tastes and expectations in entertainment were now moving in new directions.

In May 1961 Bridie topped the bill in the final week of the Empire Theatre in Belfast before it closed for demolition, in a show that included Billy Danvers, Frank Carson and the Alexander Brothers from Scotland. It had been at the heart of variety and dramatic theatre in Belfast for over sixty years, with great stars like Marie Lloyd, Charlie Chaplin and Jimmy O'Dea performing there. But cold commercialism decided that the public's tastes were changing, and that going to the theatre was fast becoming a thing of the past for most people. Bridie had the great honour of topping the bill of that show, one that was to become in many ways a watershed in Irish variety theatre. Change was on its way.

Chapter Seven

CHANGING TIMES

Goodbye, Johnny dear, when you're far away,
Don't forget your dear old mother far across the sea;
Write a letter now and then and send her all you can,
And don't forget where e'er you roam that you're an Irishman.

'GOODBYE JOHNNY DEAR' (PATTERSON, MAGUIRE)

*A*nyone who has ever run their own business in any sphere will know that coping with and adapting to change is often the difference between success and failure. Any organisation that does not adapt to changes in the environment or circumstances usually courts disaster. In a professional career of fifty years Bridie demonstrated on numerous occasions an amazing aptitude for coping with changes in business and, indeed, her private life. Over such a period very few show business performers can progress without experiencing numerous changes – new managers, new supporting musicians, new musical styles, new public tastes, new technology and media outlets, and many more. Bridie had her share of all of these and, time after time, managed to adapt her way of working to cater for the changes that were unavoidable or necessary. But importantly she still maintained the unique essence of her style and performance as The Girl from Donegal.

She had various managers and musical accompanists, most of whom worked with her for up to five years at a stretch, many going on to successes in their own right with Bridie's encouragement. She dealt with changes in show business, which evolved from concert halls and theatre shows in the 1950s through ballroom dance halls in the 1960s, and eventually to cabaret clubs in the 1970s and 1980s. Throughout she always retained the ability to perform and attract large audiences in major concert halls and theatres, which she loved most; she performed even as late as 1991 at the age of sixty-seven in the Lincoln Center in New York. All of these changes demanded new skills and new ways of performing, which she dealt with in a determined fashion and often gave a lead to others.

Poster for Lincoln Center concert in New York from 1991.

When cabaret clubs became fashionable in the 1970s, she used her well-honed stagecraft in theatres to great effect and many showband performers who had not had significant experience with theatre audiences copied her approach, one based on establishing a rapport with the audience who were close up and not distant at the back of a hall. As styles of music changed she incorporated new songs into her act that reflected more modern tastes, including country and western songs. But she refused to disavow her beloved Irish ballads and they remained her trademark to the end.

She also had a succession of different managers. She started with Nelius O'Connell who she loved dearly and always respected the fact that he was the one who had really helped to bring her to early prominence. Her manager after Phil Solomon was Joe Cahill from Dublin who actually left employment with Phil to take on the guiding role with Bridie. At his suggestion she set up a new company – Bridie Gallagher Promotions Ltd – with a suite of offices in Bedford Street, Belfast. The new company not only managed Bridie's affairs but became a major show business agency for many other artists in Northern Ireland. It was also responsible for arranging touring shows and for the next four years after splitting with Phil, The Bridie Gallagher Show became very popular and was booked for very successful tours and summer seasons all over Ireland and Britain.

Joe put his excellent management skills to good use and worked with Bridie for four years until he decided he wanted to go to America and explore other management opportunities. Bridie never forgot his support at such a difficult time in her career and they remained friends thereafter. Many years later in 1976, when personal tragedy entered her life, Joe was the manager of the London venue at which she was appearing. He cared for her magnificently, getting her home to Belfast safely to face her greatest test.

She had several other managers including Joe O'Neill and Shane Redmond in Dublin in the late 1960s who introduced her to the evolving cabaret scene. John Finnegan, also from Dublin, initially worked for Shane and took over Bridie's management for four years at the beginning of the 1970s. He proved to be versatile and committed to ensuring her status as a major Irish star was maintained in a new climate of extreme competition from many ex-showband stars who were transferring to cabaret. Sean Wallace, her manager in the late 1970s, was a relative novice to the business but quickly demonstrated considerable managerial abilities on Bridie's behalf. As John had done, for over three years he protected her position at a time when many artists experienced increased difficulties and even dangers as a result of the Northern Ireland Troubles.

In Bridie's case the Troubles brought change to people's lives like nothing before, but they never stopped her singing at concerts in Catholic parish halls, Orange halls, masonic halls, national forester halls or cabaret clubs in every part of the North, whether notionally Catholic or Protestant. Bridie had long won a reputation for being apolitical. Her fans were drawn from across the community divides that so tragically blighted the North. Indeed, it was notable that she attracted fans in Northern Ireland that included Unionist Lord Mayors, SDLP grandees like Paddy Devlin, and Sinn Féin leaders like Martin McGuinness. She regularly crossed the border in the early hours of the morning returning from engagements in all parts of Ireland and it could be become quite comical at police and British Army roadblocks on lonely country roads, which could make anyone feel intimidated, when a policeman, on more than one occasion, having identified the car's occupants would invariably invite Bridie to sing a few bars of 'The Boys from County Armagh'.

Bridie's career marched onwards through the 1960s and 1970s, embracing so many changes it is a wonder how she coped. In Ireland in the 1930s and 1940s, entertainment for most people was dancing in little dance halls. The 1950s saw the growth of theatre shows and then in the 1960s, there was the big boom in the showband scene and ballrooms were built almost overnight in every town and county. This was followed in the 1970s by the upsurge in cabaret clubs. Initially, there

Bridie in cabaret in London in 1974.

were few venues outside Dublin and Belfast with suitable facilities for cabaret performances. But in no time at all, it seemed that every pub in the country had built enormous extensions, euphemistically referred to as 'singing lounges', and publicans were suddenly running cabaret with music, dancing and visiting artists, and even, in a few cases, restaurants.

Bridie in cabaret in London accompanied by her son Jim (author) c. 1975.

Some of the pub owners had little idea about how to run cabaret venues, and indeed many of the performers, including ex-showband members, struggled to adapt their performances to the new venues, which accommodated smaller audiences who were closer to the stage and artists, and who were invariably not dancing but sitting and noisily drinking alcohol.

Bridie had, of course, in her extensive travelling in the US and Britain years before visited many of the world's best cabaret night clubs such as London's Talk of the Town, Manchester's Mr Smith's Club, and New York's Copacabana and latin quarter clubs where she saw acts like Jimmy Durante, Shirley Bassey, Pat Boone and Alma Cogan. She had a head start on many of the showband performers whose business had been hit hard by the advent of discos and regarded the new cabaret lounges as a lifeline to survival.

Many of the new cabaret venues were initially disastrous. There wasn't enough space in some to accommodate the crowds that turned up; others had good performance area space, but no changing rooms for bands or artists. But the biggest problem was that the publicans cashing in on the new trend refused to charge customers for entry. They had never charged customers for coming into the bar and did not see why they should do so now. They reckoned on making sufficient profits from the sale of drink on the night to pay for the bands and artists and still make a profit.

Many big name showbands were breaking up almost every week, instead forming groups of three and four, which were better suited to the cabaret scene; the smaller stages were incapable of accommodating six- and seven-piece bands. But they were not prepared to work for the small fees that many publicans were offering. So the bands and artists, including Bridie, did deals where they themselves charged the customers for entry and collected the takings on the door, rather than taking a fee from the owner. At first this seemed to increase the publicans' profits and reduce their risks. But when they saw the size of crowds flocking to cabaret and the money being earned by artists, they quickly changed tack and introduced a cover charge for the events and paid the artists an agreed fee. It took a while before audiences universally accepted the idea of a cover charge for entry into what they regarded as pub lounges. But a cover charge soon became the norm, and rose quickly from an initial charge of 50p to several pounds within a few years.

The transition to cabaret was difficult for many showband members, but Bridie had already learned the necessary stagecraft through theatre and concerts over many years. Although, it has to be said, she missed the large theatre orchestras and audiences along with reliable theatre sound and lighting systems that she felt added so much to the extravaganza of performance.

The 1970s brought other changes in Bridie's working arrangements. The burgeoning cabaret scene meant performing more often in smaller venues than she had been used to previously. It was a new factor that importantly affected the fees she could demand. In the 1960s her standard nightly fee was £100 (equivalent today to almost €3,000). By the early 1970s such fees became difficult to secure simply because cabaret venues could not hold more than 200 people at a time. Supporting bands could not always be relied on to have suitable sound equipment or the musical ability to accompany her on stage. From that point on she always travelled with her own amplification equipment, which was used in preference to any provided at venues. In this way she could be assured of a high-quality sound.

She always had her own travelling accompanist who would play for

Bridie alone, if the resident band was not up to providing musical backing (which happened occasionally), or lead the resident band. But even this could be problematic. The one musician that Bridie feared most in any cabaret band was the drummer. In her view they could make or break a performer, even if they were a basically competent drummer. If they played too loudly, too slowly or too fast, it could ruin the performance. She could be seen sometimes in cabaret struggling with bands that were being led in a tempo by the drummer. She would stoutly count them in and then, during the song, used hand signals to guide the drummer. Most times it was a success and her direction was effective. But sometimes it was not and led to a very disgruntled performer who had to be reassured later that the drummer had not ruined her show. To add salt to the wounds, few promoters, bandsmen and agents noticed these subtle weaknesses in musicians and could not understand what she was complaining about, which only added to her frustration. Thankfully, these were usually isolated occasions, and the general experience was of very good musicianship all across Ireland and Britain.

The business also demanded constant driving around Ireland and Britain. Bridie changed the car driven by her road manager every year, running up an average mileage of 40,000 miles annually. Increasingly, she returned to Belfast rather than staying overnight near the venue. It was not unusual to find Bridie and her roadie leaving Belfast at five o'clock in the evening to drive 150 miles to a venue (for example, in Sligo) and returning home at four o'clock the following morning. Bridie tended to stay overnight in hotels only when the venue was more than 200 miles from Belfast. She was not alone in this regard. Few, if any, artists had overnight stopovers, especially the showbands, who faced even greater costs. This was the physically demanding nature of the business that the public rarely understood or appreciated. But Bridie insisted that *'the public needs to believe that you have just stepped off a helicopter into a nearby luxury hotel, and not that you have driven for five hours down bumpy country roads in all weather conditions. That's part of the magic they pay for.'*

The changes in Irish show business were new for audiences too and some did not always adapt as quickly as others. Bridie told the story of a night at a new cabaret lounge in County Cavan where Cecil Kettles, originally from the very successful Sky Rockets Showband, and his trio were the new resident band. It was a very nice place with a full house of several hundred people. Cecil and his musicians had been playing for some time before Bridie went on to do her first spot. When she came off stage, she asked Cecil if her performance had been all right. He reassured her that it had been fine. But Bridie was not convinced. *'Well, why didn't they applaud?'*

They could not figure it out. Cecil also complained that the audience was 'bloody awful'. In fact, he was so annoyed he was reluctant to go back on for the second half of the show. It was a struggle for everyone to get through without any audience reaction at all, except at the very end of the show.

But when the show was over, dozens of people blocked the door backstage wanting to get Bridie's autograph, and the club owner appeared bubbling with excitement at what he described as 'a wonderful show'. Everyone kept shouting to Bridie that she was marvellous. She was dumbfounded and so were Cecil and the others. Cecil told the owner that he thought the audience had a funny way of showing their appreciation. To his amazement and relief, the owner explained to Cecil and Bridie that most of the audience had never been to a cabaret lounge in their lives. They were used to going to country dances where they rarely applaud, except at the end of a set number of dances or the end of the dance. They considered it rude to applaud during a show. Bridie and Cecil had a good laugh that night afterwards in the bar and prayed that audiences would adapt quickly to the new cabaret format because otherwise doing shows was going to become a nightmare for performers. Thankfully, audiences everywhere adapted, cabaret flourished and performers prospered accordingly.

In the 1980s Bridie was still touring Ireland and Britain, and played regularly in large Irish centres and city hall concerts that attracted large audiences. For over twenty-two years, she did numerous shows for one particular promoter, Jim Connell, who was originally from Ballyhaunis in County Mayo. She first worked for him in a dance hall in Manchester called Sherrocks. After it burned down, he took over the nearby Ardri Ballroom near Manchester University. She appeared there twice every year until he retired, always doing top business, and always receiving a top fee. He told Bridie years later that, of all the big names he engaged during the 1970s and 1980s, his biggest drawing artistes were Bridie and the American country and western star Hank Locklin. Bridie regarded him as a true gentleman to work with. Jim undoubtedly loved Bridie and not just because she drew great crowds to his club. He treated her as a very special person, and always made sure Bridie stayed in a beautiful hotel and was met at the airport or train station by a luxury car. He personally collected her from her hotel for the show and delivered her back, and treated her to supper and drinks after every show.

At that time her normal cabaret performance could be anything up to an hour, and often more, but at every performance at the Ardri, Jim would urge her to sing four or five songs only, which would take just fifteen minutes. At every show, without exception, after the fifth song he would be up at the side of the stage waving, *'That's enough Bridie. They're not buying any drink while you're singing.'*

Bridie would struggle to turn a deaf ear, as the audience would be calling for more, but eventually Jim would get his way and she came off, usually after thirty minutes. The ballroom was licensed, so when the large crowd rushed towards the stage, the bar area became deserted until Bridie's set finished, and the drink profits nosedived. If any other promoter had behaved like Jim, Bridie would probably have refused to return to the venue. Instead, while feeling exasperated at times, it became her running joke to see how long she could stay on stage with Jim waving at the side for her to come off. In fact, over time many of the audience became aware of the game being played every show and urged her on to stay longer, usually infuriating poor Jim.

While cabaret dominated the scene, Bridie still found herself in demand for theatre concert tours from time to time in Britain and the US during this period. The shows were increasingly set in town halls, many of the old variety theatres having disappeared as cities were redeveloped. But cabaret was now the staple diet for most performers. While it was hard work, she loved touring Britain and its numerous Irish clubs and dance halls. As well as the Carousel and Ardri Clubs in Manchester, The Irish Centre on York Road in Leeds was one of her favourites where she was always guaranteed a great reception. Others included London clubs such as the Shamrock Ballroom in Elephant and Castle owned by the great Irish sportsman Paddy Casey from Sneem, The Two Brewers in Wandsworth, Butty Sugrue's The Bush in Shepherd's Bush, Quex Road Irish Club, The Galtymore Club and The Buffalo Club in Camden Town. Many of the London engagements were organised by another old friend, Johnny Green, who escorted her to every venue and insisted she was treated to the best support and care at all times.

In Ireland, as the cabaret scene matured Bridie increasingly looked forward to appearing in many special venues up and down the country where she established strong audience support and often close friendships with owners or managers. In Dublin she revelled in the atmosphere and professionalism of the Talk of the Town in Terenure where she invariably received a thunderous welcome. The venue of the same name in Belfast owned by Norrie Sharp, where the MC was Roy Walker (who went on to great success as a comedian and television game show host), was also a great favourite not least because the resident band was so flexible and accomplished. The Bridge Bar at Dunloy in County Antrim was, in her view, the best designed and equipped cabaret club in the country despite being able to hold only a couple of hundred patrons. The Lagoon Lounge in Termon (run by Johnny McCaffrey) and the Corncutters Rest in her hometown of Creeslough (run by Danny Lafferty) were the Donegal venues that, time and again, hailed her return performances and gave her endless satisfaction by their warmth of reception and the friendship given by their owners. The Shamrock Lounge in Kilross near Tipperary town was one of the largest and best-run venues in Ireland as far as Bridie was concerned. The family-run Lepsitt's Cabaret Lounge in Collaney in County Sligo was again one of Bridie's favourites, not least because of the wonderful hospitality provided by the lovely family who owned the successful venue. And there were many more in Cork, Kerry, Roscommon, Mayo and other counties. But her single favourite cabaret venue was perhaps the least likely. It was not the biggest or the most plush. But it was the friendliest, and one Bridie always looked forward to visiting.

It was McDermott's Lounge in a tiny village called Glenamaddy in County Galway. It was owned and run by Dermott and Kathleen McDermott who also combined it with a shop and bed-and-breakfast facility. When Bridie first appeared there in the early 1970s, it held only about a hundred customers. Dermott's ambition and Kathleen's flair saw it grow into a venue capable of accommodating up to 300 patrons and it proved to be one of the most popular venues in the Roscommon and Galway area. Bridie appeared there every year for almost twelve years and each time acquired new fans and new friends. The McDermotts became firm friends, so much so that on occasions she visited them to stay for a relaxing rest away from the hurly burly of travel and work. Most of all, the McDermotts came to represent, in Bridie's eyes, the many good cabaret venue owners across Ireland in that period.

'Kathleen and Dermott, like so many other good owners of cabaret lounges, understood what hard work really was, and never lacked

Poster for Bridie's cabaret appearance in Glenamaddy, County Galway, from August 1978.

ambition or determination. They built up their business, borrowing from the bank more than once to make their place the best. But through it all they never lost their decency and warmth. They looked after me and other artists so well, in the good times and the bad. It is people like them that helped the likes of me be a success and I've never forgotten it.'

She also continued most years to do concert tours of the US and Canada, such as one organised by Senator Dan Kiely in 1972. This was a rather unique venture, which combined Bridie's performances at venues across five different states from New York to Illinois with a simultaneous tour of the Kerry GAA football team. They played local GAA teams in every city where she performed. The size of Irish-American audiences that turned up at venues was staggering. It reinforced once again the reality that, while Bridie's popularity in Ireland had diminished to some extent in the wake of the 1960s pop and showband era, in America she was still a major star. She did numerous interviews on the main Irish-American radio stations and even entertained Senator Edward Kennedy in Boston at a fundraising dinner on that tour.

Bridie was often asked about the best venue she had performed in. She played many of the world's great concert halls and theatres, as well as dance halls and cabaret clubs. But while the London Palladium was probably the pinnacle of her long career, there is one venue she played only once and it remained her favourite by far: the Sydney Opera House. She was flown to Australia specifically for one concert in that most magnificent and iconic building on Monday 11 April 1977.

She loved the shell-like structure and stood for a long time admiring its unique and beautiful shape and style. There are several different-sized

NATIONAL IRISH CONCERT

SYDNEY OPERA HOUSE

EASTER MONDAY NIGHT, 11th APRIL, 1977

8p.m.

presenting

★ **BRIDIE GALLAGHER**
DIRECT FROM IRELAND

★ **JOHN MacNALLY**

* **KATHLEEN McCORMACK**   * **THE CONNARIE**   * **SHAY O'HARA**

RANSLEY SCHOOL OF CELTIC DANCING

COMPERE **SEAN KRAMER** (STAR OF THE FILM "BARNEY")

BOOK EARLY — PHONE: 644 7806, 451 7761

TICKETS $8.00 (PLUS BOOKING FEE)

TICKETS ALSO AVAILABLE AT:
SYDNEY OPERA HOUSE BOX OFFICE
DAVID JONES, MITCHELLS & USUAL AGENCIES

'COME BACK TO ERIN'
at the

national Irish concert

MONDAY, 11th APRIL, 1977

Left: Poster for the Sydney Opera House concert with John McNally from April 1977.

Below: Sydney Opera House programme cover from April 1977.

concert halls in the massive complex, plus function rooms of all kinds. The main auditorium has a massive stage with people seated in a vast semi-circle that rises majestically to the high ceiling. That enormous stage would have been frightening to walk onto, except that most of it was occupied by a full orchestra.

The atmosphere was so electric and the applause so thunderous, it made it incredibly exciting for Bridie. She found fabulous dressing rooms like no other,

125

Bridie pictured at a party in Sydney in 1977, hosted by Leo Ward *(second from right at the back)* from Leitrim and his wife *(on Bridie's left)*. Shay O'Hara, the promoter of Bridie's tour, is on the far left. The photo was taken by radio DJ Brendan Walshe.

all equipped with showers and lounger couches. There seemed to be endless corridors, a restaurant, coffee shops, souvenir shops, booking offices and bars.

She was extremely nervous before going on stage, being so far from home, but after receiving a wonderful welcome she relaxed and performed brilliantly, according to local press and radio presenters present, who even today remember that special night for so many expatriate and second-generation Irish. Something else that helped her to relax was the fact that the MC for the concert was a man she knew well but had not seen for many years, Spanky Kirwin from Dublin. His father, Jack Kirwin, had been a very funny and successful comedian in Ireland for many years, making his name in the old Capitol Theatre in Dublin. He had featured in Bridie's summer season show to Bundoran in the early 1960s. Jack and his family emigrated to Australia in the late 1960s and Spanky had done well as an actor and had played a key role in the Australian movie scene. It was a very special moment to get together again with old friends after so many years and talk about old times.

It was Shay O'Hara, the producer of the show, who brought Bridie to Australia. He used to run a showband in Ireland before he too emigrated. He had his own television show and toured Australia doing

Bridie at Sydney Harbour on her way to rehearsals at Sydney Opera House in 1977.

concerts with great success. He told Bridie he had admired her greatly back in Ireland and knew the impact she had on Irish audiences around the world in her live performances and her records. He had promised himself not long after emigrating that as soon as he could afford it, he would bring her to top the bill at the Sydney Opera House. While she was in Australia Shay also booked her onto television and radio shows and organised three other concerts in Melbourne, Adelaide and Brisbane. It was a most successful and enjoyable trip that also allowed her to experience some of the many delights of that country – the Blue Mountains, koala bears and kangaroos, Bondi Beach and the inimitable Aussie barbeques.

She was also thrilled to meet a girl she had gone to school with, Unzie Coll, who was the daughter of the local doctor in Creeslough. They visited many exotic places and had wonderful times together, including a cruise on Sydney Bay on her husband's yacht. Shay and his friends, notably the Irish-Australian radio personality Brendan Walshe, entertained Bridie regally and introduced her to so many people at different parties, she was dizzy with delight.

But overall she remained fascinated by the beautiful edifice of the Sydney Opera House itself, and went back several times to view it, each time pinching herself to remind her it wasn't a dream and that she had actually starred on its stage. The building is on a rostrum-like platform stretching out into the harbour, with rows and rows of steps all the way up to the entrance. The final exciting visit involved a twenty-minute trip in a light aircraft around Sydney Harbour and gave her the most spectacular view of this wonderful theatre, one that she would grace only once but never forget.

Of course, she played many great venues that others could only dream of doing. The Royal Albert Hall was a building she first admired from the top deck of a bus as she passed it on her very first visit to London with James Young in 1953.

'Never in my wildest dreams did I think in those days that one night I would top the bill there and go to achieve the record for the biggest capacity crowd.'

She was credited with attracting a crowd that St Patrick's night in 1959 of 7,500 – a capacity record for the hall that was never to be surpassed. This was before new fire regulations later in the 1960s placed a lower limit on capacity.

Naturally, given its significance in rocketing her career skywards in 1959, the London Palladium, with its towering tiers of seats, its beautifully draped stage and plush dressing rooms equipped with showers, settees and telephones, held a special place in her memory. Before there were multi-channel televisions, the Internet and social media in every household, this was the theatre that every performer around the world wanted to play. It was synonymous with success and glamour, and 'treading it boards' was a dream for all but a few. Bridie was one of those few from Ireland and was one of the very first from Ireland to achieve such an honour and thereby set the standard for so many to follow.

Probably the hottest place she ever performed was Lusaka in Zambia. By an extraordinary coincidence Bridie's good friend Ray Sheils met an old friend in a Belfast hotel one day in 1985. John Allen was originally from the Cavehill Road in Belfast but by then was working as the Chief of Police in Lusaka. He was secretary of the Wild Geese Society in Zambia, which was a society for Irish expatriates living in the country. Over a drink John mentioned that the society was keen to arrange for an Irish celebrity to visit Lusaka for their St Patrick's Day celebrations. Ray

Poster for Arts Theatre Variety Show in Belfast from September 1983.

**BELFAST CIVIC
ARTS THEATRE**

VARIETY IS BACK

IN THE

BRIDIE GALLAGHER SHOW

with

VIVIENNE McMASTER DANCERS
MARJORIE REA • STUART WHITE
JIMMY KENNEDY • FRED HANNA
BIRDIE SWEENEY • JUSTIN DUFF
DORRIE MARR • MARK MITCHEL
GERARD O'RAWE AND HIS MUSI

⭐ Dancers, Music and Comedy for All the Family ⭐

MON., 12th to SAT., 17th SEPTEMBER, 1983

BOOK NOW AT BOX OFFICE   Telephone 224936

Above: Bridie and Ray Sheils (*on her right*) meet a Zambian government minister during Bridie's tour there in 1985.

Right: Bridie in Lusaka in Zambia in 1985.

suggested Bridie as the perfect choice. Ray contacted Bridie and within a few weeks a deal had been negotiated and contracts exchanged.

Bridie was incredibly excited at the prospect of performing in Africa. She had never been to any part of the continent before and was in trepidation at the thought of performing in a country where she knew no one and was unsure about musical accompaniment, or indeed the type of performing venues. She need not have worried. She flew with Ray to Lusaka and they were taken to the most beautiful Hilton Hotel to stay, in whose ballroom Bridie was to perform on St Patrick's Night. It proved to be a fabulous night. The seven-piece band was made up of local Zambians with superb musical skills. They were more used to playing pop, reggae, jazz and rock 'n' roll music, and had never played, let alone heard before, Irish ballads. But after a short rehearsal Bridie was thrilled to find that they played her music as if they had been playing it all their lives.

The audience was made up almost entirely of Irish people from all over Zambia who were working as teachers, mining engineers, architects and doctors, as well as senior ministers from the Zambian government. The reception she received was fantastic both because she performed well and also because she was the first Irish performer to travel to Lusaka. But the heat of this equatorial country was ferocious.

It was intense in the day and even the evenings. Bridie found the perspiration was running down her face and into her eyes as she prepared for the show. Fortunately there was air-conditioning in the hotel rooms but the heat in the ballroom, packed with over a thousand revellers, was severe. She rarely wore false eyelashes, but that night she happened to be wearing some bought especially for the trip. In the steamy heat, one of the lashes dropped off in the middle of a song. She looked down to the floor of the stage and saw what she thought was an exotic spider. She screeched with alarm and the band stopped and the audience was hushed in wonderment. What could be the problem with this great star? When she realised the spider was her false eyelash she was convulsed in laughter and then she just ripped off the other one. When the band and audience saw what had happened the laughter was thunderous. Another success, but she never wore false eyelashes again on stage.

The organisers of the trip brought her to the town of Livingstone beside Victoria Falls on the border with Zimbabwe for a weekend treat. She gasped at the grandeur and thrill of the falls and surrounding scenery, although she did shriek on more than one occasion when

Bridie performing at the Wild Geese Society's St Patrick's Day gala in Lusaka in 1985 with her Zambian backing group.

monkeys from the nearby bush ambled across the poolside where she was sitting. She was in Zambia for a week but before she left, there was a farewell party to see her off, comprised of the Wild Geese Society organisers, a government minister and many new friends she had made. She was presented with wonderful gifts of local copper art, wooden carvings, jewellery and precious stones. It had been a hot experience in so many ways, but one she savoured for the rest of her life.

In 1985 she encountered another change. This time it was musical video recording. It was a completely new experience for her. She had done many television recordings over the years but musical videos, which became very popular in the 1980s, allowed artists to present their songs and recordings in a visual form not previously available. This was due mainly to the advent of VHS recorders, which had quickly come to dominate nearly every home's entertainment agenda.

She was approached by a promoter, Hugh Hardy, whom she had known for many years in promoting concerts and dances. He had ventured into the new video market and wanted Bridie to help enhance the market share of his new company, Apollo Videos. She made her first video in Mosney Holiday Resort, previously a Butlin's Holiday Camp. It was recorded live as a concert with an audience. She sang ten songs with no breaks, except for a short introduction to each song and one short interlude after the fifth song. The intention was to replicate on video her typical concert/cabaret performance.

She was supported by her then musical director, George Bradley from Bangor, County Down. After the fifth song George stayed on stage and did a selection of Irish jigs on the accordion while Bridie did a quick change of dress with the help of his wife Patricia. There was a panic as the zip on her dress stuck but they got it right and she sauntered on stage at the end of George's medley as if nothing had happened. It was like doing a live television show with no 're-takes'. Then over the next three days they filmed Bridie singing four songs on location in the Donegal countryside. The four songs had been recorded a couple of weeks previously in a studio and a small cassette recorder was placed about 10 feet away from her while filming so that she could hear the music and mime the song.

'Miming was a very new experience for me and was the most difficult part of doing a video. Miming a song was never to my liking. Having to remember the phrasing of every line recorded demanded so much concentration, it was nerve-racking. But somehow I coped and it resulted in a very successful video that sold thousands in Ireland and Britain.'

With the success of the first video, Hugh asked Bridie to record a second the following year. This time she and Hugh chose a selection of songs specifically about different counties or places in Ireland with spectacular scenery. Then two weeks later she travelled to Dublin to record all thirteen songs in the studio in two sessions under the musical direction of Alan Connaughton. This was followed by a further session during which she recorded the voice-over introductions to each song. It was released some months later and proved even more successful commercially. Many of these are now available on YouTube and still attract thousands of viewings. Yet another change in Bridie's career had once again proved she was adaptable, innovative and always keen to present a fresh but recognisable image and style for Irish ballads for worldwide consumption.

In a career of fifty years she repeatedly embraced change in so many respects but still remained constant in her fundamental style and production. Her longevity as an artist owes much to her willingness and determination never to stand still. People knew that, if it was a Bridie Gallagher show or recording performance, it would be beautiful Irish ballads, well sung, brilliantly interpreted, musically entertaining and yet with fresh ideas, modern techniques of production and a wonderful mixture of energy and pathos. She coped with changes in management, changes in entertainment culture, changes in public taste. But the one constant was Bridie herself. She never changed as a person or artist and kept her integrity intact, and that is why perhaps it has been said that there are few Irish families anywhere in the world that do not have at least one Bridie Gallagher recording, record, CD or video, in their collection.

Chapter Eight

NO BUSINESS LIKE
SHOW BUSINESS

I love you, yes, I do, I love you
If you break my heart I'll die
So be sure that it's true when you say, 'I love you'
It's a sin to tell a lie.

'IT'S A SIN TO TELL A LIE' (MAYHEW, BILLY)

BRIDIE
GALLAGHER
SHOW

*C*hange is inevitable but sadly the one constant is that show business in Ireland, like anywhere else, is not always a bed of roses. The professional performer sometimes has to deal with outrageous facilities, jealous competitors, deceitful agents and promoters, terrible weather, exhausting travel, rogue journalists, and even ruthless clergy. Bridie's experience involved all such challenges.

During the 1960s, the massive ballrooms in Ireland became increasingly sophisticated and glamorous with bright neon lighting outside and glitter balls suspended from the ceilings, and some with restaurants and bars. They were a long way from the old parish halls that dominated Ireland before. But one feature remained, and indeed Bridie found the same characteristic evident in cabaret clubs when they later blossomed in the 1970s – few, if any, provided suitable dressing rooms or toilet facilities for the bands and artists, and certainly not separate changing rooms and toilets for male and female performers.

In most cases there was one big band changing room for everyone to share. While Bridie and the other female performers didn't like it, she had started her career with fit-up travelling shows and so was not as shocked as some female newcomers were to find they had to change their clothes and costumes along with the men, who were normally in the majority. The women became adept at erecting temporary curtains or screens to provide themselves with a little privacy. On one occasion in a west of Ireland dance hall, Bridie and her accompanist Sheba Kelly suspended a tablecloth between two cupboards so that they could undress, screened from the male bandsmen and passing members of staff.

To find even one sink and a lit mirror for use by all performers was very rare. Female artists often shared their personal mirrors and helped each other getting into costumes. But Bridie sometimes faced ridiculous and frankly farcical circumstances such as the time when one promoter blithely told the women performers they would have to change their clothes in the ladies' toilets in the main ballroom. She always refused such suggestions point blank and insisted that other arrangements be made. On one occasion she changed in her car, which was parked behind the hall, rather than suffer the indignity of undressing in what were effectively public places.

Ireland had a relatively unique reputation in the 1960s for organising large summer dances during local festivals in long tents. These marquees were of varying sizes and could accommodate hundreds or even thousands of customers. But in bad weather, they were a nightmare to operate and work in. They were most definitely the worst when it came to changing rooms or toilets. Normally they were erected in the middle of fields that could get very wet and boggy when it rained. The marquees were highly profitable for the promoters during the summer, good business for bands and artists like Bridie, and great fun and novelty for the public. But for the artists and bands, they were also uncomfortable, lacking amenities and sometimes downright dangerous, especially since electrical supplies could be unreliable and there were often exposed power cables for musicians' equipment.

Of course, the last people to be aware of the dreadful backstage conditions artists sometimes had to deal with were the paying customers. It was always the artist's responsibility to ensure that they presented an image of glamour borne from luxury. And invariably they did. Certainly Bridie's over-riding concern, in common with all other good performers, was to make sure her fans saw her at her best. The last thing she ever did was complain to the audience about dire facilities. She would certainly complain loudly and firmly to promoters backstage but the fans were blameless and were there to see their star, not listen to complaints about their local promoter's facilities.

In the early 1970s, backstage facilities in the new cabaret venues were meagre, to say the least, even for the most popular and commercially successful artists. To be fair, it has always been the case that many of the great theatres of the world also have tiny dressing rooms and one can still find situations where five or six men or women have to share changing facilities. But even in these small theatre spaces, artists would normally be able to rely on having sinks, convenient toilets and adequate lighting for dressing and make-up purposes.

With the new cabaret scene in Ireland at its height, a fabulous new club opened in County Limerick at which all the big acts, including Bridie, appeared. It held a thousand paying customers in a large cabaret lounge with a long bar, luxurious seating, an adjoining restaurant, dozens of staff, superb stage lighting and sound systems, and a magnificent resident band. Bridie and others loved performing there, except in one respect: the changing room for artistes was the tap-room behind the bar where all the beer kegs were stored and connected to the pumps at the bar. On the first occasion she appeared at the club, she was changing into her stage dress when, without any warning, a barman nonchalantly strolled in to change a couple of beer kegs, whistling while he worked. Bridie was dumbstruck at the interruption and stood motionless as this

Whistling Rufus (as she called him) went about his business, seemingly oblivious to the semi-dressed celebrity in the room.

After the show, on very firm instructions from Bridie, her road manager tackled the manager. He was actually hoping to negotiate a return date after the fantastic business that Bridie had brought to the venue. But her manager made clear Bridie would never be back unless something was done about providing her, and other artists, some privacy for changing. To his credit he did just that and six months later Bridie returned to a great reception. But this time, she had a small and private dressing room; a partition had been built at the end of the tap-room. She always wondered if the public would believe the conditions that performers sometimes had to dress or wash in. But she could still laugh at the idea of what a glamorous life the public assumed she lived.

As one of the pioneers of the Irish cabaret scene since her first appearance in 1968 at Clontarf Castle in Dublin, Bridie experienced many of these teething troubles. But sometimes matters were made even worse by so-called professional management agencies in Dublin who would contract performers for groups of dates in venues all over Ireland. It may be difficult to believe but they often sat in their offices making bookings over the telephone for artistes without ever seeing or checking out the venues for size, accommodation, facilities or operation. On occasions they did not even have a clue where some of the places actually were geographically, many being located well off the beaten track, and would simply leave it to the performer or band to find the right place on the night. This was long before the advent of Internet and satellite navigation in vehicles, and also a time when maps, and even road signs, could not always be relied on for accuracy.

One such Dublin agency had a peculiar little chap working for them who drove Bridie crazy. Let's call him Tommy. He was, in Bridie's words, 'a lovable little rogue' who spent most of his time socialising in a bar next to his office while he inventively filled up a date book for the boss. As long as it looked like he had done his job, he was assured of a wage at the end of the week, even though he often made one or two phantom bookings at venues that did not exist, or sent letters of confirmation or contracts to artists but not to promoters.

Bridie arrived at one such 'booking' in Milltown, County Galway, with her support group in 1975. They made extensive enquiries locally on arrival early that evening, even to neighbouring cabaret venues, but could not find the cabaret lounge that had been booked, let alone

Bridie performing at a dance cabaret in London 1974.

Bridie performing at a Christmas cabaret in one of the Irish centres in London in 1983.

anyone who had heard of the venue. Her roadie phoned the agency to be told that it was definitely in the book as Carberry's Lounge, Milltown. But there definitely was no such venue in Milltown, or indeed anywhere in County Galway. That wasted trip considerably dampened Bridie's relationship with that particular agency, not to speak of testing her temper with the little rogue Tommy. On another such unhappy night in County Mayo, she arrived in a crowded hall, only to find that there was no supporting band booked so it was just Bridie and her accompanist. Tommy had forgotten this rather crucial detail. So she and her road manager waited hours while the hall owner organised a few local musicians to do the job. Tommy's life (as an agent or otherwise) was now hanging by a thread, certainly as far as Bridie was concerned.

On the Irish cabaret circuit the ugliest place she played was in an enormous roadhouse pub near Kilkenny. Because the proprietor didn't live on the premises, the lounge was disorganised and filthy, and the room upstairs where she was brought to have tea and get changed was also a mess. She actually felt sick before she went on to do her show. But the business was fantastic and she was asked to return the following year. She accepted the date but I was tasked with making sure that the dressing room was clean. It was, and in fact the owner had by then improved the premises, possibly after hearing Bridie complain bitterly and loudly.

The coldest place she played was in the Butt Hall, County Donegal. It was in 1963 when there had been a very heavy fall of snow, which froze over and the wintry scene lasted for six weeks. With her full variety show company, she left Belfast in good time on a journey that would normally take three hours by road and expected to reach Ballybofey by five o'clock. But the roads were treacherous and almost impassable. The convoy struggled on its way and arrived in Ballybofey after nine o'clock (the show should have started at eight o'clock). Most cars did not have very good heating in those days, so they were all shivering with the cold and starving with the hunger. Most of the audience, several hundreds of them, had gone home and who could blame them. But somehow or other the show got started before ten o'clock for the remaining few hundred hardy souls who had entertained themselves during the delay in the warm pubs nearby.

'The heating in the hall had failed and everybody was going around with chattering teeth. I felt so sorry for the poor people who had stood in the freezing snow, so decided I should do my act early in the programme. I went on dressed in a glamorous gown but covered by a big thick pink cardigan that was torn but warm. The audience were fantastic and appreciated the lengths we had gone to, to put on the show. So while it was a very cold venue, it was not a frosty reception.'

There were aspects of Irish show business, particularly in the 1970s, which Bridie could never accept or like. She had gained her early professional experience in theatre and radio work in Ireland and

Britain between 1950 and 1965, and had grown accustomed to the strict discipline so often demanded by talented and renowned theatre directors and producers whom she worked for and learned to respect greatly. In 1957 she was recording a radio programme for the BBC in Belfast in which she was accompanied by the talented and highly innovative David Curry and his orchestra. David had gained a formidable reputation for promoting orchestral arrangements of Irish melodies usually played by traditional Irish musicians, and rarely on radio. These were frequently aired by the BBC across Britain to great acclaim. Bridie was scheduled to commence rehearsals with the orchestra for the recording at ten o'clock in the morning. She was delayed and arrived fifteen minutes late. She was by then a rising star, but not yet a top of the bill. As she rushed breathlessly into the studio, mouthing apologies, David looked down from his podium: *'He said "So kind of you to join us Miss Gallagher. Now can we begin our rehearsal please?" This was said in front of the entire BBC orchestra, some of whom smirked at my obvious discomfort. After that I was rarely late for any rehearsal or engagement, even when I was the top of the bill star.'*

In fact, she became obsessed with punctuality. No matter where she was travelling to for a performance she insisted on allowing for extra time in any travel plans in case of bad weather, car breakdowns or traffic hold-ups.

Perhaps not surprisingly she became very intolerant of artists on her own show or other performers and bands who turned up late. She complained frequently that the cabaret scene in Ireland of the 1970s seemed to be populated by a few artistes who assumed that arriving late was the prerogative of show business stardom. To Bridie it was an insult to the audience and fellow artists.

The show business scene in the 1970s brought other unwelcome characteristics from Bridie's point of view. Show business (like any other form of commercial business) has never lacked hype or fanciful claims made by artists and their management for great achievements and successes. But the 1970s brought a degree of hype that was often simply deceitful and untrue. It soon became the norm in entertainment columns of the press for new performers, or their managers, to make all sorts of ridiculous claims in a bid to make them appear more successful and deserving of public acclaim.

One example that was widely exploited in an attempt to fool the Irish public was the venues at which these performers claimed to have appeared. If the press reports at the time are to be believed, it would seem that virtually every Irish singer and band had appeared, or better still 'starred', at New York's Carnegie Hall, the London Palladium or Nashville's Grand Ole Oprey. The simple truth is that precious few Irish artists ever had the privilege to perform in these iconic venues. Bridie admired greatly her fellow professionals at that time who had actually achieved such accolades, like Brendan Bowyer, Dickie Rock, Daniel O'Donnell and Philomena Begley. But she regarded those who chose to use untruthful hype in their quest for greatness as unprofessional and tawdry.

The focus of her strongest dislike was the growth in the tendency of some managers and agents to buy favours of radio DJs or press journalists. At one time, to have one's records played on some radio stations required money to change hands. Radio plays could make the difference between high sales or no sales of records. In the 1950s and early 1960s there was little opportunity to influence decisions by broadcasters. The records chosen to be played were usually requested by the public or had been verified as having sold significant numbers in shops. By the late 1960s more unscrupulous agents and managers preferred to buy a guarantee of plays for their artists. These practices continued for some years until they were eventually exposed in Britain and Ireland with resultant scandals and legal sanctions.

But there were also newspaper correspondents, well known in show business circles, to whom gifts had to be offered in order to secure good reviews and positive stories about often imagined successes. On one occasion in Dublin, Bridie's manager told her he had been asked for a bottle of good whisky for a particular pressman to ensure a good write-up in a newspaper after one of her shows in the Liberty Hall Theatre: she did these shows regularly and attracted large enthusiastic audiences. She flatly refused and, unsurprisingly, got no write-up at all that week. These changes in how the business operated were possibly seen by some as a 'necessary evil' in a very commercial world. But for Bridie, who held rather traditional and, some might say, old-fashioned views, they were deceiving the public and were not acceptable. Her refusal to play ball probably contributed to a decline in her popularity to some degree, but as she often said, *'I wonder will people remember Bridie Gallagher in fifty years' time, or these so-called producers and journalists who think they are so important that they can demand money just to do a job for which they are already being paid?'*

She was not alone, with other fine Irish performers suffering likewise. But her response was to forge on, regardless of what she called 'the begrudgers', and she still managed to draw large and appreciative audiences right to the end of the twentieth century, long after many of the others who had 'paid their way' had fallen by the wayside.

Chapter Nine

PAIN AND LOSS

I remember the day when the big ship was sailing
And the time it had come for my love to depart
How I cried like a child; oh goodbye to you Teddy
With a tear on my cheek and a stone in my heart.

'TEDDY O'NEILL' (TRADITIONAL)

*B*ridie had her share of pain and suffering in her life. Whatever about the fame, adulation, money, success and glamour, she was like anyone else in this world, and she often expressed her own philosophy quite starkly: *'We all have our crosses to bear. Some do it quietly; some do to it loudly. In show business no one wants to know about your pain. You're expected always to be ready to perform with a smile and make other people happy, even when you're not.'*

Her life had ups and downs with disappointments, broken promises, missed opportunities, even forbidden love. But her life was also marked by several very painful and harrowing events and episodes.

In 1965 Bridie's marriage of fourteen years to Bob Livingstone ended and she never remarried. In the present culture, such a development is hardly noteworthy or even unexpected to many people. But in 1965, especially in Catholic Ireland, it was an event of major proportions, so much so that Bridie did not speak of it to most of her family or friends and certainly not publicly to audiences or the media.

As marriages go, it would have been regarded by many people in Ireland in 1951 as doomed from the outset: she was a Catholic country girl from Donegal, of conservative servile parents, working as a domestic servant; he was a Protestant-born boy, six years her junior, from a Belfast working-class family headed by an Orangeman, who had just finished his apprenticeship as a coachman; both earned minimal wages and neither had any formal education beyond the age of fourteen.

But there were, at the start, some important positive signs, the most significant being Bob's decision to convert to Catholicism before marrying Bridie. For a young Belfast Protestant boy at that time this was an enormous undertaking and arguably a clear measure of his love and devotion. It is also significant that Bridie insisted they marry in her hometown of Creeslough on 6 September 1951. She was clearly proud to show off her new husband to family and friends. Sadly, and inexplicably, their parents did not attend the wedding. No doubt her parents remembered that only four years earlier she had fallen in love with another young Protestant boy. But Bob knew none of this past history.

The relationship was good and quite normal for at least the first ten years in their cosy little house in Carmel Street, Belfast. When Bridie's earnings rose significantly in the late 1950s, she and Bob took several holidays to Italy and Spain. On one occasion in 1961, Bridie took me alone to Majorca for a short break. She had been increasingly worried about my childhood asthma and, when her doctor said a spell in a warm

Bob at the piano with Jim *(front)* and Peter *(back)* in 1958.

Bridie and Bob in Dungarvan, County Waterford, in 1958. © THOMAS TOBIN

Bridie's parents Jim and Biddy on Ards in 1958.

climate would do me good, we flew off to the luxurious Hotel Mediter-
anneo in Palma, Majorca, an experience I remember most for the fact
that we met one guest who introduced himself as the 'Greatest Little
Twister in the World': his factory made the little sachets of salt found in
packets of potato crisps – something only people of an older generation
would remember today.

Why the marriage failed is difficult to assess. As it happened, from
an early point in the union Bridie always earned more money than Bob.
She said much later that after a while Bob seemed to resent this, perhaps feeling a failure in not being the main breadwinner. This difference would be much less noticeable today perhaps, but in the culture of
the early 1950s, particularly in Ireland, it was the man who traditionally
brought in the money to a home. Mothers working outside the home
were very much a minority. Bridie was, as the years went by, also often
the centre of attraction wherever they went, which, according to Bridie, led to some jealousy on Bob's part. She claimed he was suspicious
of any man who would talk to her. Bob never shared his views on the
matter. If true, this jealousy naturally increased the friction over time.

Bob himself, who had a kind and outgoing personality, eventually
decided that he wanted to be more engaged in show business and tried
managing Bridie for a short time after the split with Phil Solomon. But
he did not understand show business or indeed business management
generally and soon found it uncomfortable. He had always worked for
other employers and found it difficult to be in charge. Bridie's business
suffered as a consequence and so she insisted on a change of plan,
demanding a new professional manager. So more cause for friction was
added to the simmering pot.

Bridie thought it would help to set Bob up in his own business. He
was a coach builder by trade but his ambitions lay elsewhere. He set up
a small taxi business, buying three taxi cabs and employing two friends
as the second and third drivers. As a result, he was often out all hours
of the day and night, especially the early hours of the morning, whether
Bridie was away touring or at home. This proved to be a development
that guaranteed disaster in the relationship, and the final straw as far
as their married life was concerned. Suspicions, jealousy, envy, friction
and remoteness saw them grow further and further apart.

Increasingly, there were arguments and bickering between them
whenever they were together. Soon these minor tiffs led to fights
that grew in intensity and frequency. One would accuse the other of

Bridie and Bob in happier times on holiday in Italy in 1960.

infidelities or insults. The fights were never physically violent but were very loud and nasty. Not surprisingly, perhaps, alcohol often fuelled events. Neither of the two was a heavy or even regular drinker. But both suffered from a common fault in not knowing when to stop when alcohol was in plentiful supply, such as at parties. Nor did either recognise that their behaviour was, intentionally or not, inciting the other to more and more suspicion and distrust. Both were strong willed and determined to be a success in their own right. Both were also gifted in many ways but had little common ambition except in one respect – their children.

Eventually Bob's sister Frances visited them at home and spoke frankly to them. There had been yet another verbal fight and the boys had been frightened. They always looked to their Auntie Frances for comfort and told her everything that was happening. She urged the warring couple to stop and think about their family and futures. A few weeks later, in May 1964, they sat up one night discussing their future, this time without any drink or interference from others. They decided that the best thing for them both, and the children, was a trial separation, not a divorce, and that the children would stay with Bridie but would be able to see their father regularly. There was still a hope that things might sort themselves out since they both adored the boys. After the split, Bob maintained close contact and was always available to guide and advise both his sons after he set up home back in his native Cussick Street.

Much later Bridie wrote: *'I always did my level best to be a good mother, and keep a nice home, but perhaps I wasn't a good wife. I know we both had our faults and as difficult as it was, I think we made the right decision for us and the children.'*

It took a long time for Bridie to come to terms with the separation, not least because she was very much in the public eye. It became clear within a few years that the separation was permanent. Eventually Bob began a new relationship, which Bridie learned of with great pain. She was genuinely afraid that admitting to marital failure was going to be an embarrassment to her wider family, friends and fans. In fact, she never actually told her mother or father what had happened at all. For years, until they both died, she made up tales as to why Bob didn't visit them. Ironically, despite the earlier reservations, they had grown to like Bob very much. They enjoyed his company and always found him cheery and pleasant. He even wallpapered their entire home the week before Bridie's brother Josie married Bridget Gallagher from Cashellily. More generally Bridie feared people would think less of her for being a separated woman. She never spoke publicly about the separation and avoided any questions asked by the press for many years.

'My mother and father, bless them, brought us up strictly, and I didn't want them to know about it because I would not hurt them for the world. So, for many years I suffered in silence while I carried on with life. I faced my audiences night after night and performed to the best of my ability, while concealing the heartache within.'

Bob's sister Frances, who was close to them both, moved into Bridie's home for several months to help with the children and provide moral support to Bridie. They had a very loving sisterly relationship before and long after Bob left. When Frances died in 1997, Bridie attended the funeral of her good friend and met Bob, who she had not seen in thirty years, except for a few short days in 1976 when tragedy struck the family. They hugged each other closely and many present who knew them both were struck by how warmly they embraced that day. After Bob died in 2007, his wallet was found to contain photographs of Bridie and the boys, and in his house he had copies of all her records. She kept personal letters and cards that she had sent him from abroad and photographs of Bob from their early days locked in a wooden jewellery case in her dressing-table drawer for almost fifty years despite the separation. In their final days they were reconciled. Fundamentally, their love for each other seemed never to die, just the relationship.

The greatest pain in Bridie's life was undoubtedly the tragedy of losing her twenty-one-year-old son Peter in 1976 in a motorbike accident. The loss broke her heart and she never really recovered from the shock. *'After a while, I learned to cope with the loss, but I never forgot it.'*

She was in London at the time, singing in The National Club in Kilburn owned by Butty Sugrue, a well-known Kerryman and one-time circus strongman, who had been based in London for many years. She had been booked to appear nightly at The National for six nights starting on the Monday, two days before Peter's accident on Wednesday 5 May 1976.

Peter had trained for hotel management at the College of Business Studies in Belfast and, after working a year at the Europa Hotel, he joined the Regency Hotel staff in Belfast. He was good at his job and over the next three years learned fast. As a result, at the tender age of twenty-one, he secured the job of bar manager at the staff bar of what was then the Ulster Polytechnic in Jordanstown, just outside Belfast. On the fateful day he was on his motorbike heading for Belfast city centre at lunchtime to meet his fiancée, Jane, to whom he had got engaged just ten weeks earlier. As he joined the motorway on the Shore Road, the front wheel of his powerful motorbike hit a depression in the road. This caused a serious wheel wobble and he lost control of the bike and was thrown over the edge of the motorway flyover, falling 30 feet to the ground below. He suffered severe injuries, was knocked unconscious and died on his way to hospital.

When the phone in Bridie's hotel room rang, she was settling down to watch the six o'clock news on BBC before getting ready for the night's show in The National where she would go on stage at 9.30 p.m. It was Paula, my girlfriend (and later my wife), ringing from Belfast. Bridie was naturally surprised and then quickly worried to find Paula and not me or Peter on the line. Paula, trying desperately to hide the fear in her voice, told her there had been an accident. For some reason Bridie asked immediately if it was Peter. She always hated the fact that Peter rode a motorbike and often talked of her dread that he would have an accident. Paula confirmed that it was and that he was badly injured. She lied rather than risk Bridie collapsing alone in her hotel at being told her youngest son was dead.

Joe Cahill, who was Bridie's personal manager in the early 1960s and was now manager of The National, had been contacted just minutes earlier and briefed on what had happened to Peter. He undertook to make all the arrangements necessary to get Bridie back to Belfast quickly, all without her knowing that her son was dead. He arrived at her door within seconds of the phone call from Paula. Bridie collapsed into his arms and pleaded with him to get her home that night. Bridie didn't notice that Joe was much more aware and calm about the situation. They made a mad dash for Heathrow Airport. Bridie left all her stage costumes and baggage in the hotel. Joe later sent it all on to her home in Belfast.

At the flight check-in Joe was worried how Bridie would cope alone on the flight. She had spent the previous hour on the journey to Heathrow talking and crying about Peter and her worry that he had been badly injured. By an amazing coincidence, Bridie noticed Jim Mills, her next-door neighbour and friend, queuing for the same flight. Jim and his wife Ruth had known Bridie for fifteen years. They were very close, and she was relieved to see a face from home. After Bridie told Jim the awful news from Belfast, Joe discreetly tipped him off as to the truth of the terrible circumstances. Jim knew what he needed to do: his job was to comfort Bridie on the journey and get her safely to Belfast. Two hours later, at ten o'clock, they landed at Belfast International Airport at Aldergrove.

'When we arrived at the Airport at Belfast, I immediately saw Jim with Bob standing some few yards behind him. Oddly it didn't seem strange at all to see Bob there, even though we had not spoken face to face for at least five years. I ran straight to Jim pleading to know how Peter was. Poor Jim just broke down and cried that Peter was dead. I remember just screaming and screaming. My youngest son Peter was dead. I cried and cried until I was exhausted. They carried me out to the waiting car and I slumped into the back seat and Bob put his arms around me. I was glad he was there. Why didn't God take me instead, was all I could cry. I'd had my life, Peter's was only beginning. Peter used to hate seeing me going away so much. But I think he did understand that I had to go to work. My last few words to him before I left home that week were as I said bye to him and he asked if I was going for the weekend. I explained I was going to Birmingham to do a concert and then down to London for a week.

Bridie in Scotland with Jim *(left)* and Peter *(right)* in 1963.

Jim *(left)* and Peter *(right)* with their grandfather Fred Livingstone in 1962.

I kissed him goodbye and God Bless. But I never saw him again. It took a long, long time for me to realise that Peter would never be coming back. I do hope he is happy in Heaven.'

Peter's funeral was held on the Friday and was attended by an enormous crowd. He was popular and had a large number of friends who were all heartbroken and distraught, none more so that his fiancée Jane. In addition, following extensive news reports around Ireland about the tragedy, hundreds of Bridie's friends and fellow artistes were in attendance along with relatives from Ireland and Britain.

A fascinating point of interest in the midst of all this sadness was that three very unusual groups of men were quietly and discreetly in attendance at the funeral. These men represented the Ulster Defence Association (UDA), the Official IRA and the RUC. Peter, always an entrepreneur in his short professional career, while working at the Regency Hotel had organised poker schools in the hotel bedrooms for all three groups separately. He provided drinks and sandwiches late into the night each Sunday. But amazingly, by careful scheduling and management, none of the three groups knew the others were there in the same hotel playing poker at the same time. It may be just a coincidence but it is worth noting that the same hotel, throughout the Troubles, was never bombed or the target of shootings. It was a testimony perhaps to Peter's extraordinary ingenuity, character, personality and people management skills.

Naturally, all Bridie's singing engagements were cancelled for the rest of the year. No one could be sure she would ever go on stage again. Her good friend Eileen Donaghy, another popular Irish ballad singer who was well known in Ireland, agreed to fulfil many of her engagements in the immediate two months that followed.

But after four months Bridie still could not come to terms with Peter's death. She was broken-hearted and feeling depressed all the time. Peter's death had attracted enormous coverage in the newspapers, but surprisingly there continued to be a big demand for her to return to performing. Most of her family and friends were agreed that ultimately the best treatment or therapy for her would be to get back 'on the road', as hard-hearted and impossible as that might seem. She needed to be 'active and productive rather than sitting at home with too much time to think' was the common view of those closest to her. Eventually, with much persuasion and hesitancy, she finally agreed to give performing on stage a try.

Her return to the stage was carefully planned. Two venues, at which she loved to perform, with excellent promoters who knew her well, were selected. They were both in Manchester – Jim Connell's Ardri Club and St Lawrence's Irish Club, run by a young Irish priest. The first show was in St Lawrence's and the priest fully understood what Bridie was going through. The audience, a completely packed house, was absolutely marvellous. What Bridie did not know was that the priest had ensured at the previous Sunday Mass that as many parishioners as possible were told about her son Peter's death and her attempt to return to singing. The fans fully supported her in a way that only a loving Irish community could do.

Bridie brought one of her nieces from Donegal to assist her on those two momentous dates. She was also called Bridie Gallagher. This Bridie Gallagher was her brother Josie's daughter. She had a hearty laugh and could be guaranteed to make Bridie laugh on every occasion. On this occasion her role was to help Bridie with the biggest challenge in her life and keep her smiling and positive.

She proved to be a wonderful support on that short tour. She was only sixteen years old and had not travelled too far at the time except to Dublin or Glasgow, so, in some ways, it was a fascinating and even exciting trip for her, despite the fact she was acutely aware of the pain and anguish being suffered by her famous aunt. When they checked into their hotel she shared a room with Auntie Bridie. She was tickled pink. The first thing she did was lift the telephone and started messing about pretending to order room service. She kept Bridie giggling all the while until a hotel waiter suddenly arrived at the room door enquiring if they needed room service. They both laughed uproariously and decided to order fancy cakes and tea.

When it came time for the show Bridie was racked with nerves. Could she do this? What would people think of her singing after losing a son? Would she even remember the words of songs? She was welcomed onto the stage by the parish priest, after a little hesitation, to rapturous applause and a standing ovation that seemed to last her entire thirty-minute performance. What no one knew was that wrapped around her arms under the sleeves of her dress was a set of rosary beads. It was her personal prayer for support and guidance.

The two shows were outstanding successes. Most people in the audiences knew the pain Bridie had suffered and the courage needed to return to performing. She had been worried that people would condemn or criticise her for returning to the stage after tragically losing her son, but she received nothing but support on those two nights in Manchester. No one criticised her. In fact, she received countless letters of support. Had she not performed those two shows in late 1976, it is doubtful she would ever have done another. More importantly, though, if she had not returned to the stage then, her life thereafter would most likely have been even sadder, less fulfilling and probably shorter. She said many times afterwards how she silently thanked God for the courage she found on those two nights, and the respect and love she received from her audiences and followers in return.

Given the trauma of marriage breakdown and loss of a child, it would probably not surprise many to know Bridie suffered episodes of depression in her later life. This first became manifest in the years immediately following her separation from Bob and was to continue on and off for the rest of her life. The circumstances of the time conspired to create a perfect context in which depression could take hold and undermine her mental health in a profound sense. Her career was still flourishing but her place at the top of the bill was increasingly under siege from younger pop stars and showbands in Ireland, and her records were played less on the radio. Ironically, her record sales internationally remained largely unaffected by the new youth culture of the 1960s in Britain and Ireland, reflecting her enduring appeal to Irish emigrants abroad. Many of the great theatres in which she performed were closing as variety theatre was slowly replaced by other forms of entertainment such as television. She was significantly isolated in her Belfast home. Her sisters and brothers lived in Britain, Donegal and Dublin. For some time she had very few close friends living in Belfast. She had travelled so much for so many years, she had not had the chance to develop a network of friends locally. She was also determined not to share publicly with anyone that her marriage had ended. This was through a mixture of guilt and embarrassment. In fact, for some years she frequently pretended that Bob was away on business if asked by neighbours.

These circumstances crashed together like a car accident and she crawled from the wreckage a very sad and lonely woman. The sadness was seen only by family at home and never in public. On stage she smiled and laughed as ever before, but in private her world was often dark and lacking any purpose except to ensure her boys got a good education and good jobs. Her work kept her going as her mind was occupied with new shows, new recordings, new management and new venues with the rise in popularity of cabaret in Ireland. But it was on her days off, when she was at home relaxing, that she would sometimes be found alone in the afternoon listening to her favourite Jim Reeves and Patsy Cline records and cradling a glass of Scotch in one hand and a cigarette in the other. On days like these it was best not to interrupt her solitude in case her dark mood turned to anger.

She enjoyed a drink, especially Scotch whisky, but could never handle more than two or three without becoming tipsy. As a young woman she never drank alcohol – mostly out of fear of being discovered by her mother who was fiercely against 'the drink' among her family. On the show business circuit in the early 1950s she became more and more aware of drinking by those around her but still mostly resisted the temptation. It was only when her career reached stardom in the late 1950s, bringing with it new anxieties and stresses, that she eventually began to take one or two drinks after shows when 'winding down' with others around her. But even then she never drank alcohol in the company of her mother. By the 1960s she regularly had one or two drinks after a show and was by then also a smoker, which for a woman in her forties was still quite moderate.

But by 1965, when depression took hold, alcohol was often there to ease the pain, as she saw it, or perhaps tighten its grip, as I saw it. But

Bridie's son Peter on holiday in Spain in 1969.

happily, with some encouragement and support from me, she always managed to keep herself right for business and performances on stage for her public. While her family naturally found these occasional episodes hard to cope with, it never lessened her love and care for her family. Unsurprisingly she had to fight all the harder to avoid more excessive drinking after Peter's death. While she continued to have a drink after shows, and at home from time to time, she reached a sort of equilibrium where the public rarely saw her with too much drink, and if they did she would laugh it off. She could also never manage to quit cigarettes, right up to the end (although she usually left more cigarettes burning in an ashtray than she actually smoked). She sought medical treatment for the depression and eventually decided to change aspects of her lifestyle to great effect as she entered her sixties. Regular swimming in a local pool, walking extraordinary distances in all weathers, taking up hobbies such as painting, and even joining her local parish choir in St

Brigid's, all became part of her recovery. To a large extent she managed her condition well in terms of mental health, as a struggle for sure, but one that, importantly, did not affect her work or damage her family relationships.

Bridie's physical health was also the cause of great pain and worry. As a young girl she played camogie and had good health. In later years when touring she began to smoke, although never heavily. She used to laugh with her friend Vivienne McMaster at their antics as young women on the road practising how to smoke and look sexy and alluring. When she started to drink alcohol at the relatively advanced age of thirty, she drank martinis but later graduated to whisky and soda (but never with ice). She was not a very heavy drinker but loneliness and depression occasionally lead to her drinking alone at home, often grieving over her marriage separation and later the loss of her son Peter.

She was well aware of the widespread public perception that people in show business were invariably involved in excessive drink, drugs and promiscuous sex, and generally living 'the high life'. Of course there have always been performers who have over-indulged in many different ways, usually hurting themselves and those closest to them. Promiscuity and drug-taking were never part of Bridie's world, and neither was living the so-called high life. If anything, when not on stage, Bridie's preference was to live very simply and away from the 'limelight', and she was most often to be found in her garden weeding, painting in oils, or in the kitchen preparing for dinner guests.

However, after thirty years of work-induced and personal stress, smoking and frequent dietary disturbance from travel, she succumbed to her first heart attack one morning in 1981. At first she thought it was indigestion after a curry eaten the night before with her friends Marie Cunningham and Moya Rooney. But by the afternoon it became clear that something more serious was happening. Her doctor visited an hour later and immediately rang for an ambulance. She was taken to the Royal Victoria Hospital where she received first-class treatment and soon stabilised. A few days later the cardiologist advised Bridie that she needed a heart bypass operation or she would probably have another heart attack soon, which might be fatal.

At that time, this particular surgical procedure was relatively new and much less common than today. Needless to say the family were extremely worried. But characteristically her indomitable spirit carried her through. By an extraordinary coincidence two of her old friends

157

from Belfast, Peter Gormley and James Carberry, were in the male side of the same ward, also undergoing cardiac procedures. Only days after her operation she showed amazing recovery. The staff nurse on her ward commented that she was doing very well indeed, considering the seriousness of the procedure and that *'she and her two boyfriends are shouting to each other across the ward. I've had to tell them more than once to keep the noise down.'*

Bridie was back performing only six months later but asked one special favour – that a gala variety show be organised in Belfast to raise money for the treatment of heart disease. And so in April 1982 a grand variety show was put on at the Arts Theatre. Variety theatre, other than Christmas pantomimes, had not been seen in Belfast for almost twenty years. All the popular stage artists in Northern Ireland at the time were performing in cabaret rather than theatre. Many of them were delighted to be part of the show. They included Ray Sheils, Danny Small, Birdie Sweeney, Jimmy Kennedy, Marjorie Rea, Gerry O'Rawe and many others. It was an astounding success and raised over £1,000 for the NI Chest Heart and Stroke Association.

But despite the bypass surgery, that first heart attack was a taste of worse to come. She did change her lifestyle in various respects, making some changes to her diet (reducing salt and fatty foods) and taking physical exercise (swimming twice each week and taking regular long walks). But she couldn't stop smoking or having a drink. In 2005 she suffered the first of five strokes. Over subsequent years each stroke knocked her back further and further. Gradually she was unable to walk alone and she suffered from dysphasia (where her speech was affected). Ultimately her memory began to fade and she was easily confused. It upset her greatly that she couldn't remember the words of songs, even though she had stopped performing five or more years before. Even more frustrating was how her failing memory disturbed her as she struggled to remember the many wonderful places she had visited in her life, the people she had met, and the many good times she had experienced.

This was the hardest suffering – to find that her memories were confused and difficult to recall. Memories of magnificent successes and achievements that few others could ever hope to emulate, memories of people and places she loved. She would go through her scrapbooks and photo albums searching for memories, but even then would sometimes not even recognise pictures of herself, let alone others. The only consolation for her and her family was that she never failed to recognise her immediate family, especially her four grandchildren, or nephews and nieces when they visited from Donegal or Scotland.

One day in 2009, a plastic bag filled with a dozen 16mm film reels was found in her attic. They dated from 1959 to 1964 and were mostly taken by her husband Bob. There was no projector to view them so they were sent away to be cleaned and, where necessary, repaired and transferred to a digital medium. When the family gathered to view the digitally enhanced old film they were transfixed. There was film of Bridie's sons, Jim and Peter, aged seven and five playing in her garden and on the Gallagher farm in Creeslough, as well as film of her and Bob walking in London's Regent's Park and sightseeing in Times Square in New York, Philadelphia and Chicago, and, best of all, footage of her on stage at the London Metropolitan Theatre. It was wonderful and everyone watching was overwhelmed. Most significantly, Bridie suddenly found a wonderful spark of memories revived for her. Her obvious pleasure and excitement at renewed memories of great times years before, as well as some tears, was a joy for all to behold.

A few months later, the journalist Paddy O'Flaherty made contact seeking a radio interview with Bridie. It was explained to him that her health and memory were now sadly poor and that an interview would be very difficult, if not impossible, to do. However, when he was told about the old home movies being unearthed, he was immediately excited and anxious to see them. A few days later, by agreement, he brought an independent television producer, Anna Marie McFaul, to view the film. They were ecstatic. Here was a truly historic visual record of Bridie at her peak, one that would be perfect for television. Within a few weeks a contract had been agreed to produce a television documentary built around Bridie's career and uniquely supplemented by these old and incredibly high-quality home movies.

It was almost magical when, on 18 December 2011, UTV broadcast that same documentary about Bridie's career. It was produced by Picture This Productions and was presented by her eldest granddaughter, Teresa Livingstone. It attracted the largest viewing figures in Ireland, apparently even greater than Match of the Day on BBC, made very creative use of the footage from her personal home movies, and included interviews with great friends like Eddie McIlwaine, Daniel O'Donnell, Dec Cluskey (of The Bachelors), Vivienne McMaster, her sister Maggie and sister-in-law Bridget in Donegal, and friend Joan Tobin, as well as fans from New York who had seen her perform fifty years before. Bridie watched it four times that evening, often moved to tears at the glowing tributes paid to her, and excited to see friends and family on her television in her native Donegal. For those few hours the glorious memories of this frail eighty-seven-year-old woman suddenly became alive again and she relived that magnificent career of over fifty years.

Throughout all these trials of separation, loss and ill health Bridie somehow still managed to present a smile to the world. Regardless of the heartache and suffering in her private life she never spoke about it publicly. She would mention that she had heart trouble in media interviews, and she eventually came to the point where she publicly acknowledged her failed marriage. The one thing she could never speak about was the loss of her son. It was too painful. Other parents who have suffered such a loss are the only ones who can understand how difficult that pain is to explain, let alone speak about. It was 'her cross to be carried' and she carried it with courage.

Chapter Ten

BRIDIE'S MUSIC

If I were a blackbird, I'd whistle and sing
And I'd follow the ship that my true love sails in
And on the top rigging I'd there build my nest
And I'd pillow my head on his lily white breast.

'IF I WERE A BLACKBIRD' (TRADITIONAL)

*B*y 1985 Bridie had celebrated thirty years as a recording artist. She had started simply in 1954 in the Jewish Institute on the Antrim Road in Belfast with Tommy James and his trio, recording 'A Mother's Love's a Blessing' on mobile recording equipment for Decca. She graduated a few years later to London recording studios with the then most modern and sophisticated equipment, including the famous EMI's Abbey Road Studios with full orchestra and George Martin as engineer. She always enjoyed recording, and even the hours and hours of practice and rehearsal required at home for weeks beforehand learning lyrics and melodies. She would normally do this alone with her little tape recorder and occasionally with her musical director present. While many might find the thought of repetitive rehearsal and learning songs tedious and boring, Bridie found it very satisfying. In all her years recording, she never lost the excitement and pleasure to be had in the whole recording process, both in and out of studio.

While she did receive some voice training from Hyodie Hunter in Creeslough and later Leila Webster when she first moved to Belfast, there was no 'training' as such for any singer starting to record. It has always been very much about learning through experience. But to do it well requires that a singer, even one who has never before been in a recording studio, knows what they want to sound like to the audience and listener.

From the beginning she was fastidious about getting the right phrasing of lyrics and understanding the exact meaning of every word sung. For most of her professional life she always had a small dictionary in her bag, and at home she kept a large *Oxford English Dictionary* beside her favourite chair. She never did crosswords, but if she heard an unfamiliar word on television or the radio, or read it in a newspaper or magazine, out would come her dictionary and she would not rest until she had the right meaning. Words, as much as music, were her 'bread and butter'. It was always vital to her that she understood what the writer of a song wished to convey, so that she could interpret the meaning of the lyrics and thus the song, and communicate that to her audience. For Bridie, singing was about communicating ideas, emotions and energy to others. The singer she admired most in this respect was Bing Crosby. She frequently described him as the singer who sang with the most perfect diction, even in jazz or blues songs, where syncopation and phrasing could make clarity of sound very difficult for average singers.

But it was in the actual recording process that she excelled. All her

BRIDIE GALLAGHER

I FOUND YOU OUT
TWO-FACED MOON
IT'S A SIN TO TELL A LIE
SOMEBODY CRIED AT
YOUR WEDDING

EP cover of *I Found You Out*, released by Decca Records in 1958.

record producers over the years expressed amazement at her stamina and determination in the studio. She never complained if songs had to be recorded time and again to get them right. Indeed, her own desire for perfection often made her ask for take after take to get it right. She would usually rise at six o'clock on the morning of a recording, have a light breakfast, and then do repeated voice exercises for hours to ensure that, by midday, her voice was in perfect pitch. She would then typically work in a studio until perhaps ten o'clock that night. It was hard work, very demanding physically and emotionally, but she revelled in it. She understood the importance of being in tune, keeping in time, and how to modulate her voice to reflect varying emotions in the lyrics of songs.

By far her favourite recordings were made in London with Stan Butcher as musical director. Stan was a quiet and gentle Englishman who was a wonderfully creative musician. Bridie and he hit it off from the first moment. There was, to use a cliché, a real chemistry between them. They shared ideas and never hesitated to say what they liked or disliked about anything that was tried. They collaborated to produce something fresh and new and exciting. With those four albums they did together they achieved a new sound that had never been produced before, nor indeed since. It was the sound that was to establish Bridie as a unique recording artist and singer with a fresh take on old Irish ballads, for so long ignored by most record companies.

The cover of Bridie's first LP from 1958.

The basic component of that 'sound' comprises several elements. In terms of instruments Stan's choice for Bridie was made up of old and new, traditional and modern sounds. First there were the strings – violins, cellos and double bass (never electric bass) featured in every song and provided a lush and warm background for the melodies. Drums, of course, provided a subtle beat to suit the style of each song track as needed but most significantly usually only employing brushes and rarely sticks. There was always an accordion, superbly played by a German session musician who provided beautiful melodies, improvisations and links between verses and chorus. Finally, there was an electric guitar played by a jazz session musician who produced a modern, contemporary sound but played with a quiet and gentle style. There were no backing singers, brass instruments or even a piano, which would, at that time, have normally featured on all new records.

The recording technology was not the multi-tracked digitised type familiar today. So there was no over-dubbing or double tracking so common in later years. It generated a simple but sophisticated sound that few have ever been able to emulate since. Bridie's was the only voice to be heard, crystal clear and perfectly pitched. The wonderful accordion accompaniment provided a perfectly balanced harmony with her voice and resulted in some of the most haunting and luscious interpretations of Irish ballads ever produced. Stan used the musicians'

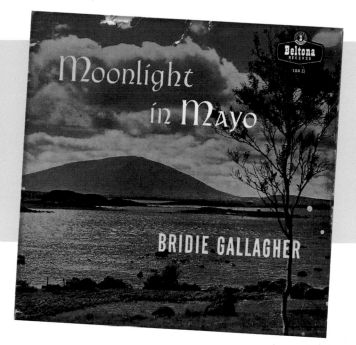

highly polished skills and techniques in his arrangements to combine Irish melody with the richness of orchestral strings and at times a touch of jazz in what can only be described as a combination of a little humour, an enormous helping of romanticism, and strong rich harmony for every song.

All of this was with Bridie's voice crystal clear and strong above the instruments, her faultless diction (in which she prided herself), invariably tune-perfect with that little 'break' to add a touch of pathos when needed. There are so many examples of these mixtures of styles and sounds. The romanticism was never better presented than in her recordings of 'Two Little Orphans', 'Teddy O'Neill', 'I Left Ireland and Mother Because We Were Poor'. The humour is best to be heard in 'When Will You Marry Me Johnny My Love', 'The Irish Jaunting Car' or 'Johnny Gray'. The sumptuous harmony can be experienced best listening to 'Kylemore Pass', 'That Tumble Down Shack in Athlone' or 'Moonlight on the Shannon River'.

Bridie recorded for a series of companies: Beltona (which became Emerald); EMI; Dolphin Records in Dublin; Outlet Records in Belfast; and Homespun Records in Dungannon. She never ceased to enjoy the thrill and challenge of recording in new studios with great producers like Cel Fay, John Anderson and George Doherty, but at the same time she never regarded any later recordings she made as surpassing or even

Parlophone LP cover of *At Home With Bridie Gallagher*, released in 1962. Bridie's sons, Jim *(right)* and Peter *(left)*, feature on the cover.

equalling the quality of her collaboration with Stan Butcher between 1958 and 1962. And in all of the hundreds of songs she recorded there was only one she absolutely hated. It was 'Ballyhoe'. She hated it for the fact that her very first note in the song is flat. She never understood how this flaw was missed and allowed to be passed for sale in the shops. As a result she never sang the song on stage. Interestingly, she said she never remembered anyone ever requesting that she sing it either.

The format of her records mirrored that of her stage performances. This involved a programme predominantly of ballads in waltz time interspersed with a few in quick-step time. These songs were invariably about the Irish home ('Tumble Down Shack in Athlone'), unrequited love ('Teddy O'Neill'), the Irishman or woman leaving or away from home ('Goodbye Johnny Dear', 'Cuttin' the Corn in Creeslough'),

LP cover of the original *Bridie Gallagher Sings Irish Requests*, released in 1963.

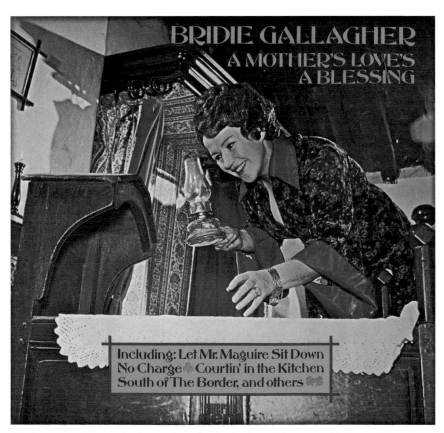

Single cover of 'A Mother's Love's a Blessing', released by Emerald Records in 1976.

167

mothers ('A Mother's Last Goodbye', 'A Mother's Love's a Blessing'), and places in Ireland ('Killarney and You', 'Kylemore Pass', 'Moonlight in Mayo', 'Cottage by the Lee' and 'Moonlight on the Shannon River').

One common feature was that many had particularly sad and heart-tugging themes. It was a formula that appealed mostly to emigrants wanting to be reminded of what they had left behind, or people in Ireland remembering their pasts. Bridie often commented that she was always struck by how many of her sad songs her audiences consistently demanded. It was not untypical to find her in any venue singing to audiences all weeping or with pained looks of grief or loss on their faces, and yet shouting for more of the same when she finished. The few up-tempo songs in her programme, which she delivered with gusto, were as much a relief to her as anyone else, set among all those songs of pathos.

'I would be a nervous wreck if I sang only those sad ones all night, even though the people seemed never to tire listening and crying along with me on stage.'

There was perhaps a subtle psychological phenomenon present in her programme, which managed to combine a series of sad songs with a fast, hand-clapping, happy song like 'Courtin' in The Kitchen' before moving back into more sad songs. This formula clearly raised adrenalin levels in her audience and possibly created a sort of 'high' that audiences came to crave. It's probably a truism that in entertainment of any kind people seek tears of laughter and sadness in appropriate proportion as some magical potion that makes most performances and even lives more bearable. Bridie certainly contributed her special formula to that magic potion for many millions over the years.

It was a distinctive aspect of her stage performances and recordings that she strove to ensure that as many counties of Ireland as possible were represented. It is a wonderful feature of Irish ballads that so many deal with love, death, emigration, marriage and courtship in the context of a particular county in Ireland. There are, for some strange reason, many more songs written about some counties than others. So it is relatively easy to compose a programme of songs to include some about Donegal, Galway, Kerry or Dublin, for example. But some counties don't fare so well.

The Irish folk singer Paddy Reilly successfully compiled an album of thirty-two songs some years ago, one for each county. But some of the songs were hardly known outside the relevant county. Nevertheless, as

IRELAND'S BALLAD QUEEN
sings
If Those Lips Could Only Speak

Cover of Bridie's
1979 album *If
Those Lips Could
Only Speak.*

Bridie learned over many years of singing to her audiences, especially Irish emigrants scattered around the globe, one of the ways of making an effective personal contact and establishing a rapport with each and every listener was to sing about the listener's place of birth or origins. And so in every performance, and every recording, there can be found a variety of songs with themes associated with particular parts of Ireland among more generic themes of love and loss.

The one thing Bridie never toured without was an accompanying musician. She had learned very early that if she relied on musicians provided at any concert venue, other than major theatres that had orchestras, she risked finding herself with ones who could not read music and so were unable to read her quite complex musical arrangements, usually prepared at great cost. It was even more common to find musicians who could not play their instruments in the particular keys that suited her voice. The average musician playing guitar or piano tends not to use keys such as E Flat or A Flat by choice because they are technically more difficult to manage. But she sang many of her songs in these difficult keys, although she did use other keys for songs where it better suited her vocal range. The keys had been determined after considerable work with musical directors and she refused to consider using a different key.

During the heyday of variety theatre there seemed to be no shortage of very accomplished musicians to choose from. But in the 1970s, when cabaret became popular, many of the clubs and lounges employed relatively inexpensive and inexperienced bands to keep costs down. Some of them, when providing backing for Bridie, would try, live on stage, to give her an easier key for them to play (for example D rather than E Flat). She would stop and turn to the band with a fierce glare the audience could not see, but which would usually make offending bandsmen wither as she would smile and snarl at the same time, *'I'll have the right key this time please, gentlemen.'*

The band would dutifully do as she instructed. As far as she was concerned the only way to do a song was the 'right way' and musicians needed to be up to the task. In her opinion the audience always deserved to hear performances at their best.

From 1957 onwards she never performed without her own musical accompaniment, most often a pianist or accordionist. Her accompanist might play alone or along with a band or orchestra, acting as the musical director for that performance. The first was Thelma Ramsey, from Larne, who toured with her from 1956 until 1958 when she married Martin Crosbie from Dublin. She was followed by Sheba Kelly from outside Dublin, a glamorous blonde and very gifted accordionist. Having an accordion was a great advantage because it meant they didn't have to depend on finding an in-tune piano at venues around Ireland, Britain or indeed the US, which was not always easy. Sheba toured with Bridie on her first four tours of the US and worked with her until 1961. Another Dubliner, Eddie Tighe, toured with her from 1962 to 1965 and was an extremely talented pianist who not only provided superb accompaniment but also constant fun and laughs.

'We had terrible snow and frost for many weeks in 1963. Eddie on piano and Pat McGuigan on guitar and harmonica were my musical backing at the time and I had a date in County Carlow. It took us ten

LP cover of
*Bridie Gallagher
Sings Irish
Requests*,
released by
Emerald
Records in 1983.

hours to get to Carlow from Belfast. The weather was so bad there were cars in the ditches all the way down. When we stopped for meal breaks, people told us we were crazy to continue our journey. But we knew "The show must go on." There were even times when I was steering while both boys pushed and heaved the car from behind, slipping and sliding on the frozen road. Eddie's language was choice. But more importantly, he kept us laughing the whole journey. We reached Carlow only to find that the show had been cancelled. The promoter, Mr Duffy, actually paid us the fee and gave us a return booking in appreciation of the efforts we had made to get there. Very few promoters were ever so considerate.'

Paud Griffen was from Mullingar and had, at the young age of twenty-five, acquired an extensive reputation for his musical ability on the newly invented accordivox. This was the first electronic accordion, which in the late 1960s became popular among a legion of accordionists. In 1966 Bridie had signed with new Dublin management under Shane Redmond and was beginning to focus less on concert hall and theatre business, which was fast in decline, and more on the new cabaret clubs springing up around Ireland and Britain. Shane assigned Paud to accompany Bridie. She was delighted to have such a talented musician working with her. He was a performer in his own right. She realised she could put Paud's exceptional talent to good use. She

171

introduced a novel ten-minute break in her one-hour performance after about thirty minutes and left the stage to Paud. He would mesmerise the audiences with his phenomenal playing while Bridie changed her dress. Then back she went to finish the final twenty minutes. It became an important feature of her act thereafter and allowed her to dazzle audiences with at least two fabulous dresses instead of just one. Paud eventually won his own well-deserved recording contracts and went to Germany to pursue a very successful musical career.

Later accompanists included John Hardin from Belfast and George Bradley from Bangor in County Down. George, who was extremely talented and great fun to tour with, became as much a close friend as an accompanist, touring with her across Ireland and Britain and on her last American tour when she performed at the famous Lincoln Center in New York in 1991. Even after she finished public performing, she said it was always a treat for her to visit George and his wife Patricia who she knew loved music as much as she did.

But what were the musical influences on Bridie, and what were her personal tastes in music to listen to at leisure?

While her mother Biddy taught her mostly old Irish ballads and folk songs, some handed down from generation to generation, the music she came to know best as she grew up was predominantly British and American songs played on friends' wind-up record players and radios. The pop songs of the time were, as for every generation since, the music that initially formed her tastes in music. She adored Bing Crosby and Vera Lynn in particular and could often entertain others with a verse or chorus of any of their recordings with ease.

She admired both singers' versatility in singing songs of many different genres, but in particular she loved their clear tuneful voices. In Vera Lynn's case she found the emotion that she was able to instil in all her songs exhilarating. In Bing Crosby's case it was his vocal dexterity and diction that she found wonderful to hear. Naturally she loved many of their songs. But her favourite Vera Lynn song was 'Yours', and it was the song she sang in that first important talent competition for Eamon O'Shea in 1942. Many of Bing's songs were not suited to her voice but she adored 'White Christmas' and 'Dear Hearts and Gentle People'. Many years later, when recording one of her last albums, she insisted that this song needed to be included, even though it was not Irish. It was always a song that had a special meaning for her.

Bing Crosby's version of the song was recorded and released in

RBA 107

RAINBOW
RECORDS

TODAY

SWINGING IN THE LANE
DADDY'S LULLABY
FADED COAT OF BLUE
BRIDGET FLYNN
OLD SPINNING WHEEL
THE ISLES OF THE ERNE
HOME TO TYRONE
LOVELY INNISHOWEN
MY BIRTHPLACE DONEGAL
THE ROAD TO MALLINMORE
DON'T BOTHER TO KNOCK
CASTLE OF DROMORE

Cover of *Bridie Gallagher Today,* which was released by Rainbow Records in 1984.

1949, the year after she left Creeslough. It was often on the radio and it registered strongly with the girl who had left her hometown only months before. The lyrics perhaps struck a special chord with her:

'I love those dear hearts and gentle people who live in my home town
Because those dear hearts and gentle people will never ever let you down.'

So rather than a Donegal song reminding her of home and family and friends, it was Bing Crosby singing a song of home (which was actually set in Idaho).

In terms of Irish ballads, which became the primary focus of her stage performances and act in 1953, her mother's teaching for many years before was obviously fundamental. Many of the songs she recorded in her first two albums were ones she learned from Biddy, including 'The Hills of Glenswilly', 'Hills of Donegal' and 'Noreen Bawn'. But, having embarked on a professional career after her move to Belfast, she toured as a supporting act with the great Delia Murphy in 1953. This introduced her to a wider repertoire of Irish songs that appealed to Bridie's sense of melody and emotion. Delia encouraged her to include many long forgotten songs like 'The Spinning Wheel', 'Queen of Connemara' and

'Slievenamon'. She also introduced Bridie to the songs of the great Percy French who had died some thirty years earlier. While he was most noted for comic Irish songs like 'Phil the Fluter's Ball', he also wrote some ballads that became the core of Bridie's act, the most important of which was 'Cuttin' the Corn in Creeslough', known originally as 'The Emigrant's Letter'. In fifty years of performing, Bridie rarely did a show without 'Cuttin' the Corn in Creeslough', or indeed 'Phil the Fluter's Ball', in the programme.

Naturally, the fact that 'Cuttin' the Corn' referenced her hometown in its title meant it was an obvious choice for her performances. But wherever she went over the years, she discovered that the simple but memorable melody and wonderful lyrics of that song, telling the story of emigration and separation from loved ones, established it as the core spirit of her act. Equally, the lightness and comedy of 'Phil the Fluter's Ball' appealed to Bridie's well-known sense of fun and laughter, and as such established that additional component of her stage performance thereafter – namely, entertainment that combined tears of laughter and sadness in good measure.

Another composer who had died some twenty years earlier was Cork man Thomas P. Keenan. Bridie was introduced to his songs by Delia and it was in his collection that she was to find two of her greatest hits, 'The Boys from County Armagh' and 'A Mother's Love's a Blessing'. Yet again both songs fitted the theme of emigration and separation from home and family, and were part of Bridie's act permanently thereafter.

Once she became better known, especially after her first album was released in 1957, Bridie was regularly inundated with new songs written by Irish composers. Many were not of good enough quality to record, and some were little more than adaptations of old traditional songs. But one writer in particular became a very fruitful source for new songs that fitted the Irish ballad genre and appealed to Bridie's sense of emotion and fun. That was Mai O'Higgins. By far Bridie's favourite was 'Moonlight on the Shannon River', but there were many others. Consequently, whether written years earlier, or newly penned by contemporary Irish composers, Bridie soon had a deep well of Irish ballad material from which to choose her performance programmes and recording hits.

However, no sooner did Bridie achieve success with hits like 'The Boys from County Armagh', than managers and advisers suggested she branch into more mainstream popular music, away from Irish ballads.

Running Order:

1. The Girl From Donegal
2. Goodbye Johnny Dear
3. Lovely Innishowen
   (Filmed on Location in Donegal)
4. Let Him Go, Let Him Tarry
5. The Boys From The County Armagh
6. The Tumbledown Shack in Athlone
   (Filmed on Location)
7. Where The River Shannon Flows
8. Courtin' In The Kitchen Part 1
   Jigs
   Courtin' In The Kitchen Part 2
9. If I Was A Blackbird
   (Filmed on Location)
10. Eileen O'Grady
11. A Mother's Love's A Blessing
12. The Road To Malinmore
    (Filmed on Location)
13. The Homes Of Donegal
14. Medley
    Shake Hand With Your Uncle Mick
    Hannigan's Hooley
    If You're Irish

Bridie Gallagher has been a legend in Irish Show-business for over 25 years. From Creeslagh in Donegal, she was propelled onto the International stage in the mid 50's with such massive hits as 'A Mother's Love's A Blessing', 'The Boys From The County Armagh' and the song that has been her theme song all down through the years 'The Girl From Donegal'. She recently completed her 21st Tour of America and ended the tour with a standing ovation in the prestigious Lincoln Centre in New York.

On this video she is filmed 'In Concert' in the Gaiety Theatre in Mosney and 'on Location' in her beloved Donegal.

Produced by Hugh Hardy

APOLLO VIDEO

The Girl From Donegal

Bridie GALLAGHER

The Girl From Donegal **Bridie** GALLAGHER

Live 'In Concert' and on Location in Donegal

Apollo Video **VHS** APV 46

Live 'In Concert' and on Location in Donegal

5 099152 001053

Cover of Bridie's first music video, released by Apollo Video in 1986.

Bearing in mind she had started her stage career singing those same pop songs rather than Irish ballads, it is not surprising that she was tempted to venture into a new style. In 1958, with encouragement from Phil Solomon, she recorded 'It's a Sin to Tell a Lie', previously made internationally famous by the Ink Spots in America, and another 1930s American hit 'I Found You Out' by the Ted Weems band (the lead singer of which was once a young Perry Como). They were recorded very much in the new contemporary pop style made famous by Connie Francis and Alma Cogan.

They transpired to be high-quality recordings that attracted much attention and radio plays around the time of Bridie's appearance at the London Palladium, and Bridie herself thoroughly enjoyed making the new style of records. But her primary fan base of Irish emigrants was evidently not impressed. The record sold reasonably well in Britain but not sufficiently to enter the charts at a high position. But more importantly, her fans made it clear in letters to Bridie and her recording company Decca that they wanted the Irish ballads and basically shunned Bridie's new venture. And so it was ever to be. Bridie decided quickly that she could not change her fundamental style or music. She was not going to become a pop singer or country and western singer. She would stay with Irish ballads. But that did not stop her from time to time introducing non-Irish songs into her repertoire or even on albums. She loved so many different styles of music, she found it difficult to ignore other influences, especially if the song was strong in emotion and story.

Songs like 'Dear Hearts and Gentle People', 'Lucky Old Sun', 'If I Had My Life to Live Over' and 'No Charge' all appeared from time to time on albums or as singles when Bridie tried again and again to introduce a little variety to her act, without fundamentally changing her style. The recording of 'No Charge', a cover version of the Canadian J. J. Barrie's hit, was released by Bridie in 1976 only a few weeks before the tragic death of her youngest son. With its very emotive lyrics about a mother's love for a child, Bridie was never able to perform the song again, and frequently regretted ever recording it.

'For the time and the tears and the costs through the years, there's no charge
When you add it all up the real cost of my love is, no charge.'

Frequently her choice of material to perform and record reflected her personal taste in music. Professionally she was always an Irish ballad singer, but any perusal of her considerable record collection revealed a very mixed bag indeed. Some artists were more prominent than others and the collection was certainly not limited to Irish artistes, and was not dominated by her own recordings.

While some people might assume that singers in show business have enormous egos and that listening to themselves on record might somehow be a daily occurrence, the fact is Bridie never listened to her own records after the recording process had ended. Visitors to her home might ask her to play one of her albums, but she usually made some excuse to avoid it. Left to choose, she rarely played her own, other than to rehearse lyrics for a show. The records she listened to for pleasure were seldom Irish ballads. Singing and recording one type of song time after time meant she needed to relax to records of a different style and culture.

In the heart of Donegal—BRIDIE GALLAGHER   emerald gem

LP cover of
*In the Heart
of Donegal*,
released by
Emerald
Records in
1968.

Her favourite recording artists gave her both enjoyment and inspiration. Their influence can be seen in some aspects of her performing and recording over the years. Undoubtedly the singer whose albums she bought time and again, and played almost daily, was the American country and western star Jim Reeves. She adored his smooth voice and once described it as 'chocolatey'. She would relax and listen to possibly two or three albums in succession either in her lounge or in her garden listening through the open lounge window. She once met his wife Mary in Nashville after Jim had been tragically killed in an air accident and told her she regarded him as not only the best country and western singer in the world but the best ballad singer in the world.

She also liked Pat Boone, Frank Sinatra, Patsy Cline, Val Doonican, Dickie Rock, Matt Munro, Vera Lynn, Bing Crosby and in her later years Daniel O'Donnell. All were solo singers. The album *Blowing in The Wind* by American folk group Peter, Paul and Mary was the only album by a group in her collection. If anyone asked her, after her fifth tour to the US in 1964, for her favourite singer and song, there was only one answer: Barbara Streisand singing 'People', the show-stopping number from the Broadway musical *Funny Girl*: *'People, people who need people, are the luckiest people in the world.'*

This held a special resonance for Bridie, and she privately spoke of how the song reminded her of the fact that as a performer, her job was to please her audiences and fans and not herself. It was these people who made her feel special and lucky. These were the people she needed. However, the song's lyrics also symbolised a degree of loneliness that Bridie experienced in her life, especially after her marriage failed. She had many good friends and a close and supportive family circle. But because she chose not to divorce Bob, and remarry, there is no doubt that Barbara Streisand's song held a special meaning for her in her later life, which she lived alone and without a partner.

She rarely performed songs in public that were not Irish ballads. When she did it was invariably in a venue where she felt the audience would appreciate something different but, most importantly, where she knew she could rely on top-class musicians capable of improvising and playing different styles. In such situations, she had several songs that she loved to perform. Some were country and western numbers and therefore immediately popular with Irish audiences, such as 'Red River Valley' and 'China Doll'. But others could surprise people. Occasionally she liked to sing Lena Horne's classic 'Stormy Weather' or the wonderful song from the musical *Showboat*, 'Can't Help Lovin' Dat Man of Mine'. They were songs that, in many respects, were as far away from Irish ballads as one could get. But they were full of emotion, which she knew how to express so well in song, and she loved the sense of freedom she got from singing in a different style, if only for a few minutes in very selective performances.

Fundamentally, she loved songs of all kinds. While she did not under-stand opera as an art, she still thrilled to listen to the great tenors and sopranos. Melody was an important factor for her in any good song. But she knew from an early stage that the lyrics were paramount. When writers sent her new songs, her first action was to read the lyrics. She never listened to the melody first. She might be disappointed if the lyrics were strong and the melody less so. But she flatly refused to sing songs if the lyrics did not appeal to her, no matter how good the tune.

Apart from variety theatre, musicals were her favourite stage shows and whenever she was in New York or London her personal treat was to catch at least one show. She saw the original *West Side Story* production on Broadway in the early 1960s and she maintained ever after it was the gold standard by which all musicals should be judged. She also loved jazz and occasionally visited Ronnie Scott's Club in London.

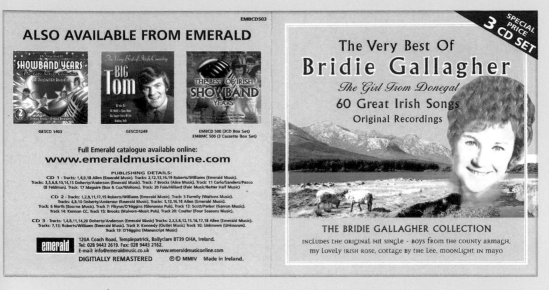

CD cover of Bridie's greatest hits, released by Emerald Records in 2005.

She enjoyed the pop music of the 1960s but never found loud electric guitar music attractive at all. But even when she didn't like the music, she could still appreciate the performance of artists. She would judge them in terms of the emotion they put into performances, their diction, their tunefulness (she hated singers who sang out of tune and there were, in her view, plenty of these in all forms of music), and their dress and stage presence (she never understood singers wearing jeans and t-shirts and regarded it as simply unprofessional).

In terms of her love of musical theatre one of my fondest memories was a wonderful evening in 2009 when I took Bridie and one of her best pals, Marie (Cunningham) Murphy, to the Grand Opera House in Belfast to see a touring show of *The Rat Pack*, a tribute to Frank Sinatra, Sammy Davis Jr and Dean Martin. By this time Bridie was eighty-five years old and Marie seventy-six. Both had suffered strokes and were frail and unsteady on their feet. But both were so excited to be in a favourite old theatre again watching a top-class show. I slowly and carefully escorted both, one on either arm, to their seats where they beamed with joy when the marvellous big band struck up and the tribute singers came on stage to give superb performances recreating the unique sounds and styles of the Rat Pack of old. At one stage I looked at the faces of the elderly entertainers beside me who each had travelled the world and themselves performed on its many great theatre stages. While glowing with joy, they were both creased in tears. At the interval I asked, out of concern, if they were okay. It was Marie who then explained that they had separately seen the original Rat Pack perform on stage in America some fifty years before. Their tears were for great memories they shared of seeing wonderful artists performing in fabulous theatres when they were young and at the height of their own personal successes in show business. In Bridie's case it was to be her last visit to a theatre show, but it was one that gave her tremendous pleasure, listening and watching excellent singers perform wonderful songs with classy style, and re-newed memories of her own times when she had topped the bill on the world's stage.

Music was inherently part of Bridie's soul and character. She sang incessantly, at home, in the car and in the garden. She appreciated good music and good musicians in particular. If someone told her they did not like music (and it happened once or twice), she thought there was something wrong with them psychologically. It was this profound love of music and lyrics that she shared with people from the stage. And it was the love of music that she communicated to her audiences that proved to be her biggest enduring asset and appeal. Bridie Gallagher and music were ultimately one and the same thing.

Chapter Eleven
FANS AND FRIENDS

I love those dear hearts and gentle people
Who live in my home town
Because those dear hearts and gentle people
Will never ever let you down.

'DEAR HEARTS AND GENTLE PEOPLE' (FAIN, HILLIARD)

*F*ans were a vital part of Bridie's life from when she started singing professionally. In the beginning her admirers were school pals, other boys and girls who knew her in Creeslough, from when growing up and singing with local bands or at parties. But for any performer most fans rarely know, at a personal level, the celebrity to whom they are devoted. They attend performances, seek autographs and photographs, buy records, collect memorabilia, write fan letters, and convince friends that their chosen celebrity is the best singer/actor/musician/sportsperson. To have fans requires some degree of fame. At first that 'fame' might be within a local community, but if it develops into a national or international phenomenon, then fans are the people who carry the performer on to greater heights. In the 1950s and 1960s, compared to the Internet-driven society of today where someone 'unknown' can achieve worldwide notice in a matter of minutes, the cultivation of fame took much longer to achieve. In fact, for most artists in that period, in whatever genre, it usually took years to build a reputation among audiences everywhere.

Widespread fame then depended primarily on radio exposure (record plays and interviews), press articles, and performances in large theatres. Television coverage was much more limited in the 1950s and only became prominent in Ireland and Britain in the 1960s. Fame rarely developed accidentally. It had to be cultivated and required constant touring, regular record releases, and seeking out press and radio

Bridie *(centre)* signs autographs for fans in Belfast *c.* 1957.

interviews. It was hard work but necessary if success and fame were to follow.

In her early years of professional work Bridie quickly attracted press coverage wherever she went. As a consequence attendances at her performances grew and grew to the point where she often sang to audiences measuring in their thousands across Ireland, Britain and north America. This was founded on the fact that she had a unique talent that set her apart from other singers, and an appeal that attracted followers.

As a result, a dedicated and enthusiastic fan base emerged between 1955 and 1965. While some were living in Ireland, most of Bridie's fans were Irish emigrants living away from Ireland. She became synonymous with Irish emigrants and ultimately was their sweetheart songstress. So few Irish singers at that time travelled outside of Ireland, she became the one who captured emigrants' hearts and they, in turn, saw her as their own. She travelled to them wherever they were when they could not travel home to Ireland. She reminded them of home, no matter what part of Ireland that might be. Time and again over the years fans told her *'you were the one who brought us back home even for a few minutes in your singing and recordings'*. A few years ago, a caller to an RTÉ radio show reminisced about a performance Bridie gave in the Holiday Ballroom in Chicago in those early years when she ended her show with the song 'Take This Message to My Mother'. The caller remembered how every person in the audience was in tears at the end of the show, including the band members.

In 2011 Bridie's granddaughter Teresa Livingstone worked with a television production company to produce a thirty-minute documentary about her grandmother's career. Bridie herself was originally supposed to present the programme but her health had by that time deteriorated badly following her fifth stroke. She could not travel and more importantly her speech had become faulty and laboured. Teresa was asked to step into the breach and she did so willingly, but also with some trepidation. She's a wonderful singer and pianist in her own right, but television presentation was a very new challenge for her.

Teresa interviewed people in London, Belfast, Donegal and New York for the programme. Daniel O'Donnell in his interview told Teresa how her grandmother Bridie had been the first to lead the way for Irish artists on the international scene. Indeed he laughed recalling how she had told him after a concert in 1985 that he should wear a little make-up on stage – something he had never considered before but ever since has taken that advice from a professional he always admired and who remained a close friend. Dec McCluskey of The Bachelors, interviewed in the London Palladium, told of how Bridie introduced glamour into Irish show business and became a role model that all other Irish artistes then wanted to emulate.

But it was when Teresa and the production crew flew to New York to interview Irish emigrants that they discovered the real essence of her grandmother's impact. She interviewed pensioners in the Queens Irish Club after she performed some of Bridie's greatest hits. One song in particular seemed to carry much meaning for the audience and she noticed several men and women, then in their seventies and eighties, weeping while they sang along with her. She later interviewed many of the audience members including one lady who was originally from County Meath. She had left Ireland as a young woman with little money, arriving alone in New York in 1960.

She was lonely, without money to travel home, frightened by the scale of the Big Apple. There were no mobile phones, no Internet, no Facebook or Skype. Communications with home were few and far between. Then one night she went to the City Center Ballroom run by Bill Fuller, a popular venue for Irish emigrants. She saw for the first time the great Bridie Gallagher. She told Teresa she cried as she sang along with Bridie singing 'A Mother's Love's a Blessing' and 'Goodbye Johnny Dear'. This beautiful, glamorous woman wearing the most exquisite frock brought her back home to Ireland for just a few minutes. This woman, like so many other people at that time living in a foreign land surrounded by different cultures, now discovered the joy of her homeland in the songs of Bridie Gallagher. As she told Teresa, *'Ever after when we heard Bridie Gallagher was due back in town we would save up for weeks to get the money for tickets to see her. We knew she would bring a little bit of home for us that night. I have never forgotten what she did for us then.'*

Right up until she died Bridie maintained a fan base across the world. She received letters and cards regularly, especially at Christmas and her birthday, from Ireland, Britain, North America, Australia, Africa and even had one regular correspondent from Romania. They came in a wide variety of types and mostly had little in common except for their devotion to The Girl from Donegal. Bridie tried to ensure that fans were always given some of her personal time, whether it was responding to letters or talking to them after shows, and for some

Bernard Purcell from the *Irish World* newspaper presents Bridie with a Lifetime Achievement Award in 1990.

special ones a telephone chat. To her, the one essential thing to do after any performance, no matter how she felt physically or emotionally, was attend to the fans. She was renowned for standing outside stage doors or dressing rooms for up to an hour, talking to every fan seeking an autograph or signed photograph, laughing loudly and warmly with them at shared yarns, and on occasions crying when consoling fans who had lost a mother or father or partner. Indeed so many fans used to tell her that they met their marriage partners at one of her shows

Above: Bridie with her friend Margo O'Donnell in July 2000.

Bridie with her lifelong mentor, Franciscan Fr Andrew *(front right)*, and two others in Kilkenny in 1979.

or dances she used to laugh and claim that the 1960s baby boom was partly down to her.

The fans came in all shapes, sizes and backgrounds, some often surprising. When she was top of the bill in a week-long variety show in the Arts Theatre in Belfast in 1982, six months after her first heart attack, audience members were filing into each show. On the second night a little old lady, probably in her seventies, was queuing up with her ticket. She had been seen the night before, arriving alone and taking her seat near the front. She was asked why she was at a second show, when the programme was the same each night. *'I'm from Sandy Row son, and I'd never miss our beautiful Bridie singing in any show in Belfast, ever since the days of the old Empire Theatre.'*

Here was a little old lady from a poor, staunchly Protestant/Unionist area of Belfast queuing up for a seat to see this Catholic girl from Donegal sing Irish ballads. It was one of the measures of Bridie's fame that became evident time and again. Irish people saw her as 'one of our own', as did emigrants across the world, and so did the people of Belfast, regardless of their political or religious background. This was a phenomenon, particularly in Belfast, that applied only to a few select performers, when the normal community divisions were forgotten and a love for song and poetry could transcend animosities. The old lady was immediately given complimentary tickets for the rest of the week, to her great delight. But even better was her thrill to be taken backstage after the show to meet her 'Beautiful Bridie' for the first time.

Her fans came from all walks of society, and Bridie learned early the importance of making them feel special. Once, when performing at a concert in Kilfinane in County Limerick, she was told the nuns in the nearby convent had been unable to get to the concert. With the local priest's help she sang for the sisters in their garden with her accompanist Sheba Kelly playing accordion while the nuns applauded excitedly from the windows above.

Many fans lived far away from Ireland and only heard Bridie perform on radio or records. One example was a priest in Africa. Fr Martin O'Connor had seen Bridie perform back in Ireland in his native County Kerry in his younger days. When he was ordained as a missionary priest he found himself sent to Kenya and later South Africa in the 1960s. His parish was located far out in the bush in the Northern Transvaal near a small town called Tzaneen, hundreds of miles from Johannesburg, and covered a vast area. He was the only priest serving a small population of whites and a much larger number of native Africans living in the poverty of townships under the oppression of the apartheid regime.

Fr Martin described it as very challenging work, made all the more difficult because of his solitude and distance from his native Ireland and the people of his own culture. He was only able to visit his home and family in Ireland for a few weeks every three years. On one early trip home he decided to bring back some Bridie Gallagher records to entertain himself on lonely evenings in his little parish home in the bush. He had seen Bridie perform in the Gleneagle Hotel in Killarney near his family home, and his mother and father adored her.

He described how he often sat in the evening watching the sun set over the horizon listening to and singing along with Bridie Gallagher on his old record player. Her songs and voice reminded him of home and family and even helped maintain his sanity in this distant parish home. One day his brother John, a doctor, visited him. The final part of his journey entailed a long drive along dirt roads by jeep far into the bush, many miles from the nearest city, Petersburg. There were no road signs and navigation could be treacherous. When he had driven for several hours he reckoned he should be near Fr Martin's house, but he could not be sure. He had stopped to check his compass and map when he suddenly heard music drifting over the trees in the darkness. It was the unmistakable strains of Bridie Gallagher singing 'Cuttin' the Corn in Creeslough'. He was dumbfounded. But then he realised it could only be his brother Martin. He headed on down the track until there emerged in the headlights a little chapel with a little house beside it. There was Martin sitting on his rocking chair on the verandah and Bridie singing beside him from the record player.

Many years later, John took a chance and contacted Bridie in Belfast from his home in Dublin. He got her private number by ringing the post office in Creeslough and reassuring the postmaster Danny Lafferty – who knew Bridie very well – that his enquiry was genuine and not mischievous. John spoke with Bridie and explained all about her distant fan. He gave her Fr Martin's telephone number in South Africa. The first thing Fr Martin knew about this conversation between his brother John and Bridie was when he answered the ringing telephone in his office only to be greeted by a lady singing 'The Boys from County Armagh'. He knew instantly who it was and, when he recovered from the shock, Bridie and he laughed and talked for almost an hour.

They became regular correspondents by letter and eventually met for the first time in Belfast in 2001, when he gratefully accepted an invitation to visit her. He was no longer just a fan. He became her good and trusted friend and, at times, mentor. They would often hold long conversations by telephone between Belfast and his bush parish home in South Africa. That friendship was reinforced when he travelled to Belfast to attend a special eightieth birthday party celebration for Bridie in 2004. She was overwhelmed and thrilled to meet her good friend again.

Sometimes she met fans in very sad circumstances. One young man in Chicago, who was originally from County Down, had not been home for ten years as he could not afford the airfare. Queuing up for an autograph, he pleaded with Bridie to visit his mother in Ireland when she returned home. It was an extraordinary request but she was deeply affected by the love for his mother and their enforced separation. Within a few weeks of returning to her home in Belfast she drove to the mother's home near Castlewellan and surprised a dumbstruck woman by presenting her with flowers and a personal message from her dear son. The woman and Bridie shared their tears and joy.

On another occasion she met the son of her Belfast accountant in New York after one of her concerts in the City Center Ballroom. Sadly he had become estranged from his parents some years before. His father often spoke to Bridie about the pain of their separation. Bridie pleaded with the son to find a way to be reconciled with his parents and spoke with him at length about his parents and their distress. Her pleas worked and some months later he flew home for the first time in five years. Son and parents were reunited.

Her reputation for giving fans time after shows to meet and talk, as well as sign autographs, soon became widespread. While many artists might hand out signed photographs, she made a point of talking with them about their lives and enjoying yarns about home. She knew that from a purely commercial standpoint her career depended on fans and that they needed to be accommodated as far as possible. But she also realised that show business fame can be short-lived and that establishing a rapport and closeness with fans would sustain her career for many years ahead. More importantly, she was genuinely interested in people, especially those living far from home. She understood from her own family history, and her own separation from family, how hard this could be and saw it as her duty to do what she could to help emigrants in particular keep in contact with family and friends in Ireland. Many years later Daniel O'Donnell, who soared to his own deserved fame and success, acknowledged how much he learned from Bridie's approach to fans. He too became renowned for giving lots of time to his fans after every performance.

Bridie met many great fans who in time became great friends.

'I had thousands of fans over the years and am happy to say still have many who keep in contact with me regularly. One in particular stands out. He told me he first saw me at his first dance and later at the summer season show in Bundoran in 1962. Apparently I spoke to him briefly one night on my way into the theatre and he maintains his legs turned to jelly – which I can never understand. Some years later I was appearing on an RTÉ television show followed by a cabaret spot at the Olympia Ballroom in Dublin. The most beautiful bouquet of flowers was delivered to my dressing room. No one seemed to know who they were from. During my performance I asked the person in the audience responsible for the flowers to make themselves known to me after the show so I could thank them personally. He did come forward later as I was signing autographs and whispered, "I'm Tom Smith, and I sent you the flowers." And so my secret admirer was discovered.'

Tom attended many of her shows and often sent her exquisite presents and cards. But more importantly they spoke at length by telephone on a regular basis sharing news of their respective families, of whom they were both immensely proud.

One night in 1970 Bridie was on her way to perform a concert in a parochial hall near Garrison in County Fermanagh. When touring Bridie was never keen on staying at expensive hotels. She would often choose bed-and-breakfast houses in Ireland that had been recommended to her for comfort and privacy. The most important thing for her was, however, food. She always insisted that she and whoever was travelling with her should eat good meals and not convenience food – fish and chips or burgers. This evening she stopped at a small but pretty hotel in Garrison and her road manager John Finnegan enquired about a table in the restaurant.

They were ushered into the dining room and seated near a window with a beautiful view of the surrounding countryside. The waiter took their order and they settled down in readiness for a good meal. But Bridie had been recognised and the news of her arrival flew round the hotel like a wildfire. They were waiting expectantly for the starter course when the kitchen doors burst open with a crash and out shot the hotel chef dressed in whites and tall hat. He was a little round barrel of a man no more than an inch or two over five feet in height, with a beaming smile, and a loud broad Donegal accent. He charged to Bridie's table, clapped his hands in joy and exclaimed, *'Aw, Bridie. God save us. It's an honour to have you in my dining room. Yes, that's right, an honour. Jesus, Bridie, I'll cook you the best dinner you ever had, girl.'*

His name was Conal Haughey. He was originally from Ardara in Donegal but had trained as a chef in London working in several of the top hotels before returning to his native Ireland in the late 1960s. He was true to his word – the dinner he served up was indeed magnificent and certainly well in excess of what was described in the menu. Conal loved all Bridie's songs and had seen her perform in London many times, including the Albert Hall. He not only loved her but was also proud of her and how she represented Ireland abroad. In the years to follow he moved to the Nesbitt Arms in Ardara as its chef where he fast became an institution, welcoming guests from all over the world and always announcing his love and friendship with Bridie Gallagher. Indeed there was rarely a night that Bridie appeared somewhere in Donegal that Conal was not in the audience, usually accompanied by some of his hotel staff. He even travelled to Belfast on occasions just to hear her sing. When he attended any performance Bridie knew instantly he was there when she heard him say, *'Aw, Bridie darling, you're great. We all love you.'*

He became a good friend of Bridie's and in her later years, especially, entertained her as his personal guest in the Nesbitt Arms Hotel where she often went for a short break from her exhausting schedule. Here she was among friends who respected her privacy but also revelled in her company. Conal famously allowed only his closest friends to sit at a big wooden table in his hotel kitchen while he worked and talked incessantly, laughing uproariously and shouting instructions to the staff. Bridie was always welcomed into that kitchen and loved the intimacy and fun she found there with her great admirer. He remained a fan who became a close friend in whom she could confide and who always spurred her on to *'keep going girl. Sure we love you, don't you know.'*

Sean and Betty McNally, whom Bridie first met in Vancouver, Canada, went to all her concerts there and eventually became friends with whom she holidayed in Vancouver and later in their beautiful home in Penticton in the Rockies. There were others who wrote regularly but whom she seldom met: one English man, whom she knew only as 'Fred from Nottingham', wrote to her regularly and sent gorgeous presents, including sapphire jewellery on one occasion; Oliver McDonnell from Dundalk wrote frequently and sent her songs and stories; Christine Hawkins from Gort in Galway never missed a birthday or Christmas and Bridie visited her occasionally; John O'Brien and family in Cleveland, Ohio, corresponded every year without fail; and many more like them. They all first met Bridie as fans at her shows. Over time they became more than just loyal fans: they became friends, friends she enjoyed spending time with, sharing her joys and woes with, and friends she came to rely on for advice, for reassurance and often for simple love.

But one fan was the most special to Bridie. She was Joan Tobin (née Connolly) from Mallow in County Cork. Like so many others, Joan had emigrated in her twenties to London in the mid-1960s. She went to every Bridie Gallagher concert in London and even travelled to other cities in England when Bridie was touring. She first saw Bridie with her mother in Mallow and immediately fell in love with Bridie's music and voice. Initially, being shy, she only ventured to get an autograph or photograph after shows. But eventually Bridie came to realise that virtually everywhere she went in London or its surrounding cities there would be this same young lady, always in the queue of autograph hunters, armed with her camera or, later, video camera.

Bridie quickly came to spot her and know her by name on every occasion. She had a particular talent for remembering people's names. She would often write notes in her diaries about fans she had met in venues all over the world in case she met them again. She understood

Bridie *(right)* with her closest fan, Joan Tobin, in London in 1995.

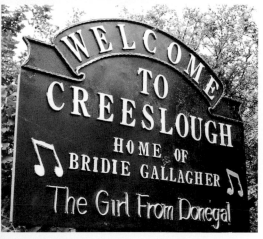

Above: The Bridie Gallagher sign erected in July 2000 by the people of Creeslough on the road into the village.

Left: Bridie heads off for Creeslough on the day the townspeople unveiled the Bridie Gallagher sign in the village, July 2000.

how important it was to the fans for Bridie to recognise them by name, even if these meetings had gaps of months or even years.

They grew closer year by year until Joan rang her one day in the 1980s, when Bridie was convalescing after her heart surgery, and invited her to stay with her in London for a short holiday. She did and, for once, flew off to London simply to enjoy its delights and not have to worry about shows and performances. Later, when she was again touring, Bridie invariably performed at clubs in London almost every year up until the 1990s. On many of these trips she would stay with Joan at her home in Finsbury Park. For Bridie, on her normally hectic schedule, and with her advancing age increasingly making her tire more easily, staying with her loyal and trusted Joan was like having a home away from home.

The one amazing aspect of Joan's devotion was her determination to have numerous photographs or video recordings of every encounter with Bridie. She would then send Bridie copies of the photos in beautiful frames or copies of the videos. Bridie accumulated a collection of hundreds of wonderful images chronicling their friendship.

Bridie is driven through Creeslough to welcoming crowds in July 2000.

Part of the vast crowd in Creeslough to welcome Bridie home in July 2000.

Left: Bridie sings on stage in Creeslough with Daniel O'Donnell and her sisters in July 2000.

Below: An emotional Bridie views the sign in Creeslough for the first time with Daniel O'Donnell and his sister Margo, July 2000.

She confided in her on every subject and Joan steadfastly protected Bridie's privacy in every respect. On occasions Bridie would visit Joan in London just to stay with her and they always went to at least one West End show, which was the very best treat for Bridie. Joan even came to Belfast to stay in Bridie's own home, especially in the later years when travel became a real difficulty for Bridie. In time Joan, once a devoted fan, became one of her closest friends, and in many ways a sister she loved deeply.

It is true that, in many ways, fans can be exploited by artists. They can be whipped up to a frenzy of expectation and delirium by shrewd advertising to buy concert tickets, records and DVDs, t-shirts, books and even products of various kinds 'endorsed' by the artist. And artists of many kinds can make a lot of money from this exploitation. In Bridie's case the truth is, except for a few short years at the end of the 1950s, she never had a slick PR operation behind her. She never endorsed products of any kind (except when she presented a half-hour radio show on Radio Éireann for Bulmers in the early 1960s), she never sold t-shirts. She sold many records across the world and her records are still played on radio stations worldwide. But the royalties she earned were tiny.

She and many other artists of the 1950s suffered a great injustice in that they were universally contracted to a standard royalty for every record sale of one shilling (or seven cent in modern currency). This was during a time of relatively low inflation. If inflation had stayed very low Bridie would have earned as much as many others. But it didn't. She was still getting one shilling per record sale when a record cost about £1. As the price of records rose quickly from the 1970s onwards, newer artists were contracted to get 5 per cent of the retail price. But Bridie was still getting seven cent for her early recordings while other younger artists were often getting up to fifty cent. In other words, despite selling millions of records, Bridie did not make millions of pounds. Apart from her earnings for shows and concerts Bridie's relationship with her fans was as much about a shared love for the music as it was making money. She did well financially, enough to keep her comfortable into old age. But in 2000, approaching her seventy-sixth birthday, Bridie discovered a richness that many show business artists never achieve.

The people of Creeslough, led by the postmaster Danny McLafferty, and spurred on by Margo O'Donnell, a great Donegal performer in her own right, decided it was time to mark Bridie's achievements in some permanent form. They settled on a large sign that was to be erected at the entrance to the town on the road from Letterkenny. It read 'Welcome to Creeslough, home of Bridie Gallagher, The Girl from Donegal'. Bridie was invited to attend an unveiling ceremony in July 2000. She did not know what to expect and readily agreed. When she arrived she was overwhelmed by the reception.

Over two thousand people had gathered in the town's square to greet her and she was driven through the town in an open-top car accompanied by her dear friend Daniel O'Donnell, waving to the crowd who lined the main street and led in procession by a local accordion band. A stage had been erected and speeches were made by local dignitaries, councillors and TDs, and artists like Daniel and his sister Margo who had played a prominent role in organising the event. It was a very emotional moment for Bridie. Her friends and fans, some of whom she had known since school days, had gathered to pay tribute to her. Notably in the crowd were Willie Kelly, her first boyfriend, and Frank, her first true love to whom marriage had been forbidden fifty-three years earlier, on a special visit from his home in Glasgow. She was truly overwhelmed to find that a large metal sign had been erected in her own hometown.

People from all over Ireland attended the event and it was reported widely in local and national newspapers. But it didn't finish there. To Bridie's astonishment she was told that she was to attend a special civic reception in the Chamber of Donegal County Council the following day, an honour bestowed on very few. She went with family and friends, and the entire council, led by Cllr Charlie Bennett, gathered to pay tribute to Bridie and her achievements. She was presented with a specially commissioned painting of her local homeland. When she went back to her home in Belfast later that day, she described herself as an emotional wreck, but a gloriously happy wreck.

It meant more to her than money, awards, manufactured or genuine praise in the press, or in fact, fame itself. To have her own people pay such a generous and unique tribute to her work was more than she could have ever dreamed of all those years ago before setting out on her professional career. The people there that day were not to know that two weeks later Bridie would perform her very last show. It was in Letterkenny's beautiful An Grianán Theatre. That night she was accompanied by her granddaughter Teresa on piano and myself on guitar. She sang wonderfully, even if at times she struggled for breath, and the audience as usual loved her. But at the age of seventy-six she decided she could do no more. She did not have the energy and she was not prepared to give her fans second-best performances. So she came off the stage and turned to me and cried gently, *'Jim, I can't do it anymore. That's the last. I'm sorry, I'm just too tired. But please don't tell anyone.'*

I held her in my arms that night and knew this was the end of performing for Mum, but somehow I knew it was not the end of Bridie Gallagher. A few months later I wondered might the end really have come when Bridie suffered the first of five strokes that she was to endure over the next ten years.

But despite her ending her public performing, her fans remained constant. Every birthday and Christmas would bring a minor avalanche of cards and presents, in addition to those from family and immediate friends. Regular letters and postcards from fans sharing their own life experiences and devotion for The Girl from Donegal arrived almost every day. Telephone calls from those she trusted with her private number were also commonplace, as indeed were calls made by her to selected fans/friends whose advice, views or just company she valued. She never forgot that it was the fans who had sustained her singing career. *'It's the fans who buy the records, tickets for shows and best of all give the applause that every performer needs. I've never forgotten that and I hope I never do.'*

They were important to her as a performer, but invaluable to her as a person. They inspired her during the times of success and helped carry her through the trauma of pain and loss that were part of her life.

Chapter Twelve
NOT JUST A SINGER

Again I want to see and do
The things we've done and seen
Where the breeze is sweet as Shalimar
And there's forty shades of green.

'FORTY SHADES OF GREEN' (J. CASH)

*B*y the late 1980s Bridie was still touring cabaret clubs, some theatres and even doing major concerts in London, Glasgow and New York. But the dates were fewer, especially following her heart surgery in 1981. She needed to slow down. One of the benefits of having more free time was that her life took on a new and more relaxed tempo and diversity.

She had always admired good paintings, whether oil or watercolour. Wherever she went she would comment on paintings hanging in hotels, people's houses or anywhere they were to be found. When I suggested to her one day that she should take up oil painting, she laughed and said: *'Don't be silly, I couldn't draw a cat or a straight line for God's sake.'*

But she needed a new interest because with fewer tours and less performing in her later years she often got bored and lonely. Eventually she was persuaded to try it out and she went to St Monica's High School in Belfast near her home to enrol in a Painting for Beginners evening class run by the Rupert Stanley Further Education College. There she was introduced to the art teacher John Ginn with whom she struck up an immediate affinity. In her usual gregarious way she got to know

Bridie at home in 1990 painting in oils, a hobby she came to late but loved very much. © BELFAST TELEGRAPH

Bridie's oil paintings.

Top left: *Sunset over Mayo.*

Top right: *Errigal Mountain in Donegal.*

Left: *Cuttin' the Corn in Creeslough.*

every single classmate that first evening. Most of them had been painting for some years, but it didn't matter. Under John's expert tutorship Bridie was totally smitten. She loved the feel of oil painting. She amazed herself with how much she could do and never missed a Thursday class from then on. She bought all the oils and brushes and got an easel. She soon turned one of her smaller bedrooms into an artist's studio. Within weeks she had produced her first oil painting on canvas, a still life of flowers in a pot. It was so colourful and expressive. She proudly displayed it to her young granddaughters when they made their regular weekly visit. The children were thrilled and excited to see what their granny had produced. In fact the whole family was frankly amazed at how good it was for a first attempt. The look on her face was magical. She had found a new talent and her audience loved what she did.

For the next fifteen years she painted and painted, mostly landscapes of her beloved Donegal taken from photographs, or more still lifes. Some of the paintings were naturally of a quality to be expected of a novice. But some of her later pieces were stunningly beautiful. As she progressed she didn't easily take criticism from anyone other than her tutor or classmates.

And frankly she was right. Beauty is in the eye of the beholder, they say, and in this case the beholder, Bridie the artist, knew what she liked. The joy she was getting from painting did not need assumed expertise from critical amateurs to dampen her enthusiasm. The only 'criticism' she would ever accept on her paintings was from her art teacher John Ginn, who in his class would often be heard to exclaim, *'Gallagher, less of the talking and more painting please.'*

Painting gave her joy, relaxation and a feeling of real achievement and purpose. She also made many new friends in the classes over the years – none less than Aileen Midgeley, with whom she formed a close bond that never broke. She never regretted attending that first class. And now, many of her family and friends have the pleasure of looking at her paintings hanging on the walls of their homes and offices.

Bridie always loved her garden. It was a love she probably inherited from her father. After she married in 1951, her first home, in Carmel Street, Belfast, was a small terraced house with no workable garden apart from a tiny space at the front. By 1959, with her growing success in show business, she acquired the money to afford a bigger house and chose a lovely home in the Stranmillis area, insisting the house must be one with a big garden. In fact, the house she and Bob chose had the biggest garden in the area. It had a small plot at the front but a large extensive garden to the rear, backing onto a school hockey pitch. The garden became her refuge during years of touring, stress and worry. She spent much of her spare time digging, weeding and planting, pruning, and sometimes just admiring the colour and variety. She loved roses and shrubs and her garden always seemed to be in some form of bloom regardless of the season. She even dug a section of the garden up herself so she could turn it into a vegetable patch. She delighted in showing family and friends how to till the soil and build 'drills', long built-up mounds of soil, so she could plant potatoes. For many years she delighted in growing her own vegetables as well as flowers of all kinds.

Bridie playing in her garden with grandson Peter and granddaughter Nuala in 1991.

In later years, when her health failed, she hired gardeners to do the heavy work. But even when she was quite frail, more than one such gardener would gasp at the unexpected vision of this little elderly lady trying to reach up to prune her apple trees or rhododendrons. If the garden was untidy or overgrown (as it often was when she was away for some weeks abroad) she would get very frustrated and tetchy and could not rest until it had been put back in order. It was her private paradise and she could not bear to see it unkempt. When, by 2010, her health had worsened considerably following multiple strokes, her favourite pleasure was to sit in her garden wrapped in a shawl with a cigarette and cup of tea beside her on her garden table. While her carer Linda was busy in the house cleaning or making her a meal, she would sit for ages in the garden savouring the colour, the birds, the fresh air and the beauty of her creation, now tended by her regular gardener.

Bridie was taught to cook first by her own mother in Creeslough, but some years later, shortly after she got married, it was her sister Sarah living in Dublin who introduced her to the delights of baking. Within the family, and among friends and visitors to her home, she became renowned for fabulous home cooking and baking, especially delicious sweet and savoury tarts. There was hardly a dish or recipe she would not try. Growing up, her family did not appreciate what a good cook

Bridie *(centre)* at Jim and Paula's wedding in 1978.

Right: Bridie with sons Jim *(right)* and Peter *(left)* in Bundoran in 1960.

Facing page: Bridie posing for press while painting her windows in 1975.

© BELFAST TELEGRAPH

Left: Bridie (*left*) visiting brother Josie and family on Ards *c.* 1985.

Below: Bridie and her brothers and sisters in 1986 at a family wedding in Creeslough, *back row (l–r):* John, Jim and Josie; and *front row (l–r):* Sarah, Grace, Rose, Nellie, Mary, Maggie and Bridie.

she was. It was only when the children's school friends came to visit that they realised she was something special in the kitchen. Their friends all marvelled at the dinners and snacks she produced and used to beg to be invited for tea.

In later years her special delight was to entertain her grandchildren for Sunday lunch. It was always a marvellous treat for the kids to go to Granny's for lunch or dinner. She cooked enormous turkeys, sides of beef, legs of lamb or stuffed chicken. Her stuffings for every type of meat and joint seemed to change by the week as she experimented with new variants – stuffing with peaches, with lemons and even sometimes with fruit no one could identify. The one thing everyone could be sure of, apart from being served a delicious meal, was that there would be plenty of it. She seemed to be able to generate mountains of potatoes and vegetables and, on occasions, more than one meat dish. One time, she presented a sumptuous whole poached salmon to the dinner table with adults and children waiting excitedly. But knowing the younger children didn't like salmon, she produced a stuffed chicken as well. No one ever left Bridie's house hungry.

At the same time, her culinary tastes were very traditional and simple. And she had one enduring rule: as far as she was concerned, no meal was complete without potatoes. She would serve chicken curry with rice, but with the addition of boiled potatoes on the side. Her personal favourite was the simplest meal of all, reminiscent of her early days in Creeslough – boiled potatoes with a large dollop of butter melting on the top, and if she was being very extravagant, a fried egg.

Her baking was traditional, but always light and tasty. Everyone's favourite, and especially that of her grandchildren, was her mince steak tart. It was tender mince steak, cooked in an onion gravy, in a pastry case. Most could eat more than one big slice and savoured the meal with home-made chips and garden peas: simple but delicious. Her granddaughters just loved it, almost as much as the enormous and juicy trifles smothered in fresh whipped cream that she made in a dish so big it was a real effort to carry it from the kitchen to the dining table. To the children's delight it was always topped with sponge biscuits, which they would devour.

Unfortunately, as she grew into old age and increasing poor health, she cooked less and less, but still tried to please. One day when her teenage granddaughters visited, she announced she had made some tarts and asked if they would like to take one home. They all looked at each other and shrieked 'Yes, please!' I rang my wife Paula at home and told her not to worry about getting something for dinner that evening as Bridie had done one of her mince tarts.

Paula was relieved but also equally delighted because she, like me, loved the mince steak tart. We later settled down to have the meal, savouring the thought of the juicy meaty tart. As the pastry was cut to serve the first helping, there was shock and disappointment around the table. It was an apple tart, not a mince steak tart. We realised immediately that Bridie, with her increasing forgetfulness, had made a selection of tarts, some with fruit and some mince steak, but forgot which were which when she froze them. We laughed and laughed at our misfortune. But all agreed not to mention the mistake to Bridie. It would embarrass her too much. So we had some boring sausages instead and rang her that evening to tell her how good the mince tart was, hoping silently that she would produce another one very soon.

On 16 May 1982 Bridie was relaxing in her garden. She'd just returned from a tour in England and as it was Monday she'd just finished her weekly clothes wash. White sheets were now flapping languidly on the washing line over by the vegetable patch. She was looking forward to a couple of weeks resting after a busy spring schedule. Suddenly drops of rain started to plop down from the dark ominous clouds that had crept across the sky. With annoyance at her sunbathing being interrupted she gathered her bits and pieces and trotted into the house. The rain became heavy and insistent and she resigned herself to an afternoon indoors. To pass the time she switched on the television and settled down with a copy of the magazine *Woman's Own* and a cup of tea. At first she concentrated on the magazine with its mixture of celebrity scandal and homely advice and largely ignored the television.

She suddenly became aware of cheering crowds on the television and looked up to discover that a snooker match was about to begin and the crowd in Sheffield's Crucible Theatre were welcoming Alex 'Hurricane' Higgins into the arena to commence combat with the reigning World Champion, Ray Reardon. Up to that very day Bridie had never watched a game of snooker. She didn't know any of its rules or players and had never ever expressed any interest in the sport. But just a month before, she met a very famous snooker player. They stayed at the same hotel in Manchester when she was performing two nights in the Ardri Irish Club for Jim Connell – a regular engagement at least twice every year in the 1970s and 1980s.

She had returned to the hotel after midnight and, while passing through the lobby on her way to her room, she heard raucous singing and laughter from the bar. Her name was called out. It was Jim Kennedy, an Irish-born building and demolition contractor who was a millionaire businessman in Manchester. He called her into the bar to meet some people. At first she declined, feeling tired from the night's performance. But with a little coaxing she followed Jim into the bar to loud cheers from an assembled group of Manchester Irish expatriates. He urged her towards the bar where a slim, wiry man wearing a fedora hat sat perched on a stool drinking. She was introduced to Alex Higgins, the snooker player from Belfast. Alex was fast becoming the most popular and successful snooker player in the world. Although he had won the coveted World Championship in 1972, his television fame had only recently become a phenomenon. Alex whooped with delight. Being himself from Belfast, he knew of Bridie but had never met her, yet he threw his arms around her. For her part Bridie had no idea who Alex was at all.

'This is The Girl from Donegal, folks. She's OUR star.'

Bridie spent a few noisy minutes with the small group, enjoying a late nightcap, but tiredness won out and eventually she excused herself and went to her room for much-needed sleep. But the young, flash Belfast snooker player had made an impression on her.

And now here he was on television playing the World Championship final. Bride was immediately transfixed and remained glued to the set for the next few hours. She revelled in the drama, skill, excitement and razzamatazz that professional snooker provided. She watched every single frame, hardly daring to leave her seat in case she would miss something. Her vigil culminated late that night in the emotionally charged and thrilling win by Alex 'Hurricane' Higgins. He was her favourite player, with Jimmy White coming a close second. Every single year thereafter she religiously watched every televised snooker competition. The World Championship from the Crucible in Sheffield was eagerly awaited and planned for every year. She even once declined an engagement to perform because it clashed with the final.

She soon knew every player, the intricate rules and even techniques of the game such as 'putting side on a cue ball', 'touching ball' and 'back spin'. She spurned telephone calls and even visitors in the middle of matches, and on occasions actually took her telephone off the hook to avoid unwanted interruptions. Even with her health worsening in her later years, she still insisted on watching the snooker. She might watch tennis and football occasionally, especially Gaelic football, but the snooker was her real passion. It was, for her, a magical world of drama, entertainment and joy that gave her enormous pleasure.

The Lily Comerford Irish Dancers from Dublin were contracted to appear in her London Metropolitan Theatre show for one week in 1959. At the end of their stay one of the little girls presented Bridie with a thank you gift – a large Crolly Doll, which she treasured for the rest of her life. Indeed, she began gathering dolls from each of the countries she visited thereafter. She eventually had a collection of fifteen dolls from far and distant places – Australia, Canada, Spain, Italy, France, Zambia, India (bought on a stop-over in Mumbai on the way to Australia), Scotland, England, Wales, Jersey, the US, Newfoundland, Cyprus and, of course, Ireland. The Crolly Doll was her favourite and very special to her because it was made in a little factory in Crolly near Gweedore in Donegal, 25 miles from Creeslough. She visited the Crolly Doll factory several times to see them being made and was especially sad when it closed owing to financial difficulty. She even recorded a song about the Crolly Doll. The manager there told her about a little nun who had bought a doll one day. He explained with a smile that she called at the shop and announced that she had come to collect her 'Bridie Gallagher'.

This was the beginning of Bridie's enthusiasm for collecting memorabilia. Wherever she travelled she brought back an extraordinary variety of mementoes. One day she was in the Gresham Hotel in Dublin for a meeting with Phil Solomon, her manager. They were being served coffee in the lounge. It was presented in exquisite, tiny coffee cups and saucers monogrammed with the hotel's name and insignia. Before leaving she complimented the manager on the beautiful little cups. He immediately offered this famous star, who regularly stayed as a guest in the hotel, a set to take away and keep. She adored its fine porcelain and delicate design. And so she started another collection. She soon acquired similar coffee cup sets from hotels all over Ireland, Britain, Europe and the US, proudly displaying them in a glass cabinet at home. She was asked one day how she had managed to persuade so many fine hotels to part with their precious coffee cups and saucers. With a glint in her eye, she giggled and said nothing in response. Were they all collected in an entirely legitimate manner? It's probably better now not to judge too harshly.

Her other passion for collection was, strangely, furniture. She loved fine-quality furniture, and especially if she thought it was a bargain. She bought one of the first PYE radio gramophones in 1959 and it adorned her living room for sixty years. It was housed in a large mahogany cabinet and played vinyl records in stereo. She polished it almost every week to sustain its shiny beauty. She announced one day she had seen a grandfather clock in a shop near Sandy Row in Belfast (one of her favourite shopping haunts) and felt sure she could get it for a good price, always convinced of her prowess in negotiating. When I visited a few days later to see the clock, she beamed and reported she had got an even better deal than she expected, and so had bought a grandmother clock as well. It was the first time anyone in the family had ever seen a pair of grandmother and grandfather clocks together in one room. She always had a charming ability to convince herself that she had bargained hard and got the best price. But her family knew that negotiating had never been her best skill and realised that furniture stores in Belfast probably just loved to see Bridie come through the door.

By coincidence, in 1960, at the height of her fame, she was contracted by one of the major furniture retailers to open their new stores around Northern Ireland. Each opening event attracted very large crowds, keen to see the big star. This only added to Bridie's enthusiasm to have fine furniture of all types. Among other items she rejoiced in acquiring (some in auctions and some in retail shops) were a mahogany cabinet cocktail bar, a Waterford crystal chandelier, a traditional Welsh dresser, numerous coffee tables, and a varied selection of footstools. All were acclaimed to be bargains of course, which some actually were. They gave her great pleasure, although as the years went by her house became filled with furniture of many kinds and styles in every room.

Bridie first became a grandmother in July 1979 with the birth of Teresa Tynan Livingstone (the name Tynan was given to her in honour of the father of her mother Paula, Sean Tynan, who died in 1976 just weeks before Bridie's youngest son Peter was killed). My wife Paula and I had three more children: Shauna Margaret followed in 1980; Nuala Frances in 1983; and finally Peter James in 1988. Bridie discovered a new and wonderful joy in her life – her grandchildren. When Teresa was born, Bridie helped to look after her for several months when her mum Paula returned to her teaching job. This was while still having concert and cabaret commitments from time to time. But this could clearly not continue indefinitely as she was still in frequent demand for shows and tours. Eventually Paula and I made more permanent child minding arrangements but Bridie still revelled in her new-found role as a granny.

Although, it has to be said, at first she baulked at the title 'granny'. This was mostly due to a sense of what such a title implied about her age, something she was always reticent to reveal publicly. It was always a cause of amusement within the family, and a little irritation to Bridie, when journalists asked Bridie what age she was during interviews. Many press articles in the 1950s and 1960s gave an age about ten years younger than she actually was at the time. Indeed, even in her own writings in the 1980s she referred to herself leaving Donegal 'as a young teenager to go to Belfast to find work in 1948', when she had in fact been twenty-four years of age. She was quaintly determined to perpetuate the idea publicly that she was considerably younger than she actually was, perhaps in response to the growing youth culture of the late 1950s and the 1960s. It took a little time for her to get used to the idea of being called a granny while she was still a relatively young woman of fifty-five. But from 1979 onwards she relished being a granny and having her grandchildren around her.

She loved the fact that from an early age Teresa was a talented and enthusiastic musician who sang and played piano, always described by her granny as 'a born performer'. Sometimes, to Teresa's embarrassment, but also delight, she would proudly announce that 'this girl will be a star one day'. She adored Shauna's chat and love of animals. In many ways Shauna often reminded Bridie of herself as a young girl. She was musical too and played the clarinet, but her main focus was having fun learning to ride horses. She displayed a constant brightness of attitude and was always ready for fun and games, the crazier the better, much to Bridie's delight but sometimes consternation. Nuala was the quietest and youngest of the three sisters, although just as playful and musically talented on her cello. Bridie recognised this was a girl who loved her books and was always amazed and wonderfully entertained at her storytelling ability.

The three girls gave Bridie constant entertainment and joy. She loved going to their dancing festivals, urging them on to success, or going to their school concerts, where she beamed with as much pride as their parents at their singing, musical performing and acting. But best of all she loved having the girls for 'sleepovers' in her house, which they in turn regarded as major treats. They would put on little concerts

Above: Bridie with her granddaughters Teresa *(left)* and Shauna *(centre)* seeing Santa in a department store, Belfast, in December 1983.

Left: Bridie with her three granddaughters *(l–r)*: Teresa, Nuala and Shauna in 1986.

Below: Bridie going for a walk in the park with her granddaughters in 1987, *(l–r)*: Shauna, Teresa and Nuala, with Jim's wife Paula in the doorway and dog Benji waiting patiently to the left.

213

Bridie with her grandson Peter in 1991 *(above)*, in 1993 *(right)* and at Christmas 2005 *(below)*.

for her, tape themselves singing on her tape-recorder, play for hours in her garden, and gorge themselves on her heavenly cooking and extra-special trifles.

When Peter was born in 1988 with serious medical complications, she comforted the girls in their home while Paula and I maintained a vigil at his incubator in Belfast's Jubilee Hospital. It was obviously a time of great concern and stress for everyone in the family and Bridie, as a granny and mother, was a constant support during this difficult time. Thankfully Peter survived several traumatic years of sickness and hospitalisation.

As he was named after his deceased uncle Peter, he naturally captured Bridie's heart in a very special way. He was born with physical and learning disabilities, but Bridie simply glowed with pride and joy every time he would charge into her house on a visit and jump onto her chair for a cuddle. Sometimes he brought a couple of his chums from his special primary school and they played in her garden. One day, when Paula called to collect Peter and his gang to take them home after a visit, she found Bridie squeezed into a little play tent on the lawn sharing in a feast of buns, chocolates, crisps and lemonade with Peter and his friends.

She stayed with us and the grandchildren every Christmas, helping to cook the turkey as well as playing games and singing around the piano. She was often involved in helping Paula organise birthday parties and christenings, usually by cooking and baking, and even entertaining gangs of her grandchildren's friends in party games. She was the true granny (the children knew her as Granny L and Paula's mother as Granny T), playing, encouraging, offering unsolicited parental advice (as grannies do, of course), doing the girls' hair and letting them dress up in her stage gowns, and try out her make-up (a particular treat at nine years of age), often with hilarious outcomes.

As the children grew into adulthood she enjoyed listening to their tales of travel, going to dances for the first time, and achievements at school and university, and was always ready to give advice and encouragement. Whenever she had visits from other family and relatives she invariably waxed lyrical about her own grandchildren, their exploits and achievements. In particular she was always keen, often to the girls' minor embarrassment, to hear if they had a boyfriend or one in prospect.

Gradually the children came to realise that this granny was a little different from other friends' grannies and was actually very famous. They frequently glowed with pride when people asked *'Is your granny really Bridie Gallagher, the singer?'* Even when they moved away from home to go to university and pursue their careers in Scotland, Spain and Australia, they kept in touch, sending cards and presents and telephoning Granny from time to time. The closeness she had with them never faltered, even in her final years of frailty, and she was a permanent feature of their lives, showering them with endless love and support as any granny would.

There was pride and joy in her face when Teresa appeared on a local television programme singing her own composition in 1994; when Peter made his First Communion in 1996; when she sat dressed in her finest silk sky-blue suit in the Good Shepherd Chapel in Belfast, with tears on her cheeks, witnessing Shauna's marriage to Stuart Baldwin in 2007; and when she posed with Nuala on the day she graduated with a PhD in Psychology in 2008. Sadly, she would never live long enough to meet her first great-grandchild Ciara, who was born to Shauna and Stuart in Sydney, Australia, on 25 January 2012. But she remains a granny who was loved and admired by her very proud grandchildren.

Of course for me, she was simply my mum. Time and again over the years, people would ask me what it was like living with a famous mum. Frankly, most of the time, I found the question strange. Growing up she was simply 'Mum', not 'Bridie Gallagher'. When she came home from tours, she didn't arrive with a fanfare or roll of drums. After welcome-home hugs and kisses, she was more likely, as any mum would, to scold my brother Peter and me for having an untidy bedroom, to want to know if homework had been done, and at times to listen patiently with a stern look as we brothers complained about the other's antics while she was away. She never stopped being a mum, and a great one at that. She continually encouraged us to work hard at school, reminded us of the need for manners and consoled us gently when things didn't go our way. This motherly concern carried on well into our adulthoods when she never relented from correcting us if we misbehaved or did something she regarded as unacceptable.

On one memorable occasion I was with her in London in 1974 on tour. I was twenty-two and viewed myself as an adult, no longer in need of scolding by my mum. It was her birthday and I had arranged to take her to her favourite nightspot in London, the Talk of the Town in Leicester Square, for a dinner cabaret show starring The Bachelors.

This was London's premier nightclub – previously it had been the Hippodrome Theatre and was converted by Bernard Delfont in 1958 into a plush and exotic cabaret venue that attracted all the top stars like Sammy Davis Jr, Tom Jones and Judy Garland, to name only a few. It was a night I was always to remember, when I effectively entertained both Bridie Gallagher and my mum simultaneously. Throughout our dinner before the cabaret started we were constantly approached by many celebrities in the club who recognised the great singer Bridie Gallagher dining out. After the show we were invited backstage to meet her old friends The Bachelors and were entertained well into the wee small hours by comedian Roy Hudd and the boys. Bridie was the centre of attention and I was in awe at how much all these celebrities held her, my mum, in such respect and admiration. But earlier in the evening I experienced the motherly side of the great star.

When the cabaret started, what had been a small dance floor for the diners was suddenly raised 4 feet to become an extension to the stage at the rear, ready for the floor show to begin. With great fanfare the dancing girls came on to do their high-kicking fan dance. Their exotic sequined-blue costumes, covered only the bare essentials, and they wore large feather plumes on their heads. They were gorgeous and with our table being right by the stage I had the closest view possible of the beautiful creatures. Naturally, as a young adult male, I was mesmerised. We were still in the middle of our main course of roast beef. I sat transfixed and open-mouthed, with my knife and fork poised in mid-air, never having seen such exotic beauty before. Suddenly, I was slapped on the wrist and heard Bridie scold, *'Eat your dinner. Stop ogling those girls.'*

Bridie Gallagher had reverted to Mother, obviously regarding her son's dubious behaviour as unacceptable and worthy of reprimand. I did as I was told, like any dutiful son, but still managed, painfully, to squint sideways to catch more views of the extravaganza on stage. I still laugh at the thought of being scolded at the age of twenty-two by my mum who herself had been in numerous adult nightclubs watching glamorous floor shows all around the world. It is one of my favourite memories and epitomises for me the great qualities of this show business star, revered by millions, who never stopped being a mother.

There was only one memorable occasion on which I flatly refused to obey her instruction. It was 1982 and the Troubles were at their height. Thankfully Bridie escaped any real danger or threat during these awful years of suffering but one night criminality came to her door: her car

Bridie *(right)* with her sister Rose *(centre)* and sister-in-law Bridget *(left)* on Horn Head in 1999.

was stolen from her driveway. The police surmised it was probably destined for use in a robbery or some other outrage. Fortunately, the thieves were confronted en route to their target by a police patrol and the gang abandoned the car in the middle of a little terraced street in Belfast. Bridie was woken by police in the morning, unaware of the theft during the night, and was invited to come and identify the vehicle as her own. She rang me in a panic and I immediately drove over to bring her to where her car had been found.

We arrived to find the street blocked at both ends by British Army troops and police. Because the car had been abandoned with the doors left open, they could not be sure it did not contain a bomb. The police inspector at the scene explained that the army were preparing to use their robot bomb disposal machine to open the bonnet and boot to view their contents with a remote video camera. Before doing so he calmly advised Bridie that, if she felt so inclined, she could reclaim her car first, but he advised against it. She immediately turned to me and, with

Celebrating Bridie's eightieth birthday in 2004, *back row (l–r)*: Fr Martin O'Connor and Bridget Doak (Maggie's daughter); and *front row (l–r)*: Bridie, her sister Maggie Curran and her sister-in-law Bridget Gallagher.

supreme innocence, said, *'Jim love, please go and get my car before they blow it up.'* I was dumbfounded: she clearly did not understand the potential risks and was simply focused on retrieving her stolen property. With a little trepidation I replied with a firm *'No'* and bade the police and army do what they needed to do. Poor Bridie cried and shook as the army team fired shots at her beautiful new car. The boot lid and bonnet flew open, revealing nothing suspicious or dangerous. The fear and dread experienced by onlookers at the prospect of a bomb was nothing to what I felt having just said no to my mum. She hardly spoke to me for the rest of the day. After a little while, however, she realised her mistake, made in the midst of panic, and thanked me. The memory has never left me of saying no to Bridie. But it still makes me smile.

So Bridie Gallagher, The Girl from Donegal, famous around the world for her singing, was also Bridie Livingstone – a mother, wife, painter, cook, snooker fan, gardener, collector and a very special granny. It seems an obvious point to make that she was more than just a singer, albeit one of international renown. But it is important to recognise the many different facets of character and personality that made up this fascinating woman. She had a diverse range of interests and talents that she developed outside show business, and got great pleasure from these important aspects of her life. On occasions these were a healthy diversion from the stresses and pressures of show business, introduced her to new friends and pleasures, and ensured she remained throughout her life a woman of great character and interest.

Chapter Thirteen
THE FINAL CURTAIN

Love her as in childhood
Though feeble old and grey
For you'll never miss your mother's love
Till she's buried beneath the clay.

'A MOTHER'S LOVE'S A BLESSING' (THOMAS P. KEENAN)

*T*he Thursday night Mum was admitted to the hospital after her fall was a long one. None of the family slept much. My wife Paula and I had phoned our daughters Teresa and Nuala to tell them what had happened. They came straight to the hospital to see their granny. Our son Peter, of course, was always by our side. We rang our daughter Shauna in Australia that morning knowing that by that time her husband Stuart would be home from work and with her. She was eight months pregnant with her first baby. They all loved their granny and wanted to help any way they could, even at a vast distance.

The next day the doctor told me that a fractured hip was a serious issue for a woman of her age. She needed surgery and it was scheduled for the following day. We knew there were risks, but she was strong and we equally knew there was really no alternative. Back in the ward Mum was awake, although still a little groggy from the effects of the morphine she was getting for the pain. She held my hand tightly, in a grip so common among all the Gallaghers, and in a tiny voice asked where she was and what had happened. I reassured her gently, whispering that she would be having an operation and would be as right as rain and home with us in a few days. She looked up at the painting on the wall and asked if it was The White Gate on Ards. When I told her it was, a smile rose in her face. She then closed her eyes and went to sleep muttering, *'Isn't that just lovely?'*

Her operation went ahead on the Saturday and was a success. Dr Heyburn, the physician, was pleased with the outcome and described Mum as *'an amazing woman with great resilience for an 87-year-old. That was a big operation and she came through well.'*

The key concern now was to monitor her closely and guard against any infection that might set in. Sunday brought a Christmas Day with a difference. For years it had been the family tradition for Mum to come and stay with us for a couple of nights over Christmas and she would invariably want to get involved in preparing the Christmas dinner. She was a great cook and we used her recipes and tips for producing the most delicious meals. That morning in the hospital, we were all excited to see her more alert than in previous days. She was especially pleased to see her grandchildren.

We all chimed 'Happy Christmas' in unison as we gathered round her bed and kissed her one at a time. Peter couldn't wait to push forward and deliver his Christmas present first. Mum smiled at his eagerness and thanked him for a lovely gift. She smiled again as each of the girls presented their gifts. It was a ceremony that had been conducted every Christmas for thirty years between Bridie and her grandchildren, and one she always looked forward to with intense pleasure. Now, of course, it was a little different. We were all in a hospital ward. She had just come through serious surgery. And Shauna was not there, but in Australia. But for a few short minutes it felt like we were at home again, by the Christmas tree, with presents littering the floor all around us, a roaring fire feeding us warmth, and not a care in the world.

In the days following Christmas, the doctors expressed relief that she had come through the procedure well, but she was weak and not eating much. She couldn't engage in any chat for more than a few minutes, tiring very quickly. We were now looking ahead to discharge in a week or two, knowing she would need permanent nursing care. As a family we made sure that throughout each day at least one of us was at or near her bedside. I headed in for my early morning visit. As soon as I entered the ward and saw the staff nurse's face I knew something was wrong.

She explained that there had been a setback during the night. Mum's repaired hip had somehow dislocated. She was in considerable pain but had been put on morphine again and was now reasonably comfortable.

I was stunned. How could this happen? Her physician explained that it was uncommon but not unknown following hip surgery, but it was now critical she had another operation as soon as possible to repair the dislocation. Needless to say this second operation was going to be an even higher risk than the first, especially given her weaker disposition but, as before, it was unavoidable.

The second operation went ahead the following day and was successful from a technical point of view. Mum had now been moved into a single side-ward room because an infection had set in. It's what we and the doctors had feared most. It was late in the evening and I was sitting by her bed. Now and again Mum would open her eyes and look to see who was there. Each time I would hold her hand a little more firmly and chat away about anything and everything, making sure to watch for any signs of pain or discomfort. Then she mumbled something while looking straight at me. I put my ear close to her mouth and could just detect the word 'water'. I reached across to the jug of iced water on the bedside cabinet and, holding one of her hands in mine, used the other to hold the plastic cup of water to her lips. I held the cup at what I thought would be a sensible angle to pour a little water in between her lips. But it became clear it was not enough. Mum grunted and for once held my hand tight as if to admonish me. She wanted more water than I was pouring. I laughed to myself quietly that here I was, a man approaching sixty, and my mother was still admonishing me as if I were nine years of age. I smiled at the evidence before my eyes that Bridie was certainly not finished just yet. She still had that spark of determination and was ready to let her big son know if he had done wrong. It was a good feeling and welcome, but only a temporary one.

By Friday Mum's condition had deteriorated further. She had now developed pneumonia and her physician warned me to prepare for the worst. While we were not surprised, given what she had gone through in her frail condition over the previous two weeks, we were, as a family, devastated to realise that her death might be imminent. I had complete trust in the medical and nursing team, and had watched carefully as they had fought to keep her alive, but it was obvious that she, despite putting up an incredible fight, was now too weak to fight any longer.

We immediately arranged for a priest to give her the Blessing of the Sick. Sometime later a priest, who was from Wexford but based in the nearby parish, arrived. He was a gentle man with a soft brogue and he asked me about Mum and her history. He gasped when he discovered she was the singer Bridie Gallagher. *'My God, I have her records and my whole family adored her.'*

She was sleeping at first but then woke. When she saw the priest sitting by her bed she seemed to acquire newfound strength from somewhere and insisted on shaking his hand. She smiled that wonderful smile known to us and thousands of her friends and fans. She kept shaking his hand and thanking him for coming. It was as if in her heart this was what she had been waiting for. The old priest took out his missal and began to recite the prayers of the blessing. He anointed her with oil and blessed her forehead. She stayed awake through the whole ceremony. She recited the 'Hail Mary' with the priest, still smiling. I had not seen her look so comfortable and peaceful for two weeks.

The staff nurse rang me just after three o'clock on the Monday morning to advise that Mum's condition was now critical. We had left her bedside just a couple of hours earlier. We dashed back to the hospital and went to her room with dread. The nurse greeted us with a look of deep concern and gently advised that Bridie didn't have long to go.

As we entered her room I noticed again the painting of The White

Facing page: *The Irish Times* obituary for Bridie in January 2012.

14/1/2

Obituaries

Bridie Gallagher

Singer known as 'girl with a tear in her v

Bridie Gallagher valued domestic recognition far more than successes abroad

DONEGAL SINGER Bridie Gallagher died in Belfast last Monday after a short illness. She was 87.

Gallagher was born and reared in Creeslough, the ninth of 10 children. Her father was James Gallagher, from Ards and her mother was Bridget Sweeney from Creeslough, who played the melodeon.

Many of her siblings (six sisters and three brothers) enjoyed singing. But she was the only one to pursue a professional career in music which in the 1950s was a career choice few women pursued.

Gallagher attended Massinass

1950s, she moved to Belfast. Gallagher later married George Livingstone (no relation to Bill) who managed her career briefly. They went on to have two sons, Jim and Peter. One of the great traumas of her life was the death of her son, Peter, at the age of 21, in 1976, as a result of a motorbike accident.

Gallagher's range was distinguished by a quality which led to her being known as "the girl with a tear in her voice". Her first big success came in 1956 with *A Mother's Love's A Blessing*. She was an affable woman, known for her quick wit and developed a reputa-

the largest audience to fill the famed auditorium: some 7,500 attended prior to the venue becoming fully seated.

She enjoyed further success with performances in Carnegie Hall, New York, and Sydney Opera House. Much of her audience was drawn from the extensive Irish emigrant populations in North America, the UK and Australia. Such were the crowds who came to hear her in venues across Ireland that on at least one occasion, she abandoned the venue (in Tipperary) and performed instead on the back of a lorry, to the delight of

225

Gate on the wall. It seemed all the more poignant and appropriate right now. I wondered if she could see her favourite place, her birthplace, looking down on her as she lay there weak and approaching the end of life.

We gathered around her bed as she lay breathing slowly and deeply. A short while later she breathed her last, and we all wept quietly and each said our own goodbyes.

We got back to the house about seven in the morning, sat around the kitchen table drinking tea and started to plan Bridie's wake and funeral. Soon we began ringing the wider family circle and relatives, especially those in Donegal. We also rang her closest friends so they would hear the news from us first.

By mid-morning the news bulletins on BBC and RTÉ were already reporting the breaking news of the death of The Girl from Donegal, Bridie Gallagher. Bulletins were repeated hourly throughout the day. That first bulletin was the starting pistol for a veritable flood of telephone calls from friends and media from around the world. *The Irish Times*, *Irish Independent*, *Belfast Telegraph*, BBC, RTÉ, *Daily Mirror*, radio stations in the US and Australia, and many more were in contact over the next two days, all wanting the story of her final hours and quotes for their news editors.

Of course, friends and relatives were the priority. But among them were some surprises. Our son Peter answered the telephone while we were having some breakfast and shouted that it was Martin McGuinness. I had worked for Martin when he was Sinn Féin Minister of Education. Of course we had one important thing in common in that both our mothers were from Donegal. He expressed heartfelt sympathy for the loss of mine, which was greatly appreciated by all the family. Other politicians, Unionist, Nationalist, from north and south, followed, each paying glowing tributes to Bridie and offering sympathy to us as a family. For someone who knew or cared little about politics it was amazing to see how many diverse politicians recognised Bridie Gallagher as an important figure in Irish culture.

In the days that followed we were equally delighted and humbled to receive a lovely letter of condolence from the President of Ireland, Michael D. Higgins. In it he wrote, *'In a long and distinguished career, Bridie's wonderful musical talent brought enormous pleasure to audiences at home and around the world. You can take great pride in knowing that her outstanding legacy to the world of Irish music will always be remembered.'*

The Taoiseach, Enda Kenny, wrote a personal letter to me, expressing deep sympathy for my loss, just as he had experienced with the death of his mother in preceding months: she too came from Donegal. Both he and the president sent emissaries to Bridie's funeral two days later, an extraordinary tribute, which was greatly appreciated by the family and her many friends and relations.

Condolence letter received from President Michael D. Higgins following Bridie's death in January 2012.

UACHTARÁN NA hÉIREANN
PRESIDENT OF IRELAND

10 January, 2012

Mr. Jim Livingstone
c/o Fr. Edward O'Donnell
St. Bridget's Church
40 Derryvolgie Avenue
Belfast
BT9 6FP

Dear Mr. Livingstone

I was greatly saddened to learn of the death of your dear Mother, Bridie

I would like to offer my sincere sympathy to you and to all of your wider family circle as you come to terms with this sad loss. During a long and distinguished career, Bridie's wonderful musical talent brought enormous pleasure to audiences at home and around the world. You can take great pride in knowing that her outstanding legacy to the world of Irish music will always be remembered.

I hope that the happy memories of your mother that you and your family share will also offer some solace at this difficult time.

Bridie's passing will be felt by all those who had the privilege of knowing her.

Yours sincerely

Michael D. Higgins
Uachtarán na hÉireann
President of Ireland

Irish Independent
Tuesday 10 January 2012

6 NEWS

'Girl from Donegal' and 'first global pop star' Bridie Gallagher dies at 87

Greg Harkin

THE singer described as Ireland's first international pop star" and the idol of a generation of emigrants died yesterday aged 87.

Bridie Gallagher was known as the 'Girl from Donegal' but she conquered many of the globe's most famous concert venues.

As news spread of Ms Gallagher's death at her home in Belfast, tributes were paid last night by fans who went on to carve their own careers in show-business.

A native of Creeslough, Co Donegal, she inspired many modern acts, including Paul Brady and Daniel O'Donnell, and was once the darling of RTE radio.

Ms Gallagher became famous in 1956 after being spotted by a talent scout in Belfast and releasing the hit single 'A Mother's Love's a Blessing'.

Radio

She was later given her own show on RTE radio and went on to play London's Royal Albert Hall, the Sydney Opera House and Carnegie Hall in New York.

She made Belfast her home in her 20s but she travelled the world as her career took off.

Ms Gallagher was caught up in the booming pop music scene of the late 1950s and '60s, and tapped an Irish emigrant audience in the US.

In an interview recently, she recalled: "I always loved New York and I always remember going to Times Square, you know, and I felt I've really made it now."

Clockwise from right: singer Daniel O'Donnell and his sister Margo with the late Bridie Gallagher at a function for her in her hometown of Creeslough, Co Donegal; Gallagher in 1955; and a publicity still during her career.

EOIN McGARVEY

Irish Independent article on Bridie's death in January 2012.

The telephone calls continued from near and far. Daniel O'Donnell rang early. He had been a close friend for many years and was deeply upset. He had been praising Bridie's contribution to Irish music for years and, in particular, her enduring influence on his career and on many other Irish stage artists. When I told him the funeral service would be in Belfast followed by burial in her home town of Creeslough he was audibly moved. *'I'll be there, Jim. And so will be all of Donegal.'*

Daniel's sister Margo rang within minutes, weeping and expressing deep love for her friend. The Derry singer Dana, record producers John Anderson and George Doherty, television producer Anna Marie McFaul, Bridie's dearest friend Fr Martin O'Connor in South Africa, her greatest fan and friend Joan Tobin in London, her old pal Conal Haughey in Ardara, her school pal Anna Kelly, and many more phoned, all offering sympathy and professing love and admiration for The Girl from Donegal.

The relatives from Donegal started to arrive, by the dozen, led by Bridie's dearest relative, her sister-in-law Bridget Gallagher, her brother Josie's wife. It was the same Bridget who, as a young girl of twelve in her family's home at Cashellily, had played those records on the old record player sixty-five years earlier for Bridie and her pals. Then the coffin with Bridie's remains arrived at the house in the afternoon. The wake soon commenced in traditional fashion. There were sandwiches, cakes, tea and coffee on a conveyor-belt-like kitchen table, wine and spirits for those who wished, and the rosary at nine that evening.

With the funeral service organised for St Brigid's Chapel in Derryvolgie Avenue and the burial in Creeslough, it was obvious that, because of the time of year, the burial would need to be before three o'clock that afternoon. The funeral service was scheduled at the unusual time of half past nine in the morning. But I realised we were faced with a major logistical problem: traffic. For a funeral service so early, the remains would need to leave our home in Ravenhill at about half past eight. I contacted the police to advise that the funeral would be crossing the city commuter traffic early on Wednesday morning. To my amazement they decided to provide police motorcycle outriders to escort the cortège. Wednesday morning duly arrived and there were four outriders lined up outside the house beside the O'Kane hearse. As we settled into the funeral limousine I smiled at Paula beside me, *'Imagine, a police escort for her funeral. Bridie's travelling in style yet again.'*

The chapel was packed to overflowing. Hundreds of mourners were there – both known and unknown to the family. There were people from

Irish Daily Mail article on Bridie's death from January 2012.

show business, fans, friends and family, and numerous journalists and photographers along with television camera crews from UTV, BBC and RTÉ. Bridie's grandchildren all played their part in her farewell. The music was beautifully arranged by Teresa. Nuala and Peter handled the spiritual readings with ease. And a devastated Shauna, confined to Sydney in Australia where her first baby was due in a matter of days, had a Mass said for her granny. Her baby was born twelve days later and she was named Ciara Bridget. The funeral service itself was led by Fr Eddie O'Donnell, the parish priest, with Monsignor Ambrose Macaulay, a good friend and pastor to Bridie in her later years, concelebrating.

At the end of the service, as Bridie's coffin was escorted from the chapel, the organist struck up with the air from 'The Homes of Donegal'. Bridie had ended every stage performance with this one song, which was dear to her heart. No singer sang the words today. It seemed so right that this final appearance of Bridie Gallagher should end just as she would.

After a short break for refreshments in the parish hall, the cortège began the long final journey back to her home county of Donegal and her final resting place at Doe Cemetery outside Creeslough. The funeral hearse was met there by hundreds of people lining the main street as a guard of honour to welcome back the town's most famous daughter. Daniel O'Donnell was waiting with Creeslough's local councillor and Bridie's friend, Noel McGinley. The hearse moved slowly through the town followed on foot by Peter and myself, with Daniel, Noel and a procession of cars behind, and with people lining the main street applauding for Bridie. It was an extremely emotional but uplifting sight. At St Michael's primary school all the pupils were lined up along the road standing respectfully with their teachers.

At Doe Cemetery there were already hundreds of people waiting respectfully in the drizzling cold rain. There were friends and relatives from Belfast, Dublin, Donegal, London and Glasgow. Fr Briody, the local parish priest, conducted the graveside ceremony, at the end of which Bridie's grandniece, Donna Sweeney, played an Irish air on the tin whistle. In the wet and windy graveyard, with hundreds of mourners standing in sadness and respect, watched by television camera crews and press photographers, the people of Donegal and Ireland laid their Girl from Donegal to rest beneath the towering Muckish Mountain, just a mile from The White Gate.

In the days that followed there was phenomenal media coverage of

The White Gate, Bridie's favourite place in the world, half a mile from where she was born.

events. In Ireland every radio and television station reported extensively on Bridie's passing and her funeral. Every newspaper carried photographs and reports about the funeral and her career. Hundreds of Mass cards, sympathy cards and letters from all over the world arrived for weeks after the funeral.

The *Belfast Newsletter* commented that '*she was credited with being Ireland's first pop star*'.

The *Belfast Telegraph* described her as the '*singer who packed out the world's biggest concert halls*' and commented that '*she paved the way for a generation of Irish singers to appear on the international stage and she brought a touch of magic and glamour to Irish show business*'.

The *Irish Times* described her as the '*singer known as the girl with a tear in her voice*' and commented that '*she was an affable woman, known for her quick wit and developed a reputation for her glamorous wardrobe and stylish coiffure on stage*'.

Belfast's *Irish News* commented that *'she melted the hearts of millions, particularly those Irish who had emigrated to Canada, America and England'*.

Ireland's *Sunday Independent* commented that *'in a spectacular six-decade career, she opened the door to the world for a generation of Irish artistes when she conquered the stages of London, New York and Sydney'*.

Donegal's newspaper, the *Tirconaill Tribune*, wrote *'she achieved fame all over the world but her heart remained back in Donegal'*.

The *Irish Independent* mourned the death of Ireland's *'first global pop star'*.

The *Daily Mirror* described her as *'the performer who took the world by storm in the 50s and 60s'* and also as *'a trailblazer who lit up a room'*.

The *Irish Daily Mail* called her *'a shimmering star who drew thousands to her shows, many of them emigrants living abroad desperate to hear the familiar songs they had left behind'*.

All the many press articles chronicled her career, quoting friends' and colleagues' tributes, and emphasising the pioneering and trailblazing role she had played in Irish show business. Many also noted the fact that her life had been hard and not without pain and loss, especially the death of her son Peter. Every single newspaper and television report was full of extraordinary praise and tribute, which was wonderful to read.

After some months I started to deal with Bridie's estate. She had collected numerous awards, gifts, paintings, sculptures and jewellery from places as diverse as New York, London, Sydney, Lusaka in Zambia and Creeslough. These were distributed among family members. Then I faced the biggest conundrum: what to do with her stage dresses and gowns. There were almost a hundred, all carefully stored in customised wardrobes in her house. They were mostly from the period 1955 through to 1980; twenty-five years of exquisite style and glamour that had been valued by one expert as worth €70,000 or more at auction. I balked at the idea of selling them. It felt cheap and tawdry. My three daughters chose one gown each to keep. But what was I to do with the rest?

A few months after the funeral, I passed the Lyric Theatre in Belfast. This newly rebuilt theatre stands on the banks of the River Lagan and was only half a mile from Bridie's Belfast home. She often went to productions there to what she called 'legit theatre'. She loved the theatre

Bridie's dresses on display over a weekend in August during the Creeslough Festival in 2005 to raise funds for Donegal Hospice.

just as she loved all the theatres she had ever graced around the world. Theatre was without doubt her natural home. I eventually met with the Lyric management and agreed to donate the entire collection of gowns to the Lyric Theatre for use in productions in perpetuity.

A month later all the dresses (including a beaver fur coat) were handed over to the theatre. The director Ciaran McCauley had instructed that a special wardrobe be constructed to house the dresses, henceforth to be referred to as the Bridie Gallagher Collection. The theatre management was thrilled at the acquisition and promised that every time one of the costumes was used in a production the Bridie Gallagher Collection would be acknowledged in the production programme.

I was very satisfied and thrilled that Bridie Gallagher's name would live on in perpetuity in the setting she most loved – the theatre. I was doubly delighted some months later when one of the dresses was used in a production of one of Marie Jones' plays. I knew then that Bridie's name would be a part of Irish theatre for years to come.

Chapter Fourteen

LEGACY

Now go where you will upon land or on sea
And I'll share all your sorrows and cares
At night as I kneel by my bedside to pray
I'll remember you, love, in my prayers.

'I'LL REMEMBER YOU LOVE IN MY PRAYERS' (THOMAS P. KEENAN)

*S*o how might we define Bridie's legacy? The answer, I think, lies under two headings: Bridie Gallagher, the Irish ballad singer, and Bridie Livingstone, the mother, grandmother, sister and friend.

As a singer coming from a small town in County Donegal she achieved enormous popularity and acclaim around the world, especially among Irish people. She did this at a time when fame rarely came quickly or easily, as so often appears today with a culture that spawns overnight celebrities on television talent shows, reality shows and gossip magazines, a culture where some even become famous for just being famous. She journeyed thousands of miles to perform for her audiences around Ireland and Britain, and across oceans by air and by sea at a time when travel was expensive, relatively slow and arduous by today's standards. Her records sold in millions; her concerts attracted enormous crowds numbering in their thousands, at a time in Ireland when 'big crowds' usually meant hundreds.

But is this the stuff from which legacies are made?

Times have changed with the advent of modern social media, multi-channel and global television, stadium concerts, and instant stardom from television talent shows, so much so that Bridie's record sales, radio plays or theatre capacity audiences of the 1950s might appear modest now to some, and it is perhaps difficult for a younger generation to appreciate their significance. Perhaps a legacy is something more memorable and lasting than simply fame, which in reality lasts only a lifetime. It is something that has an impact in today's world and beyond. I would suggest Bridie Gallagher's legacy lies with her contribution to Irish show business and musical culture, which laid the foundations for following generations to build on.

She made Irish ballads popular after many years of neglect by Irish recording artists. But she also made them more modern and relevant by introducing musical arrangements in her recordings that reflected a new era of record production. Her records were among the first in Ireland to use full orchestras instead of small ceilí or dance bands. In particular her records with arrangements by Stan Butcher established a level of sophistication and musicality that had never been heard before in Irish music and set a standard for many artists that followed in her wake. Few ever fully acknowledged or realised her contribution in this regard at the height of her fame in the 1950s and 1960s.

But looking back it is now very clear that the quality of recordings

This photo was taken at Derby Castle Theatre in Douglas on the Isle of Man in 1959 for promotional material *(l–r)*: Gertie Wine, Pat York, Cy Brent (pianist), Bridie, Frank Carson, Billy Livingstone and Frank McIlroy.

by other artists in Ireland improved significantly from the time that Bridie's records dominated the charts and radio broadcasts in the late 1950s and early 1960s. Most Irish artists that followed realised that, to be successful, especially internationally, their quality of record production and stage performance needed to be better. Recording techniques, quality of musical arrangements (no matter what genre) and quality of musicianship (including singing) needed to match the best on the international scene. Bridie began that evolution and today we can see the evidence of the success of so many great singers and bands of all kinds that have emerged from Ireland onto a world stage like never before.

Her style of performance set a new standard that has become an accepted norm in today's theatres and stadium concerts by Irish artists. She wore exquisite gowns when others were going on stage with 'nice dresses or suits' and often said that her greatest influence in dress style was American star Doris Day. She spent enormous sums ensuring her dresses were spectacular and her wardrobe of many styles became one of her signatures. Indeed, it was often said that many of the women in her audiences were as keen to see what Bridie was wearing as to hear her sing. And she took extraordinary steps to avoid wearing the same gown in the same venue, even twelve months apart. Her hair styling and make-up drew on American influences and created a new focus on the importance of visual image for stage artists, especially female singers. Dec Cuskey of The Bachelors said, just before she died:

Bridie with her granddaughters Teresa (*left*) and Shauna (*right*) in 1980. © BELFAST TELEGRAPH

'She introduced glamour to Irish show business, which had never been there before. She showed us what could be done and Irish artists were inspired to follow her example.'

She introduced a new dynamic into what could be called 'stage presence'. She created a new approach of moving about the stage holding a handheld microphone. Many today may be surprised to learn that prior to this time singers, male or female, invariably stood centre-stage at a microphone on a static stand. She told me her initial inspiration in this regard came from that performance she saw of Judy Garland in Dublin's Theatre Royal in 1951. Bridie made the then bold step of using a handheld microphone, just like Judy. This meant moving about the stage using hand gestures to emphasise lyrics in an artistic manner and thus communicating even better with all parts of the audience. She sang to people in the audience as individuals. She often singled people out and directed her singing to them, and so engaged everyone personally and with real meaning. This legacy to stagecraft has already been acknowledged by many of the great stars like Daniel O'Donnell, Margo, Phil Coulter and many journalists like Eddie McIlwaine of the *Belfast Telegraph*. As Eddie said: *'She made every member of her audience feel special.'*

She also inspired a new generation of singers and performers. In her touring shows of the early 1960s she introduced many young up-and-coming artists to wider audiences around Ireland and Britain, and they in turn, went on to great success. Comedians like Jackie Wright, who joined Benny Hill and realised international success, and Frank Carson, who became a household name in the 1970s, owe their success to Bridie. Daniel O'Donnell never forgot the encouragement she gave him as a young singer coming from Donegal. She showed aspiring Irish artists that it could be done and how to do it. As Daniel said, *'She opened the door to international performing for so many Irish artists. She led the way and we followed in her wake.'*

Since her death, it is gratifying to see that her professional legacy is now recognised as one that inspired Irish singers and performers to look beyond Ireland's shores and achieve greatness internationally. It showed the way for many to present an act on stage in a way that could truly engage an audience. And she established a quality of singing, musical arrangement and sound that was to make Irish recording production one that eventually would lead the world – a wealth of musical talent that is now almost taken for granted.

Of course, for all her fans and admirers, it is her distinctive voice that will endure. At an early stage in her career it was often commented on that she had a 'break' in her voice. This was a feature that could best be described musically as a trick of the voice where she would sing a note in a pure tone and then falsetto, an octave higher. It was described as sounding like she had 'a tear in her voice', particularly appropriate perhaps for one who sang so many songs that were sad. It set her apart then from other singers and ensured that whenever her records were played, listeners immediately recognised who it was – a very valuable asset for any recording artist. But she had a strong and versatile voice that was always in tune and that she used skilfully to suit the tempo and sentiments of the song. It was always imperative to her that each song deserved its own tone and colour. No two songs were ever sung the same. The voice was used to give each song a unique identity.

This was well demonstrated in 1962 when, as requested by her recording company Decca, she recorded two pop songs – 'It's a Sin to Tell a Lie' and 'I Found You Out'. It was the company's attempt to widen her appeal beyond just the Irish market and to some extent was very successful. These were definitely not Irish ballads but more in line with recordings then by artists like Max Bygraves. She adapted her voice almost effortlessly, and these recordings are still regarded by many fans to be as important as her Irish melodies. Bridie herself, however, took the decision to stick with the Irish ballads, but in this brief detour had proven that her voice was as powerful in any style, and is the enduring aspect of her performing that can be claimed as a legacy.

Perhaps one of the key aspects of her legacy lies with her enormous impact on Irish emigrants around the world, especially in the 1950s and 1960s when emigration from Ireland was at its height. Countless fans have written and spoken of the fact that for them Bridie Gallagher was so often their link back home. Her recordings and performances were always carefully adjusted to suit her audience. As was so often the case in those days, Irish people from a particular county would predominate in certain cities or venues. In Philadelphia it was Donegal; in clubs in Manchester it tended to be people from Connacht; in Toronto it was Ulster counties; in London it tended to be Cork and Kerry emigrants. In each performance she made sure to include songs in her repertoire from the relevant counties to make that particular audience feel special and engaged. When her record sales declined in Ireland in the 1960s, they hardly faltered in the US and internationally. She was undoubtedly very special for Irish emigrant families and played a role in keeping them in touch with their birthplace.

There was one extraordinary event when, on holiday in 1969 on the island of Majorca, some years before it became the popular holiday destination, Bridie was walking down a little street in Palma with my brother Peter and I, admiring the quaint whitewashed buildings and ancient architecture. Suddenly, we could hear the strains of 'The Boys from County Armagh' coming from somewhere close. It was a little bar with a Spanish name. Peter and I looked inside and there was just a barman and three local customers chatting. Peter went inside, leaving Bridie puzzling outside, and asked the barman if he was Irish. He replied he was from County Armagh and welcomed Peter loudly on hearing his Northern Irish accent. Peter asked him if he knew the singer whose record was playing on his jukebox.

'*Of course I do. That's the one and only Bridie Gallagher. The guys here never heard of her, but I play her from time to time to remind me of home. Come on in and have a drink young man.*'

Then Peter asked him if he had ever met Bridie. He just kept polishing his drinking glasses and replied, '*Sadly no. I saw her sing in Portadown Town Hall once, but that's as close as I got.*'

So Peter asked if he would like to meet Bridie. He scoffed and said: '*I'd pay good money to meet that lady, but I'm hardly likely to here in Palma, Majorca.*'

So out Peter went and urged a reluctant Bridie to come in and meet the barman from Armagh. As soon as she entered, the barman cried in astonishment: '*Holy Jesus. It's Bridie. In my bar.*'

We stayed for a short while and Bridie chatted away to him as if she had known him for years – and in a way she had. He was like so many emigrants she had met before, keen to talk of home and beguiled by The Girl from Donegal.

Her professional career lasted fifty years and had countless highlights and achievements, from her early appearances at the Theatre Royal in Dublin in 1956, through record-breaking seasons in London's Metropolitan Theatre, touring her variety show around all the major city theatres of Britain and Ireland including the Empire Theatre in Belfast, starring twice at London's Albert Hall to a record-breaking capacity audience, playing New York's St Nicholas Arena, the London Palladium, San Francisco's Fillmore West and Sydney Opera House, to her last major concert in the Lincoln Center in New York in 1991.

She recorded many albums, dozens of single records and videos. She appeared in virtually every town and townland in Ireland, performing in small and large halls, cabaret clubs, marquee tents, and even on the back of a lorry to an audience of 6,000 in Kilmainham Wood.

Her career had one key disappointment, though. Inexplicably, she was never given her own show on Irish television, despite frequent demands from the public and newspaper columnists. She did make several guest appearances on RTÉ's *The Late Late Show*, *The Pat Kenny Show* and other productions, always to great acclaim, but was overlooked by producers as probably being, in their eyes at least, by the 1970s, past her peak. She was hurt by this dismissal and often said privately that because she was not living in Dublin and an active, and perhaps sycophantic, part of the show business establishment scene there, she would be largely ignored, as she undoubtedly was until she died.

But such disappointments aside, her career was not just immensely successful commercially over many years; it also established her with a special and unique place in the history of show business in Ireland. During a period in which the country was still coming to terms commercially, politically and socially with the aftermath of independence and the Civil War, when thousands of people were emigrating annually for work to Britain, the US and elsewhere, when people relied on newspapers and the radio for news and entertainment and only a handful had televisions in their homes, Bridie brought her singing and her shows direct to the people wherever they lived. In small halls, large theatres, open-air concerts, she engaged up close with the people. Unlike some celebrities today she was not remote, seen only on television or film, or in gossip magazines. She was the Irish star who belonged to the people and went to them in their cities, towns and townlands, across four continents. She spent time with her fans and related to them as a friend, helping many to retain their links with home. This must surely be her greatest legacy.

Her legacy as Bridie Livingstone is no less important to her family and friends.

She demonstrated to all her family the importance of hard work, ambition and determination to achieving success. She was always encouraging her grandchildren to sing, play music, perform, dress up, practise and work hard at school, and she always revelled in their successes. Today, they have each gone on to emulate that philosophy and success in their own right. She taught her family the importance of entertaining friends with good food, wine and music. Livingstone

Bridie and her granddaughters at Teresa's First Communion in 1986, *(l–r):* Shauna, Nuala and Teresa.

parties are now never without a sing-song around the piano and invariably one or two of Bridie's songs will feature – usually a fulsome rendition of 'The Boys from County Armagh' which is guaranteed to get everyone singing.

She proved that, even in the midst of the pain, suffering, grief and hardship life brings to everyone, you can still smile if you choose to, and make others happy. In doing so it is always possible to receive back a little of that same happiness and keep life worth living. There were many times when she admitted life did not seem worth living – when she lost her husband and her son Peter, and when her health deteriorated. But she kept smiling that lovely smile and sharing her infectious laugh while she struggled on.

Her laugh, for many, will be a characteristic that is missed most. Every radio or television interviewer would usually at some point comment on her laugh, which she expressed often, freely and loudly. But it was not just a stage laugh, delivered in some contrived way. She loved chat, and swapping old yarns and silly jokes with friends. Indeed she had certain turns of phrase with which she repeatedly raised laughter among others, such as 'the craic was good in Cricklewood', 'as I said to the Bishop' and 'up she flew and the cock flattened her'. I for one was

Above: Bridie with her granddaughters Teresa and Nuala on the day in 2005 that Nuala graduated from Queen's University Belfast with a degree in psychology.

Right: Bridie with her grandson Peter in 2006.

never sure if she really understood the nuance of some of these phrases or why sometimes people, who did not know her well, would at times look a little shocked. Her laughter was from the heart and always genuine, never forced. But I think it was also a blanket to cover underlying pain and sorrow, as well as an expression of the joy and fun that she always sought. It truly is a part of her legacy to be remembered and cherished.

As a family we experienced many times, when strangers were present, how she would 'put on her performance' and become, even briefly, the star again. She could never let her public down or let them see her depressed. Being that star helped her survive great adversity. It continued to give others pleasure. For her it was never lost, even as it took increasing effort to shine. She combined being a mother, grandmother and show business star in a way that many might think impossible, and in doing so demonstrated great courage and humanity that many others would find incomprehensible.

She was a complex human being with talents, weaknesses, diverse abilities and countless successes as well as her share of failures. Her life was different to many others in terms of stardom, business success and being in the public eye. But equally it was the same as many others, enduring sadness, tragedy, ill health and personal failings. She was demanding of herself and others. She always wanted things done right and could show a temper that was volcanic if they were not. In performing on stage, some musicians, directors, managers and promoters could suffer her sharp tongue or stern look if the sound system was not first-class, musical accompaniment was faulty, advertising was weak or production was flawed. At the same time, every record producer or stage director in Belfast, Dublin or London that she worked with invariably praised her willingness to work long, hard hours and take direction when needed in order to produce a perfect performance, even in her later years. George Doherty of Emerald Records recalled with admiration how she was one of the few performers who could walk into a studio and record a track in one take. He also never forgot how, after recording an album, she would take the entire team out for dinner to celebrate, not something that happened often with many other artists, according to George.

She valued the many friendships she made throughout her life. She developed an amazing network of friends, not just business acquaintances, around the world. In Belfast she had good neighbours who, like Ruth Mills and Sheila Tomb, became good friends. She had her favourite show business pals like Marie (Cunningham) Murphy and Vivienne (Stewart) McMaster with whom she shared many evenings, as well as Danny Small and Ray Sheils and his wife Vi, who were loyal and caring friends from the business over many years. She had more distant friends like Kathleen McDermott in Glenamaddy, County Galway, Christine Hawkins from Gort, and Conal Haughey in Ardara, with whom she would occasionally stay for a few days' quiet relaxation. There was, of course, Joan Tobin in London, with whom she spoke every month by telephone as well as visiting from time to time. There was the O'Brien family in Cleveland, Ohio, Bridget O'Hare in Vancouver, Sean and Betty McNally in Penticton in the Rockies, Fr Martin O'Connor in South Africa and many, many more. She corresponded regularly with all of them, and visited most for short breaks to get away from the pressures and hurly burly of show business life. She worked hard at maintaining all her friendships and valued them greatly, especially in her later years living alone, suffering increasing ill health, and adjusting to a life without performing on stage. Her friends still cherish the memory of their friendship with The Girl from Donegal, or just Bridie.

There was one person above all who was her closest and most trusted friend. That was her sister-in-law Bridget Gallagher, the wife of her late brother Josie. She was that young girl who kept the record player well stocked and wound-up when a teenaged Bridie and her friends danced and sang at Bridget's family home in Cashellily in the middle of Ards Forest. Bridget and Josie brought up their family of seven in the Gallagher home at Aghalattive while also caring for Bridie's ageing parents Biddy and Jim through their final years in Ards. Bridie had a close relationship with her nine sisters and brothers, but Bridget was the person in whom she confided most and turned to for comfort in hard times. She revelled in Bridget's company, chatting over cups of tea by a roaring log fire about family exploits and local news, and sharing many wonderful times socialising with her around Creeslough. Bridget was often entrusted to look after me and my brother when we stayed on Ards for summer holidays while Bridie was touring the world. Both of them visited and stayed with each other many times and telephoned frequently. Bridget was always her rock, her closest and best friend, and the woman who Bridie said inspired her most as a mother.

Bridie's love of Ireland, and especially Donegal, was profound and unending. She lived in Belfast for sixty-three or her eighty-seven years, but as one might say 'you can take the girl out of Donegal, but not Donegal out of the girl'. Aside from hundreds of trips to perform all over the county in halls and cabaret, she visited her home county frequently for relaxation and renewal when her spirits were low. She loved the mountains and the beaches, its wild scenic beauty, but most of all, its people.

She would often be teased that when travelling from Belfast to Creeslough, crossing the border at Lifford or Derry, her accent would change almost in mid-sentence. Naturally, she usually spoke with a

Left: Bridie with grand-daughter Shauna at her wedding in 2007.

Below: Bridie with her family at Christmas in 2008, *(l–r):* Bridie, her son Jim, her granddaughers Teresa and Nuala, Stuart Bald-win (who married Bridie's granddaughter Shauna in 2007), her granddaughter Shauna, her daughter-in-law Paula and her grandson Peter.

soft Irish accent that had been cultivated by various influences such as many years living in Belfast, travel abroad, and her well-practiced diction developed in recording, television and radio studios. To her it was essential that her speech was clear and understandable to audiences everywhere. But once she crossed that border, suddenly her accent broadened and she would talk of the weather being 'wild', start most sentences with *'Ayyyye'* and her pitch would lower to one commonly heard around Donegal. It was an amazing but attractive transformation to witness, which underlined that this woman was always going to be, first and foremost, a child of Donegal.

She was fanatical about following Donegal football, the careers of fellow Donegal performers like Daniel O'Donnell and Margo, and the local news from Donegal newspapers, which she purchased regularly in Belfast. Seeing her watching the Donegal team win the All-Ireland football final in 1992, seated in front of her television at home, was both comical and worrying. She jumped up and down, screaming at the screen and shouting instructions to her team. I thought that day she would have a second heart attack. But she was just overjoyed at their success and immediately sent a message to Brian McEniff offering hearty congratulations. She also loved to see artists like Daniel O'Donnell and others doing well. To her it was further reinforcement of her long-held view that Donegal possessed so much talent that had for too long been overshadowed by Dublin-centric or Belfast-centric show business news and opinion in Ireland. Her home was festooned with Donegal paintings, pottery, and even plants. The trees and shrubs in her garden were all taken from cuttings in Ards forestry near Creeslough.

She also took every opportunity to promote Donegal wherever she went, especially abroad. In the US she went out of her way in interviews to explain where Donegal was in Ireland and what a special place it was. For many years Americans in particular only appeared to be aware of Dublin, Killarney and Galway as places worth visiting. Bridie made sure they heard about Donegal, tucked away in the far northwest, but worth any journey to see and experience. She would speak lovingly of places like Barnesmore Gap, Glenveagh Castle, Killybegs harbour, Glencolmcille, and naturally her beloved Creeslough and Ards. Years later commentators would often say she 'put Donegal on the map' internationally. Perhaps she did, but for Bridie, her love of the county and its people was deeply personal and very real. It sustained her in so many ways that one could say it was Donegal that helped keep her on that same map.

Her generosity was legendary. She gave her time freely and willingly to perform for many charities every year, raising large sums for hospitals and children's homes in particular. For many years in the 1950s when TB was still prevalent she made a particular effort to visit and perform in hospitals and sanatoriums, especially at Christmas time. She never forgot visiting one in Cappoquin, County Waterford, in 1957, where she met a little girl who was dying with TB. She was very near to death, but still wanted to meet this stage star and hear her sing. Bridie came away very disturbed, but determined to do more to help however she could.

On a second visit to the same hospital the following year, to talk and sing to the patients, she cried like any mother when she learned the little girl had died. The doctors presented her with a most beautiful handmade rug, which she treasured ever after and displayed proudly in her dining room.

Another time she visited an orphanage in Belfast. There was this big room in which the children gathered round, sitting on the floor, while the nuns collected requests for their favourite songs. Amazingly, the most requested one was 'The Two Little Orphans'. It was a struggle to get through the song as she wanted to burst into tears. The one thing she never did was talk publicly about her charity work. To her it was a private matter and not one for self-promotion.

She was generous too with her time, hospitality and support for her own family, never forgetting the birthdays of her four grandchildren and numerous nieces and nephews, and always lavishing gifts and treats in large measure. In later years, when failing health meant she couldn't go out to shop at Christmas, she would send me to town to get the grandchildren's presents. Every time, I returned laden with bags and boxes, but no matter what had been spent, she would ask, *'Are you sure that's good enough? Is it the right style for the girls? Could you not get a bigger toy for Peter?'* When her parents were still alive, she used to send large luxury hampers every Christmas from Belfast to the Donegal home on Ards, a special treat that was never forgotten by the children. That generous spirit was reciprocated many times by her nieces and nephews over the years that followed. Indeed, Bridget and Josie's children became an extension of her own family in Belfast. When they were young they always roared with excitement when 'Auntie Bridie' visited Ards. In return, as her health declined, they would often visit her in Belfast (including the last week of her life in hospital), bringing news, yarns and endless laughter – potent medicine that Bridie thrived on. She also enjoyed visits from her many other nieces and nephews, all wanting to show their love of Auntie Bridie. To her they were all family, to be proud of and loved.

It may surprise many to know that she rarely ever knew how much money she had. In the early years of her career she had business managers and accountants whom she trusted and by and large they managed her affairs well. From the early 1970s, it was my job as her eldest son to manage all her financial affairs, and make sure she was secure and always comfortable, including taking steps to ensure that the taxman got his fair share. Money was not of any real importance to her. It was a means to an end. Indeed one task she refused to do was settle up with promoters after shows. Her various managers had to do all the financial negotiations and dealings in money. She could not cope with the stress of negotiation, nor indeed, understand some of the complexities of money management. While she lavished gifts on others, she told me one day, *'Just make sure there's enough to give me a decent burial when I go.'*

As it was, she lived comfortably in her own beautiful home in a peaceful and lovely area of Belfast for all but her final two weeks on this earth, financially secure, with many memories and mementos from around the world that were priceless. At the end, whatever about her worth in her heyday, she was not a multimillionaire.

Neither was she a saint, but yet she clung to her Catholic faith with a quiet fervour. One of her great joys was travelling with my wife Paula and her sister Margaret to see Pope John Paul II celebrate an enormous open-air Mass near Drogheda in 1979. She frequently sought advice and guidance from the Franciscan priest Fr Andrew, whom she first met in Creeslough, even after he moved to Kilkenny. In later years she valued enormously the advice and counsel of her good friend Fr Martin O'Connor in South Africa. When she eventually became too frail to attend Sunday Mass she was always delighted to receive regular visits from Fr Ambrose Macaulay in Belfast. The year her son Peter died, I took her to Rome and, with a lovely Sister Anne who worked in the hospital beside the Irish College, she visited various holy sites where she prayed fervently for her young son. She wept many bitter tears that week in Rome, and yet benefited greatly from the solace and warmth given to her by Sister Anne and her devotion to her faith.

Inevitably, while Bridie was always the 'Singing Star', she could still be wonderfully ordinary and homely. One day, when she was in her seventies, a new neighbour, who had recently moved into the house opposite, was out walking his dog passing her house in Hillside. He stopped in his tracks with astonishment and came over to speak with her. She was dressed in old jeans and an anorak, wearing plastic gloves, and painting her front gates with white gloss paint, streaks of which adorned her arms.

'Aren't you the famous Bridie Gallagher?' he asked.

'Yes I am,' she laughed heartily. *'Sorry, I can't shake your hands. They're covered in paint.'*

'But you're painting a gate,' he cried incredulously. *'You are a big star. Surely you could get someone to do that for you?'*

'These are my White Gates. See the nameplate on the house over there,' she pointed. *'It's where I'm from in Donegal. Why shouldn't I paint them myself? I'm fit and able to do it, so I might as well,'* she explained, smiling without a care.

He bid her good day and went on his way, no doubt having learned that this particular star was one that never flinched from hard work and ordinary chores. Her grandchildren were coming to visit the next day and she was determined to welcome them to her White Gates home, gleaming bright and fresh as the home in Donegal she remembered.

So The Girl from Donegal made her mark on this world. She left a great and diverse legacy to Irish show business and her family, which will endure for many years to come and of which many of us can be proud and grateful. She had a good and long life, but also suffered sadness and tragedy without ever seeing her star really fade away. The songs she recorded and made famous among Irish people across the world have been re-recorded by many other artists since. But there are many that will forever remain synonymous with the name Bridie Gallagher – 'A Mother's Love's a Blessing', 'Goodbye Johnny', Cuttin' the Corn in Creeslough', 'Teddy O'Neill', 'Two Little Orphans' and not least 'The Boys from County Armagh'.

So as a legacy she left us with great riches, which will last for many years to come – inspiration to achieve our best through hard work and a determination to overcome all adversity; musical quality and a stage presence that has helped lead others to greatness in Irish show business; a love of family, friends and birthplace that reminds us what is most important in life; and a memory of how laughter can lift the spirit and make life worth living. It is fitting to end the biography of this wonderful woman the way she ended every show:

> *Now the time has come when I must go, I bid you all adieu*
> *The open highway calls me forth to do the things I do*
> *And when I'm wandering on my way I'll hear your voices call*
> *And please God I'll soon return unto the Homes of Donegal.*

'The Homes of Donegal' (S. McBridie)

INDEX

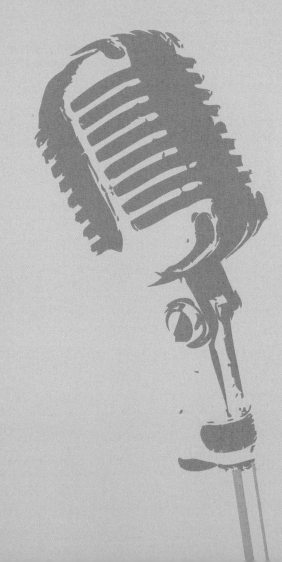

Note: illustrations are indicated by page numbers in **bold**.